THE THEORY OF
CHRISTIAN
EDUCATION PRACTICE

THE THEORY OF CHRISTIAN EDUCATION PRACTICE:

How Theology Affects Christian Education

RANDOLPH CRUMP MILLER

Religious Education Press
Birmingham, Alabama

Copyright © 1980 by Religious Education Press

No part of this publication may be reproduced, stored in a retrieval system, or transmitted, in any form or by any means, electronic, photocopying, recording, or otherwise, without the prior written permission of the publisher.

Library of Congress Cataloging in Publication Data

Miller, Randolph Crump, 1910–
   The theory of Christian education practice.

   Includes bibliographical references and index.
   1. Christian education (Theology)   I. Title.
BV1464.M53   207   80-15886
ISBN 0-89135-049-7

Religious Education Press, Inc.
1531 Wellington Road
Birmingham, Alabama 35209
10 9 8 7 6 5 4 3 2

Religious Education Press publishes books and educational materials exclusively in religious education and in areas closely related to religious education. It is committed to enhancing and professionalizing religious education through the publication of significant scholarly and popular works.

PUBLISHER TO THE PROFESSION

DEDICATED TO OUR
GRANDCHILDREN
DANIELLE, DAVID, DUDLEY,
DEBORAH, "PAC," CHRISTOPHER,
JAY, VAUGHAN, ELIZABETH,
"V," RANDY, JENNIFER,
NATHANIEL, EMILY, KATHERINE

Contents

Preface

My teaching over the years has dealt with the theory of Christian education practice. It seeks to provide the intellectual framework for understanding what Christian educators try to do. It is primarily a theological endeavor because the theory I am concerned with is related to the nature of God and what it means to be human. I think my theology is sufficiently empirical and pragmatic to be workable as a basis for the educational ministry of the church.

H. Richard Niebuhr spoke of the need to be theoretical. A theological school, he wrote, "deals with the theory of preaching, of Christian education, of social action and of worship as well as with the theory of divine and human nature, of God's activity and [human] behavior. So its work is theoretical through and through."[1] Niebuhr was concerned with what we can know and placed the emphasis on the *relation* to God and neighbor, which is a complex and many-sided problem. The minister or other teachers bring an understanding of Christianity to the educational ministry. Niebuhr sees the minister as a teacher and teacher of teachers, as well as the head of the educational organization of a congregation as a leader and not just a manager.[2] Thus the theory of practice is carried over into experience on which one reflects, and this in turn improves and corrects the theory for future action.

1. H. Richard Niebuhr, *The Purpose of the Church and Its Ministry* (New York: Harper & Row, 1956), pp. 125–126.
2. Niebuhr, *Purpose of the Church*, p. 83.

1

This theme has been worked over in a variety of ways in books and articles, but there is an opportunity now to bring together some aspects of this approach to Christian education. There is a theory of educational practice which is theologically based, which does not abrogate the findings that come from educational philosophy, the studies of human development, or the social sciences. With this proviso, I have insisted that Christian education is a theological discipline and method.

This book is divided into two sections. The first eight chapters face the question, How does theology affect Christian education? Starting with a brief introduction to a theology that is empirically based and process oriented, we move to consider questions about nature, method in theology, the authority of scripture, what it means to be human, the nature of value, and the place of ethics in Christian living. In each case the theory points toward practice and there are suggestions for educational procedures.

The final eight chapters turn the argument around and ask, How do Christian education theory and practice reflect theology? It begins with a basic statement I made in 1952 when I began my teaching career at Yale. It was a statement that marked a turning point in my move from theology to education, and it had a relevance for the kinds of questions being asked at that time. I claimed then, and would continue to do so, that theology is the clue to Christian education. This became the theme of most of my books in the field and remains so in this one. But theology must always be in dialogue with educational theory and practice as developed in secular educational philosophy. I have been helped in understanding this dialogue by the contributions to educational thought of linguistic philosophy, as briefly summarized in chapter ten.

The most practical chapters in the book are those on worship, the use of the Bible, and anxiety. In these chapters I seek to demonstrate three ways of dealing with crucial questions. We have not solved the problems of worship, and we need more information relating to both theory and practice. We are still fighting old and new battles on the proper way of teaching the Bible at various age levels, and we are in danger of losing some of the advances we have made in the past forty years. We are discovering that a certain kind of anxiety arising out of interpersonal relations can hinder the learning process at any age level.

Religion is taught in independent schools and at public universities. It will broaden our views to consider both of these problems within the framework of the theory of practice. Then we consider the situation today and look in the crystal ball. My guess is that my crystal ball is no better than yours, and perhaps we need more dialogue and less guessing or even the projecting of sociological charts. The future is always open.

In writing this book, I have made use of a number of articles and chapters previously published. They have been rewritten, expanded, updated, and put in inclusive language, so that they become parts of a single theme with variations that are consistent with my view of Christian education today. I am grateful to those who have granted permission to reprint some material or to re-create it in new forms: "Empiricism and Process Theology: God Is What God Does," copyright 1976, Christian Century Foundation. Reprinted by permission from *The Christian Century*, (March 24, 1976), 284–287; "Process Thinking and Religious Education," *The Anglican Theological Review* LVII, No. 3 (July 1975), 271–288; "The New Naturalism and Christianity," *The Anglican Theological Review* XXII, No. 1 (January 1940), 25–35; "Authority, Scripture, and Tradition," *Religion in Life* XXI, No. 1 (Autumn 1952), 551–562, copyright 1952 by Pierce and Smith; "The Relevance of Christian Ethics," *Religion in Life* XIV, No. 2 (Spring 1945), 205–215, copyright 1945, by Whitmore and Stone; "Images of Man and the American Scene," from Randolph C. Miller and others, *What Is the Image of Man?* (Philadelphia: United Church Press, 1959), pp. 1–13, by permission of Pilgrim Press; "Christian Education as a Theological Discipline and Method," *Religious Education* XLVIII, No. 6 (November–December 1953), 409–414, and from *Who Are We?* ed. John H.

Westerhoff III (Birmingham: Religious Education Press, 1978), pp. 110–122; "Some Clarifying Thoughts about Religious Education," *The Living Light* 13, No. 1 (Winter 1976), 487–498; "Anxiety and Learning," *Pastoral Psychology* (February 1964), 11–15; "How to Use the Bible," *Resource* (November 1969), 9–11, and (December 1969), 5–8, also *The South East Asia Journal of Theology* 11 (Spring 1970), 77–82; "The Discipline of Theology in the University and the Divinity School," reprinted with permission of Macmillan Publishing Co., Inc., from *Does the Church Know How to Teach?* edited by Kendig Brubaker Cully. Copyright © 1970 by Macmillan Publishing Co., Inc., pp. 289–313.

I have quoted from various translations of the Bible, which are identified as follows:

E   *What Jesus Taught* by Burton Scott Easton. Copyright 1938 by Burton Scott Easton. Nashville: Abingdon Press.

G   *The Complete Bible: An American Translation* by Edgar J. Goodspeed and J. M. Powis Smith. Copyright 1939 by the University of Chicago Press.

KJ   *King James Version*

M   *The Bible: A New Translation* by James Moffatt. Copyright 1922, 1935, 1950 by Harper & Row.

NEB   *The New English Bible.* Copyright by the Delegates of the Oxford University Press and the Syndics of the Cambridge University Press, 1961, 1970

P   *The New Testament in Modern English* by J. B. Phillips. Copyright 1947, 1952, 1955, 1957 by the Macmillan Co. and 1958 by J. B. Phillips.

RSV   *Revised Standard Version of the Bible.* Copyright 1946, 1952 by the Division of Christian Education, National Council of Churches.

TEV   *Today's English Version of the New Testament.* Copyright 1966 by the American Bible Society.

20   *The Twentieth Century New Testament.* Copyright 1900–
        1904 by the Fleming H. Revell Co.

I am indebted to these and other publishers in cases where
they have given me permission to quote copyrighted material,
indicated in the footnotes.

Randolph Crump Miller
The Divinity School
Yale University

1

God Is What God Does

The primary resource for understanding Christian education is the theological position implicitly or explicitly held. One's theology determines crucial decisions about the nature of the learner, the content to be taught, and the methods to be used. Because theology is related to all the information one has in the secular field, the educator makes use of the best knowledge coming from education as a discipline in itself, from the psychology of learning, and from the other social sciences. Theology is not used to undercut other ways of acquiring knowledge and it does not have an authority which denies knowledge otherwise achieved. We make use of theology to provide an overall view of the nature and function of an education which can be called Christian. The data on which theology builds are not the private insights of experts but are public and available to all.

The Christian faith is based on the Jewish and Christian movements in history. It claims to be based on a revelation that centers on the events surrounding the birth, life, death and resurrection of Jesus Christ, who becomes the focal point of Christian education. Revelation is a theological position, interpreted in many different ways throughout history, and how it is interpreted determines one's approach to education. If one believes that revelation is contained in the contents of the Bible, and that the propositions derived from the Bible are a summary of revealed theology, both the contents and the method of education will be affected by this presupposition. If one assumes that revelation centers entirely in the events surrounding Jesus

Christ, so that the proclamation of Jesus Christ is the heart of education, the use of content through proclamation will be the primary approach. If revelation turns on a transaction by which Christ bought humanity out of its sins, the emphasis will be on the sinfulness of the learner at the expense of stressing the learner's worth in the sight of God. Horace Bushnell many years ago reacted against a conversion formula in favor of a nurturing formula.

If, with William Temple, revelation is interpreted in terms of the coincidence of a revealing event and an appreciative mind, which goes on all the time, education becomes an ongoing process based on a deeper understanding of the events of daily life as well as on the history of revelation in the Christian tradition. All events are not equally revealing, and experiences of human beings vary tremendously. All existence is to some degree a medium of revelation. But some events are more conspicuous than others, and some minds are more sensitive than others. "From all this it follows that there is no such thing as revealed truth. There are truths of revelation, that is to say, propositions which express the results of correct thinking concerning revelation; but they are not themselves directly revealed."[1] The greatest revelations come from the most significant persons responding to the most significant events. The interpretation of these events can be appreciated by the learners as they are exposed to the story of how God acts in the cosmos, in history, and in personal and social experience.

Christian education in recent years has been based on one or another interpretation of revelation. Traditional theology, on the whole, has stressed the contents of the Bible and propositions interpreting it. Neo-orthodoxy, although greatly varied in its position, insists that there is no criterion of revelation except the

1. William Temple, *Nature, Man and God* (London: Macmillan, 1934), p. 317.

revelation itself; there is no external, rational, or empirical test. This leads to an emphasis on the revelation of God's attitude toward us rather than of knowledge of God's nature. The liberal view, held by many religious educators in the 1930s, frankly equated revelation with discovery as an ongoing human enterprise. Thus, theology could emerge out of the educational process.

The emphasis in this book is on revelation as the coincidence of God's action and the human response. It assumes that God is at work in the world and can be known by human beings. There are disclosures which come to human beings and as these disclosures are assimilated there is new knowledge. Such disclosures need to be tested for their validity by some kind of empirical procedure and rational analysis. They are followed by a new or renewed commitment to that which or who is disclosed. The central figure of this disclosure for the Christian is Jesus Christ. Thus, education stresses the need for insight or disclosure as essential to the process.

This view of revelation leads to theological procedures which are empirical, pragmatic, and sometimes pluralistic. As we will see, process metaphysics can become a basis for theology, naturalism can become a basis for a natural theology that includes revelation, and an analogy of organism can be illuminating for both theology and education. The primary question for theological discourse becomes, What does God do?

HOW WE GOT HERE

We pick up the story in 1932, when *The Christian Century* published each week for twenty-five weeks a series of articles on "Is There a God?" The participants were two empirical theologians, Douglas Clyde Macintosh of Yale and Henry Nelson Wieman of Chicago, and the cheerful atheist, Max Otto, of Wisconsin. Otto made positive statements about the nonexis-

tence of God, and the two theists criticized each other. Both
Macintosh and Wieman believed that by the empirical method
of observation, experiment, and reason one could establish belief
in the existence of God. Macintosh accused Wieman of being
like "a tight-rope walker at a circus. At one time it almost
seemed as if he were going to come down on the side of theism."
What irked Macintosh was that Wieman talked about God as
"the growth of meaning and value in the world" and saw no
evidence pointing to God as a person, while Wieman thought
that Macintosh, although starting with empirical evidence, pro-
ceeded to interpret God in terms of human wishes rather than
the facts. Furthermore, Macintosh was guilty, said Wieman, of
relying on the religious consciousness, with results that were
subjective.

Nothing was really established by these conversations except
the need for even more careful use of empirical methods. Both
Macintosh and Wieman went on to write much more fully about
their respective positions, and empirical theology continued to
be considered an important discipline for a few more years. But
with the rising pessimism about human goodness and the threat
of war this kind of theology was largely ignored from about 1939
until its revival in connection with process theology in the
1960s.

In 1939, *The Christian Century* printed thirty-five articles on
"How My Mind Has Changed in the Last Decade." Sixteen of
the writers mentioned Karl Barth, but only three admitted a
favorable reaction. The emphasis was still on some brand of
liberalism. Halford Luccock entitled his article, "With No
Apologies to Barth!" At this time, Charles Hartshorne was making an impact with his process thinking and especially with his
logical analysis of the ways in which we may think of God as both
absolutely and relatively perfect, so that God is unsurpassable
except by self; this analysis opened the door to thinking about
God as one who suffers and therefore changes in response to the

world. The empirical theologians leaned toward such process thinking, but at this point they had not worked out the implications.

With the coming of World War II there was a Barthian blackout of empirical theology. The emphasis was placed on the revelation of a wholly other God. Natural theology was at least suspect and in some cases it was ruled out altogether. Macintosh characterized Barthian theology as "reactionary irrationalism," but as a younger generation took over theological discourse, Barthian ways of thinking predominated. Slowly the whole of theology was permeated by what is called neo-orthodoxy.

The effects were seen almost immediately in the field of religious education. Harrison Elliott wrote what was probably the last significant treatment of religious education based on liberal theology, *Can Religious Education Be Christian?* The changing theological climate was illustrated by H. Shelton Smith in 1941 with his thoroughgoing attack on all forms of liberalism in education in *Faith and Nurture.* A committee under Luther A. Weigle was already modifying the position of the International Council of Religious Education with a 1940 pamphlet, *Christian Education Today.* In 1944, Paul H. Vieth headed a committee that restated the theological and educational insights of the Council in the direction of the prevailing winds. An attempt was made in 1950 to bridge the gap between content and method by understanding the place of theology in Christian education in my *The Clue to Christian Education.*

During this time, most churches held to traditional biblical orthodoxy which was only slightly swayed by developments in either neo-orthodoxy or liberalism. Yet there were disturbing changes taking place. The emphases of the culture as a whole were influenced by secularism, scientific discoveries, and technology. There were criticisms of theology from within as theologians began to take account of these secular forces. John A.T. Robinson's *Honest to God* in 1963 was a reaction to standard orthodoxy rather than to neo-orthodoxy or liberalism, and the response of lay people in both England and the United States revealed that there were many unanswered questions.

We were ready, then, for the "death of God" movement. Paul van Buren's *The Secular Meaning of the Gospel* in 1963 pointed directly to Barth's concept of God. The logical positivists with their demand for verification addressed themselves mostly to traditional supernaturalism. Many concepts of God were dead, but that did not mean that God was dead. Henry Nelson Wieman looked at the carnage and concluded that no one was talking about *his* concept of God, for an empirical approach required the kind of verification that the logical positivists were demanding.

Certain developments in theology pointed to a recovery of belief in God. Following Bultmann and Heidegger, Schubert Ogden moved toward an existentialist approach in *Christ without Myth* (1961). However, Ogden was also steeped in the thought of Wieman, Hartshorne, and Alfred North Whitehead; in *The Reality of God* (1966) he moved toward an empirically based process theology, although with the pointedness of existentialism. About the same time, John B. Cobb, Jr., building on Hartshorne and Whitehead, developed *A Christian Natural Theology* (1965). When in 1969 Bernard Meland edited *The Future of Empirical Theology*, it seemed that there had been both a recovery of empiricism and an enrichment of it. The specifically Christian developments became evident in *The Spirit and Forms of Love* (1968), by Daniel Day Williams, which Cobb called "the first systematic process theology."

If we broaden our historical perspective, we will see that there have been constantly changing viewpoints throughout the history of Christianity. The biblical faith came into contact with Greek thought, and this cross-fertilization led to a new perspective on the world. When Thomas Aquinas adopted Aristotle for his philosophical framework, another world view replaced the earlier one. Kant, Hegel, and Kierkegaard provided new ways of looking on things. Today we have modern physics and process philosophy. Each paradigm that evolves not only determines the data we select but also the way we interpret them. In each change of paradigm, data previously ignored have forced themselves upon human consciousness, effecting a conversion to the new paradigm. It has occurred in science as well as in theology, and it is through such a process that human knowledge is advanced.

THE PROCESS PARADIGM

The common paradigm in secular knowledge today is determined by developments in science, technology, communication, political procedures, and, ultimately, a world view that comes not only from recent discoveries but also from new ways of looking on old data. Wittgenstein once said that "the problems are solved, not by giving new information, but by arranging what we have always known."[2] So we are called to reexamine data from the biblical and historical traditions and our common everyday experiences as well as to interpret new data.

Given a process paradigm, we see reality as a process of becoming and perishing, with new beginnings building on what has perished. The model is that of the human body, with its interrelationships whereby plural activities constitute a unity; the constant process of becoming and perishing is the key to understanding it. The process paradigm evokes a picture of the world that is consistent with the findings of modern science and yet is specifically religious in its orientation.

Within this framework, the starting point of theology is the study of the relationship between human beings and a superhuman reality we call God. But even to assume such a reality as

2. Ludwig Wittgenstein, *Philosophical Investigations* (New York: Macmillan, 1958), p. 47[c].

God leads to a careful examination of our experiences to determine how we can know how any thing or entity can be known to exist. We reflect on these experiences and make sure that our concepts are coherent with other concepts understood within this paradigm, and then build a world view that includes our religious beliefs as part of a coherent system.

This approach makes use of radical empiricism, pragmatism, and a pluralistic world view. Radical empiricism, as derived from William James, is based on an analysis of our experience of objects and the relationships between objects, between fact and value, with a testing process to check any conclusions. The pragmatic aspects, which involve us in checking whether our ideas work, also include value judgments; for a tree is known by its fruits, and faith without works is dead. Unless we impose a premature unity on our interpretation, there are always some loose ends in this kind of thinking. All experience is seen as being within the process of becoming and perishing, with God as an active entity within the process working toward value, and as a transcendent factor who is everlasting.[3]

Such a theology becomes biblical when the methods are used in dealing with the biblical record. The Bible provides a historical statement of religious development, a dynamic and vital interpretation of the search for God, and primary data for any normative approach to Christianity. It is the basic source for Christian beliefs. All the diversities of Christian theology claim the Bible as their source, and this claim places upon us the responsibility to deal intelligently with all that we can know about the Bible.

Seen in this way, the Bible is not centered in humanity. Although it is a record of the human search for God, the emphasis

3. These views are spelled out in detail in the writings of the process theologians and summarized in my books, *The American Spirit in Theology* (Philadelphia: Pilgrim Press, 1974) and *This We Can Believe* (New York: Hawthorn-Seabury, 1976).

is on God. It provides historical data open to human interpretation, but the theme is the acts of God. The message from God is received by the men and women of the Bible, sometimes muted, sometimes distorted, and sometimes with amazing clarity. It speaks to a different view of the nature of the world, and therefore we need to see how it fits into our paradigm.

LOOKING ON GOD

When empiricism is used to seek out and interpret the data about God, we begin with the statement that God *is* what God *does*. Revelation has to do with events and not propositions. Therefore, we identify God with the creative order of the world, a process which transforms human beings, brings values from a potential to an actual state, and works to overcome evil with good. God is that process by which we are made new, strengthened, directed, comforted, forgiven, saved, and by which we are lured into feelings of wonder, awe, and reverence. This may not be all that we can know about God, but as Daniel Day Williams suggested in reference to Wieman, this view of God as creative order "actually stated what has become the practice of people in wide areas of our culture, including much of the practice of religious institutions. When we ask what [people] actually put their trust in as revealed by their actions, we see that we may require something like 'creative interchange' to describe the operative process to which we give our attention and even our devotion."[4]

Beyond the empirical findings as part of this approach to religious knowledge, there are what William James called "over-beliefs." Here we move into the area of analogies, models, and metaphors. We use words normally restricted to human relations

4. In *Charles Hartshorne and Henry Nelson Wieman,* ed. William S. Minor (Carbondale: Foundation for Creative Philosophy, 1969), p. 56.

to describe our experience with God. We think of God *as* holy; we experience God *as* just and righteous; we construe God *as* persuasive and steadfast love; we see God *as* good. These are ways of looking *on* God *as* having certain characteristics, and as long as we don't take them literally and make God in our own image, it is a helpful way to think.

Process theologians think of reality as becoming and perishing, and this process could degenerate into chaos if there were no limits. God is thought of as dipolar, as having both an abstract and a concrete nature. As abstract, God is the principle of limitation, the source of potentialities waiting to be born, the primordial reality which structures what would otherwise be chaos. The aims or purpose of God reside in the abstract nature.

God is also the concrete process which works in and through nature and humanity. Thus, when we think of God's consequent nature, we are pointing to the immanent process which is the persuasive love of God at work. It is God's grace, God's free gift of self, God's concrete presence, which we experience. God's abstract nature is everlasting and does not change, while God's concrete nature participates in the life of the universe and is affected by it. God suffers, enjoys, changes. So God affects history and is affected by the joys and suffering of humankind. Insofar as we share in the subjective aims of God, we are on the right track. We will return to this theme.

God is not the all, as in pantheism, and God is not separate from the world, as in deism. God is both cause and effect, is independent as primordial and involved as consequent, is good and yet suffers from evil. "In God we live and move and have our being" (Acts 17:28). This is sometimes labeled *panentheism*. This dipolar diety is one God, for the abstract nature is included within the consequent nature.

The emphasis on God's love suggests an approach to the problem of evil. Whitehead was adamant that the "brief Galilean vision" pointed not to a monarchial deity but to God working through persuasive love and therefore not in complete control.

There was no doctrine of predestination, and evil was beyond God's purpose as something to be overcome with good. Evil is a brute motive force, and "the fact of the instability of evil is the moral order of the world."[5] If chance, novelty, and freedom are seen as existing independently of God's aims, they may either be aligned with God's aims or be opposed to them. Every possibility of good opens up an equivalent possibility of evil. Thus evil is opposed to God as external, and God has an environment. We can account for the world we live in and still have faith in God.

IMPLICATIONS FOR CHRISTIANITY

The implications of this concept of God for Christianity are significant. It is a theology that is both incarnational and sacramental. God comes into human life at all times, for God is immanent and is capable of ingression. There is a basis here for understanding how God was present in and worked through Jesus as the Christ and how the spirit of God or Christ may be present in the sacraments of the church. God draws us into community, and this act becomes a basis for understanding the church.

Because this kind of thinking sees the individual in relation to society, keeping the independence of the actual entity and yet seeing reality as societal and organic, religious beliefs lead to faith, worship, and action. Religion may begin with solitariness, but it expresses itself in community. It may begin with an experience which needs to be interpreted within the framework of a process paradigm, but its fruits are in achieving personal and social values. And because God is "a companion—the fellow-sufferer who understands," the concern for the oppressed is central. Thus, social action fits into this overall view of Christianity.

The future is open. There are no guarantees that God will take

5. Alfred North Whitehead, *Religion in the Making* (New York: Macmillan, 1926, renewed 1954 by Evelyn Whitehead), p. 95; see also David Griffin, *God, Power and Evil* (Philadelphia: Westminster Press, 1976).

over. If "God's power is the worship that he inspires," we find that great responsibility is thrown on human beings. If chance and the emergence of novelty are operating principles of the universe, and if human freedom is a crucial factor, the future is not known even to God. There is a "creative advance into novelty," and in this advance God may surprise the world and the world may surprise God. Thus, there is hope of liberation for the oppressed, of strength to achieve values, of comfort to face unsurmountable obstacles, and of wisdom to distinguish which is which. "Beloved, we are God's children now; it does not yet appear what we shall be" (I Jn 3:2,RSV).

One reason for the great variety of religious beliefs is that at the center of all religious experience there is mystery. This mystery remains such, to be pointed at or shown but not to be explained. The limitation of language is that words can only point or show. Words can become an invitation to share an experience or even to share a paradigm, and in some cases they may be very persuasive, but meaning is found in those words only after there is recognition of a shared experience. The heart of religion is still the holy or the numinous, to which we respond with awe, even dread, as well as reverence.

Thus, one of the most significant empirical anchors is the shared experience of worship, but this sharing depends to some extent on common perceptions, feelings, and beliefs. We still have to participate in the use of words if our beliefs are to be meaningful. Often we see the meaning for ourselves and others when these beliefs lead to commitment and action, for faith without works is dead.

We start with a paradigm that accounts for the data of our experiences in all areas of human endeavor. If the paradigm is based on an empirical and process methodology and a philosophy of organism, the resulting Christian beliefs will be something like what we have briefly described. At least they point to the reality of the world as many people perceive that world today. It is a way of viewing things with a respectable history supported by some outstanding thinkers who are devoted Christians. It has implications for the way we think about and employ religious education in our churches and schools.

RELIGION IN EDUCATION

Alfred North Whitehead wrote that "the essence of education is that it be religious."[6] He meant by this that the inculcation of duty and reverence was central. We have potential control over events and we have responsibility to be knowledgeable, all within a framework of reference that includes the whole of nature. Because all of nature is interrelated, we have an ecological model for our world view and for our education. Thus, to be religious is to be concerned for all entities that are interrelated with each other and with God. The learners come to an understanding of their world as a space which has room for other living beings and inorganic entities as well. There develops a reverence for life that carries over into all their relationships.

Although Whitehead has much to say about precision in education, along with romance and vision, he warns against premature precision or closure. He advises us to seek simplicity but to distrust it. Particularly in the field of religion, he reminds us, rigidity of belief is deadly and simple solutions are bogus ones. Logic may be an exact instrument, but it needs the backing of common sense, and the exactness becomes a fake. There is a tentativeness about all knowledge, and especially religious knowledge. This is as it should be, for the crucial factor in religion is the relationship between the worshiper and deity, which is a matter of certitude rather than certainty. Ian Ramsey put it concisely: "Being sure in religion does not entail being

6. Alfred North Whitehead, *The Aims of Education* (New York: Macmillan, 1929, renewed 1957 by Evelyn Whitehead), p. 14.

certain in theology."[7] Thus we may grow in our knowledge of God without being threatened by the loss of our commitment to the reality for which the word God stands.

Whitehead has good advice to give on many aspects of religious education that will emerge as our argument proceeds. We may note some overall observations. The human mind is an active, participating, delicate, and responsive function which lives in the present. "The present is all there is. It is holy ground; for it is the past and it is the future."[8] The one subject matter of education is all of life, which is why Whitehead can speak of all education as religious. But when specialism in education is excluded education is destroyed, so we need to note the special interests and skills of individual learners and to take steps to promote their potential specialties.

Knowledge as such does not have value. "That knowledge which adds greatness to character is knowledge so handled as to transform every phase of immediate experience."[9] This can lead to freedom, which is a dominant note; but along the way there needs to be discipline and even "a certain ruthless definiteness" in order to provide for direction and pace, so that the learner learns at a suitable speed and attains precise knowledge for immediate use so that it may be retained. This combination of freedom and discipline can lead to a wisdom beyond knowledge. One cannot be wise without some knowledge, but it is possible to have knowledge and no resulting wisdom. "Wisdom is the way in which knowledge is held."[10] Religious education in particular has sought this goal, but it has frequently failed to achieve it, chiefly because it has been caught up in petty moralism and rigid

7. Ian T. Ramsey, On Being Sure in Religion (London: Athlone Press, 1965), p. 47.
8. Whitehead, Aims of Education, p. 3.
9. Whitehead, Aims of Education, p. 32.
10. Whitehead, Aims of Education, p. 30.

dogmatism. Such petty morality "is the deadly enemy of religion." Rigid dogmatism has been used in religious education at the expense of recognizing the stages of growth. "No part of education has more to gain from attention to the rhythmic law of growth than has moral and religious education. Whatever be the right way to formulate religious truths, it is death to religion to insist on a premature stage of precision. The vitality of religion is shown by the way in which the religious spirit has survived the ordeal of religious education."[11]

Seen from this perspective, there are many motives behind the human search for religious truth, but probably the ultimate one is the sense of value. The response of awe in the presence of the holy includes an overarching sense of the value of the religious object. Wonder at the mystery of life calls for some sort of deity as an explanation. Reverence operates in those who are aware of beauty, truth, and goodness in other people and in God. Curiosity is aroused in most of us as we are faced with the teachings of the historic religions and with the advances of modern scientific knowledge. There is a need to belong that makes fellowship with God and community with other human beings central to a religious outlook. This sense of value emerges partly in the aesthetic response to beauty, but it is found also in high morality and the incredible labors of those who have found a meaningful goal.

These educational insights come from Whitehead as a philosopher of organism, a position which interprets all entities as interrelated in a pluralistic organic whole. Other educators may reach similar conclusions, and they may be consistent with Whitehead's position even when not derived directly from it.

We need to look again at process theology and further educational implications in the next chapter.

---

11. Whitehead, *Aims of Education*, p. 39.

2

Process Thinking

The opening chapter has brought us into the manner of process theology and some of its implications for religious education. We need now to probe a bit more deeply into some of the concepts of process thinking and its relation to other theological questions, especially those posed by developments in what is known as liberation theology, including the ways in which blacks, feminists, and those from the undeveloped and developing countries seek for answers to their probings in the light of their social and political conditions.

Process thinking is a natural outcome of the revolution in cultural assumptions and expectations, as derived partly from mathematical physics but also from advances in genetics, medicine, and the social sciences. At the same time, there is a rejection of the current materialistic and deterministic assumptions of some scientific endeavors.

Theology sooner or later tends to reflect the secular ways of thinking. Indeed, one of the primary functions of theology in its search for truth and the means for communicating it is to give an understanding of the secular, everyday world from a Christian standpoint. If today's thinking is derived from experience and reflection on it, from pragmatic tests of what works or makes sense, and from speculation about the nature of the cosmos that is pluralistic and processive, then theology must relate its historical and biblical insights or revelations to this perspective.

This approach assumes the close relation of theology and philosophy, a relation that has been consistent throughout the history of Christian thought, with very few exceptions. The approach moves from philosophical analysis to natural theology, which includes revelation as something available to the human mind. This is distinguished from supernatural revelation that may either be built on the findings of natural theology, as Thomas Aquinas built on Aristotle's philosophy, or it may be developed by ignoring natural theology or even denying that natural theology has a right to exist, as in the case of Karl Barth.

The approach in this book, as we indicated in the opening chapter, is by means of a view of revelation that operates in the natural realm and leaves open the possibility of supernatural revelation. As we indicate in chapter four, the empirical method moves comfortably within the domain of revelation as described by William Temple in *Nature, Man and God*, but it does not move beyond the overbeliefs that are consistent with the data.

THE WORLD WE LIVE IN

Process philosophy provides a world view or metaphysics leading to a framework for thinking about the nature of the religious object. It interprets God as being the central and all-encompassing entity related to all other entities. It gives a view of the cosmos that accounts for the working of God, for the development of novelty, chance, and freedom, for the experiences of suffering and evil as well as those of transformation and joy, for the meaning of living in community and for the validity of being an individual, for understanding that all existence is a matter of becoming and perishing in the context of a continuity underwritten by God, for grasping the meaning of the past and present as they point to an open future—open even to God himself. It reflects many biblical insights, although it questions such accretions of classical theology as the doctrines of predesti-

nation, omnipotence, and immutability; it sees God as persuasive and suffering love rather than as a dictator so separated from
the human condition that God is incapable of change or suffering. It implies a rethinking of Christology and an enriching of
the doctrine of the Holy Spirit.

These claims may be questioned, but the difficulty lies in
deciding whether they can be assimilated to the Christian tradition. Even this difficulty, however, may be bypassed, for one may
ask how process thinking fits into a non-Christocentric Christianity (as among some Unitarians) or how it can be taken up by
Jewish thinking and education. It may be, as others would insist,
that process thinking provides a way of understanding the claims
of other religions, especially Buddhism, and therefore Christianity is to be seen as only one among many cultural claimants
to human loyalty. The approach of this chapter, however, stays
within the confines of the Christian tradition.

Let us look at process thinking. It begins by considering the
nature of the human body as an analogy. The human organism
functions as a whole and yet has many parts, and each part makes
its own contribution to the health of the total organism (see
I Cor 12:12–20). This human body is in a constant process of
becoming and perishing, and its new becoming is the outcome of
its previous perishing. Yet within this change, there is a self-
identity. Just as a baby keeps developing, it remains the same
person, even when there are transforming experiences that make
one refer to "a new person."

Human beings relate to their environment through their
senses. They survive because of their capacity not only to use
their strength but also because they have the capacity to reflect
on their experiences and to act accordingly. But the human
body, furthermore, has a strong sense of the whole: there are
experiences which draw in the whole body rather than just the
senses in particular. We experience the whole body in action as
it responds with an act of commitment, as it enters an aesthetic

experience, as it worships God. We do not sense such events piecemeal but as a whole.

Human beings have a kind of empathy for others, a feeling of their feelings, a mutual interpenetration. The use of the word "know" in the Bible refers both to Abraham's sexual relations with Sara and to his experience of Yahweh. Such an experience has been called a "prehension," which is a vague affective tone, a feeling or concern or grasping by which the whole body becomes related to another whole body. In this sense, we can prehend God and God can prehend us. "You will know that I am in my Father, and you in me, and I in you" (Jn 14:20).

The body analogy points also to the social nature of reality. Mental and spiritual health depends on belonging, and among human beings the will to belong may be stronger than the will to live. Alienation can lead to suicide. We become persons through interpersonal relations, and when these relations break down the result is one or other defect in the development of potential. But the ideal remains: "If one member suffers, all suffer together; if one member is honored, all rejoice together" (I Cor 12:26, RSV).

When this analogy is applied to the universe as a whole, it proves remarkably apt. The solar system is a process, and neither the earth nor the sun is the center of the universe. Many different systems are related in ways we do not yet understand. We may not understand modern physics, but we become capable of living in a universe which is pictured by the theory of relativity and the development of nuclear energy. When the astronauts read the story of creation from somewhere behind the moon, and it has meaning to them and to us, we are the richer for gaining a new understanding of the myth of the Garden of Eden.

Quantum theory may be equally mysterious to most of us, but it helps to know that none of us has seen an electron. Yet we accept the principle that the behavior of groups of electrons can be predicted even if the behavior of a single electron cannot.

This leads to the insight that there is an element of chance or indeterminacy at the center of things. Such statistical knowledge helps us to understand human responsibility in the world, and it allows a place for freedom, but it also provides for future shock when predictions do not work out.

Process thinking helps us to understand the theory of evolution. Because of the view of process, we do not get caught up in automatic progress or continuous development toward the good. When we hear of the amount of utter waste in the evolutionary process, the relation of the suitability for survival to chance variations both within organisms and in the environment, the mutations of genes, the tinkering today with natural processes, we are appalled at the great cost of evolution. Creativity is at work, governed not only by a principle of limitation to guard us from chaos but subject also to chance and the development of unpredictable novelty. Yet there are principles of survival other than animal strength. Ants, bees, and chimpanzees survive because they form communities. Organisms, whether animal or human, create their own environments and have the power to destroy them.

Human beings emerged from such a process as this, probably because of the development of mind as the capacity to think, to invent, to imagine, to control the environment, and to do new things. The Bible claimed the establishment of human control or lordship over nature, which has turned into one of the more dangerous doctrines that threaten our continued existence. Modern science, when it has no moral controls, can lead to the discoveries in biology and medicine which culminate in the dehumanizing of persons. Yet, through it all, human beings developed a proper sense of worth which rose to the level of morality and ultimately to faith in God.

One does not ask a kitten what kind of cat it wants to become. But one does ask children what they expect to be and assumes that they will have answers that reflect unrealized ideals. In the purpose and commitment to ideals leading to action, we discover the distinction between human beings and other animals; it may be only a difference of degree, but it is what the understanding of human beings is all about.

GOD AND PERSUASIVE LOVE

If what we have described so briefly reflects the kind of world most people live in, it has implications for religion. An over-simplified gospel will not do. Religion is based on a vision of what is all around us, something real and yet pointing beyond our farthest reach. We can know something, but the farther we penetrate into its meaning, the more it dissolves in ultimate mystery.

For process thought, the most important claim is that a God of persuasive love is working for us and with us for the coming of the kingdom. Such a deity does not have coercive power. God inspires our worship and persuades us through love. We respond to God in our freedom and take on ourselves the responsibility of relating our purpose to God's more general purpose (our "subjective aim" to God's).

Most process thinkers agree that classical Christianity moved quickly from the loving deity portrayed by Jesus to the models derived from Egyptian, Persian, Greek, and Roman monarchies, with the emphasis on power rather than love, and therefore lost the capacity to come to terms with the place and meaning of evil, with the idea that God as love can suffer, and with the insight that there can be change and development in God, who shares our enjoyments and sufferings.

As we explained in chapter one, God is thought of as dipolar. God is both beyond the world and in it. God is not the world (pantheism) but the world in some sense is in God and God in the world, without being identical with the world (panentheism). God has an abstract and primordial nature that does not change and is the principle of concretion or limitation that guards against chaos. We do not literally know God in the abstract nature, but God is understood as the necessary factor and the chief exemplification of all the principles of life. This is one pole of God's dipolar nature.

The other pole (which includes the abstract nature) is the concrete one, known to us by our experiences of God in action as persuasive love. This is God as fully actual, who takes into this nature the meanings of the perishing past so that the becoming future emerges. What happens does not fade from God's memory, but God shares in our joys and sufferings. God is conscious and personal, patient and loving, and the source of all our values. In God's tender wisdom, God seeks to save the world through the attainment of value.

But there is opposition to God's aims. Evil is real, and God is not responsible for it. This limitation of God's power marks off process theology from traditional concepts. There is no all-powerful and all-good deity who permits or even wills evil; evil is not good in disguise or the absence of good or the work of the devil. Evil is opposed to God's love; it is due to freedom, chance or accident, the emergence of novelty, and the sheer malevolence of human beings. God's persuasive love cannot eliminate it, although evil is unstable and does lead to its own destruction. However, even in God there seems to be an ultimate point at which there is a certain ruthlessness, which may be God's judgment on evil. Some process thinkers would insist on a degree of coercion at this point, as a function of the principle of limitation.

How does this view of evil affect God's perfection? The process theologians claim that perfection means that God is unsurpassable in most aspects and surpassable only by self in other aspects, and therefore God is a deity capable of change in the light of God's "prehension" of what occurs. Because God's perfection is that of love, and love is open to both joy and suffering, God shares with us in the effort to overcome evil.

But if and when human beings do not align themselves with

God's "subjective aim," the results are evil, and God does not coerce them or outflank them. They must accept their own responsibility and cannot blame God for moral evil. Human beings discover that God's intention for them is to live together in community, functioning together but in diversity as a single body. Because there is chance, because there is novelty, because there are processes opposed to God's purpose, there is evil in the world—both that caused by humanity and that which can be called fate or luck. There may be illness or suffering or death which has no connection with morality or human intentions. What insurance companies improperly call "an act of God" is precisely where God does not act, except to "prehend" the meaning of an event.

Religious persons, from this point of view, are those who become aware of God's presence (Whitehead's consequent nature of God) and who may be transformed by God's love to align themselves as best they can with what they conceive to be God's purpose. In this way, they become responsible persons, within a community of responsible persons, and the members of the community seek in their freedom and autonomy to make decisions and take actions which are consistent with what they perceive as God's "subjective aim."

God's "subjective aim" may be understood as God's purpose for history. Insofar as human beings align themselves with God's purpose, the events of history have positive meaning, but when humanity fails to perceive or agree with God's aim, the results are evil. Process theologians are not in agreement as to whether God's aims are general or specific, but certainly they are embodied as specific in individuals or groups, and thus become personal or interpersonal both as cause and effect. Daniel Day Williams claims that this creative advance in human experience is the work of God. "We experience the weaving together into one community of being of many strands of action, feeling, pain, language, memory, and expectation. [Humanity] is in the weaving, but [it] is not the weaver."[1] Whitehead refers to this as the kingdom of God among us. Whatever is taken up into God is transformed and then becomes a new influence on humanity.

It is not simply up to human beings, although humanity has great responsibilities for insight and action. Persons are dependent on other human beings and on God. Bernard E. Meland speaks of living "upon the grace of one another."[2] God's creative goodness works for us, and when we resist God this creativity works against us. God is both creative and redemptive and is the source of our energies.

RELIGIOUS EDUCATION

As we look at the implications of process theology for religious education, we need to remind ourselves of the number of theologians, both Protestant and Catholic, making use of process terms today.[3] We could deal exclusively with Whitehead,[4] but it may be wiser to widen the scope. Whitehead has reminded us that all education is religious, and that religion points to the rightness of things. It leads to a combination of duty and reverence, not just to a mystical vision. Such education deals with us as total persons by offering us some interpretations of our experiences and of our commitment in the light of our worth as persons and of our awareness of God's presence.

Remember that the response to the religious vision is wor-

1. Daniel Day Williams, in Bernard E. Meland, ed., *The Future of Empirical Theology* (Chicago: University of Chicago Press, 1969), p. 190.
2. Bernard E. Meland, *Faith and Culture* (New York: Oxford University Press, 1953), p. 177.
3. Besides Whitehead, Charles Hartshorne and Bernard E. Meland are in the vanguard of first generation thinkers. Schubert M. Ogden, Daniel Day Williams, John B. Cobb, Jr., William A. Christian, and Norman Pittenger are outstanding members of a middle group. Then there are David Griffin, Delwin Brown, Gene Reeves, Lewis S. Ford, Eugene H. Peters, Gregory Baum, Ewert Cousins, Peter Hamilton, and many others.
4. See my "Whitehead and Religious Education," *Religious Education* (May–June 1973), pp. 325–332.

ship.[5] The beginning of religious education, therefore, may very well be through participating in a worshiping congregation, even at a young age, and then reflecting on its meaning in terms of the capacity of the learner. There may be a kind of social conditioning or enculturation, for certainly those who do not share in the nurturing process of worship from the beginning of their lives have difficulty later on when they face worship as a foreign experience.

In worship, the organic relatedness of all creation with God should become obvious. Here we find a sharing by human beings in some degree of social solidarity reaching out to a deity whose power is simply the inspiring of this worship. It is an end in itself, an expression of awareness leading to deeper and more profound awareness as we reflect on its meaning. This is not something that is automatic, however. Like any other aesthetic experience, we approach it with some kind of theoretical expection and see its deeper meanings as we reflect upon and then return to it. Educationally, worship provides an experience upon which we reflect, using our powers of analysis and appreciation to bring about greater sensitivity and deeper understanding.

We also have experiences in our solitariness. These are even more difficult to talk about than a shared corporate worship, but because they are individualized they tend to be self-validating. Yet error can creep in, and we return to the community for verification. In almost any group we could gather these solitary experiences, much as did William James in *The Varieties of Religious Experience*. They may not seem religious in any traditional sense, but they may be moments of wonder, awe, or simply the sense of the rightness of things even though we are in the wrong. This, says Whitehead, is not a direct vision of a personal deity, but is an alignment of our aims with the subjective aim of God. If we can "prehend" God, there is an immediacy, a profound feel-

5. See *Science and the Modern World* (New York: Macmillan, 1925, renewed 1953 by Evelyn Whitehead), p. 276; Mentor edition, p. 192. See chapter 11 on worship, below.

ing, a mutual interpenetration which must be accounted for. The experience may be transforming or supportive, and it may illuminate the issues of life in terms of commitment, decision, and behavior.

But human beings do not remain in solitariness; we must return to the community, and if we are able to share our experience the community judges whether it may be considered valid. Thus we are protected from hallucinations, private forms of self-pity, projections of our own wishes, and other distortions which may seem real enough to the individual at the time. The community of faith is bound to take seriously any claims that are made, but it also is committed to make a responsible judgment on the report.

Many people, I have suggested, have experiences like this which they do not identify as religious. They are so caught up in traditional language and concepts that they are not open to the "lure of feeling" which Whitehead mentions. They need "a suggestion from without" in order to see and grasp what has been given to them by grace. The educational process is a way of making suggestions from without, providing structures by which we can see the meaning of a seemingly unstructured experience, enabling a person to grasp the dynamic nature of God against the background of an inherited view that is more static.

The raw material of theology is experience, either our own or something we can appropriate. The beliefs that develop must be consistent with such experiences or capable of evoking them. A sterile dogma is religiously useless. God as an available companion, as persuasive love and a fellow sufferer who understands, becomes a reality when experience is understood in process terms.

This is interpreted in terms of duty and reverence, which is a biblical combination. When Moses is overcome by his experience of the presence of God, he seeks to do what is required of him. When the crowd at Pentecost hears Peter's sermon, they ask what they should do. Isaiah's response in the temple is to ask the Lord to send him. Jesus in Gethsemane accepts God's will rather than his own. Concern for social justice, for the poor, for prisoners, for the sick and oppressed is correlated with reverence in both the Old and New Testaments.

AREAS OF RELIGIOUS CONCERN

Process thought does not give us any new insights into the nature of religious education, but it selects certain emphases already current and applies them in terms of its theological insights. We can take the predicaments of today and correlate them with insights derived from process theology as a way of explanation. In a prior study of the significance of process thought for black theology,[6] I identified seven areas which can serve us conveniently without any claim that the list is exhaustive: (1) theodicy, (2) suffering, (3) liberation, (4) freedom, (5) reconciliation, (6) the worth of human beings, and (7) Jesus Christ.

(1) *Theodicy.* Most religious thought asserts that in the beginning human nature was good; some assert a historical fall; others claim that every human being starts life with an inheritance of good potential, however quickly this potential may be destroyed by what happens. It is evident that oppression, injustice, evil, and suffering are dominant notes in all experience, regardless of the moral quality of a person. This can be accounted for if God is for some people and against others, or if God is indifferent to both suffering and morals, or if God is so different in goodness that human analogies do not hold (as in the case of Job). But in the Christian tradition it has been assumed that God loves all creatures, regardless of any conditions such as color, sex, or economic or political condition; and yet the results are not consis-

6. See *Black Theology II*, ed. Calvin E. Bruce and William R. Jones (Lewisburg, PA: Bucknell University Press, 1978), pp. 267–285.

tent with such a conclusion if God has any power, especially all the power. When one people or race suffers inordinantly, as in the case of the Jews, it can lead to a denial of their position as a chosen people and of the existence of the God who chose them.

Individual suffering needs a similar understanding. It occurred for me when I was a junior in college. My mother was suffering from multiple sclerosis and was to spend the next twelve years in a wheel chair. The issue was sharp in my own mind, and I had to challenge either the power or the goodness of God. In my course in philosophy of religion, we read the works of William James and I began to see how a pluralistic universe, with God having an environment which included various kinds of evil, could provide an answer. I have seen no reason to change my point of view since then. For me, there simply is no other viable approach to the reality of evil.

The issue turns on the reality of love as a force other than ourselves. This claim has been at the center of the Christian tradition. "God is love, and he who abides in love abides in God, and God abides in him" (I Jn 4:16b, RSV). There is a constancy in God's love, so that God is not subject to the whims of the moment. Love is dependable. Therefore, we rely on our understanding of natural law and expect the universe to show some degree of consistency. But any combination of natural factors may lead to evil results, and we need to recognize the element of risk as we seek to live according to God's aims. Furthermore, it is clear that in the process of life there are elements of chance and the emergence of novelty, so that complete predictability is impossible.[7]

In religious education, we struggle with certain interpretations of experience. If we start, as most people do today, with a view of the universe as governed by natural law, which is an adequate enough explanation for most events, we come quickly to excep-

7. See my *Living with Anxiety* (Philadelphia: Pilgrim Press, 1971), pp. 157–162; also my *Live Until You Die* (Philadelphia: Pilgrim Press, 1973), pp. 141–147.

tions. We discover that chance is a factor in all our judgments and expectations, sometimes leading to unexpected goods and other times to fatal evils. We see the emergence of novelty not only in history but also in daily events. Natural catastrophes are always a shock when they contradict our expectations. It is not very helpful to explain this piously as "the will of God." What is needed is an attempt to relate our understanding of God's love and power to the reality of evil along the lines of process thought.

Because all reality is a process of becoming and perishing, with what perishes being the basis for moving toward new frontiers, we can see ways in which evil may be overcome and goodness may be achieved. If God grasps the feelings of the goodness and the evil that we experience, something like a computer that stores everything in its memory, except that in God evil may be transformed, if God, in Whitehead's terms, is "the fellow sufferer who understands," then we can hope to be "transformed by the renewing of our minds" and to seek a better world. But the future remains open, both to God and to humankind, so that what we do makes a difference.

(2) *Suffering.* There is a great deal of suffering due to illness, but the focus here is on the suffering that human beings inflict on each other. An adequate theology for today must come to terms with black suffering, with what happens to oppressed people especially when the selection is due to ethnic, racial, or sexist distinctions. This is the kind of suffering that leads some people to deny the existence or the goodness of God. If the Jews are God's chosen people, why were they destroyed in concentration camps? If blacks are loved by God, why was not something done about slavery or poverty or the destructive influence of discrimination? What does God do about it? The Bible is full of accounts of the evil human beings inflict on each other, and even Jesus was a young man when he was put to death.

We can make a distinction between negative and creative suffering. To some extent this is a purely pragmatic conclusion.

The suffering is evil in itself, but out of suffering good may sometimes come, although this is not predictable. The suffering of Jesus was genuine and seemed to end in his being forsaken, but the process was reversed through the resurrection experiences. In such a case we say that suffering may be and has been redemptive, as it becomes the cost of something greater. Martyrdoms are often in this category. If God is persuasive love in action, we may discover this through our understanding of or experience of suffering.

But most suffering is not redemptive. It is meaningless and leads to a dead end. God seems to be powerless to do anything about it. Yet among the oppressed (as long as they survive) there may be a rediscovery of purpose. This is what black power is striving for; it starts with a sense of worth, which as Whitehead suggests leads to religious insights. Paulo Freire has suggested ways of accomplishing this sense of worth through education; it releases power by which some of the evils of oppression may be overcome, and promises liberation.

I think it is significant that the Gospel has usually been heard first among the oppressed. It has provided an element of hope in an almost hopeless situation. In some cases, the situation was so bad that hope was transferred to another world, and yet even the other worldly spirituals of black folk had a way of building up their hopes for a new world, via the underground railway or rebellion, and we have a black church today that provides motivation for social and political movements.

The church has a responsibility to continue its ministry to the oppressed, not by providing the values of the oppressors, but by giving them the educational tools to come to an understanding of their own worth as human beings. This is why Whitehead could write, "the kingdom of heaven is with us today."[8] Educationally,

---

8. Alfred North Whitehead, *Process and Reality.* Corrected Edition, edited by David Ray Griffin and Donald W. Sherburne (copyright 1929 by

this points to a responsibility to make sure that the church reaches all oppressed groups, supports their yearnings for a better life, and opposes those who stand in the way. Thus, the radicalness of the Gospel can be supported by this understanding of process theology.

(3) *Liberation.* This is the major theme of black, feminist, Third World, and youth-oriented theologians. They are emphasizing an aspect of the gospel that is easily overlooked among more affluent groups. It stands at the center of process theology, for it points to freedom to be ourselves through the alignment of our subjective aims with that of God. The social nature of reality makes it clear that no one is free until all are free, and this is the vision of what liberation is all about.

As we examine the positions of various kinds of minorities, including the nations that lack power, we see that the state of society today (although an improvement for certain groups over previous conditions) is far from providing the kind of liberation that oppressed groups desire. The just society would provide for the human rights of all its citizens, and this the United States has failed to provide except for some white males and a few others with exceptional ability and luck.

If reality is primarily social, with everything related to everything else within the whole of society and nature, it should be evident that each entity has a purpose of its own in relation to other entities, and survival depends on its own health in relation to others. This is what community is supposed to mean, especially when interpreted in New Testament terms as community of the spirit or of Christ. We can believe that this goal is consistent with God's subjective aim.

Religious education needs to work in this direction. There

Macmillan Publishing Co., Inc., renewed 1957 by Evelyn Whitehead. Copyright 1978 by the Free Press, a division of Macmillan Publishing Co., Inc.), p. 351 (p. 532 in 1929 edition).

have been some moves in terms of new understandings of the nature of the group, in Reuel Howe's insistence on theology understood in terms of relationships, in the concern for the issues of life as a basis for curriculum building, in the development of worship in community as the congregation in action and in relation to God and others. Christian faith has looked upon Jesus Christ as the liberator, and through faith in him we can expect the gift of freedom and understanding, for he came to free the captives and heal the sick and draw in the outcasts, and to announce the year of the Lord.

(4) *Freedom.* Liberation becomes a possibility only when freedom can be established as a means. Process thought builds on the principles of relativity and indeterminacy and allows for chance and novelty as essential in the process of becoming and perishing. Thus, metaphysically, there is room for a genuine freedom as human beings move from where they are to where they can envision themselves as being, guided by goals which they are capable of developing and implementing. There is some degree of freedom even for lesser creatures but it becomes greater for human beings.

Freedom, however, is a gift, not only from God but from various elements in society. It needs to be exercised or it will be lost, and unless it is nurtured by society it can wilt very quickly. Yet, even under the duress of severe oppression, the elements that make freedom are never completely destroyed. Freedom can exist in a concentration camp, a prison, or a ghetto. Paul's or Martin Luther King's letters from jail indicate they though they were locked up they were still free, but this was a freedom based on their relation to God and not to society. A law-and-order society, whether fascist, communist, or pseudo-democratic, fails to provide the social conditions for moral and political freedom.

But freedom does require a structure, even if it is something other than law-and-order. Process thought sees God working as a principle of limitation lest creativity sink into chaos. So also there are restraints in society, in the church, and in the structure of the moral conscience, so that freedom becomes a live option within a structure of possibilities. Nothing is completely determined in process thought, so adventure and risk occur within a structure through which creativity operates.

God does not overrule human freedom. This marks off process thought with its persuasive grace from any kind of irresistible grace. It places responsibility on human beings because God has neither predestined what is now happening nor determined how to outflank human choice in fulfillment of God's subjective aim. This places an awesome responsibility on human beings, although they know that they can turn to God for forgiveness, acceptance, and renewal as well as guidance in their efforts to achieve worthy goals.

One way of implementing a new understanding of freedom is to practice it in the church. Many of our churches have a democratic structure, even when their inheritance is monarchical, and there is a certain amount of freedom in administrative decisions. But many have forgotten that, if we are to create a society in which freedom is an actuality, we need educational institutions which permit the practice of freedom. Some Sunday schools are known for their anarchy, but few for genuine freedom. The concern for persons in terms of their capacity to make responsible choices, the practice of making such choices in ways that count, and a structure in which this freedom cannot degenerate into chaos or become phony because it is abused, are essential elements in the church's program of education. This is something different at each age level; we have achieved it in some instances with younger children, occasionally with elementary age in open classrooms, and rarely in any responsible ways with youth groups. Adults are frequently regimented into lecture or sermonic situations in which dialogue is impossible. So where is the freedom we cherish? Just to seek to understand what freedom means in relation to God and other human beings might be a good starting point.

(5) *Reconciliation.* One of the major goals is the bringing together of humanity in mutual acceptance and understanding in spite of previous enmity. Process thought makes use of the concept of "prehension," whereby one feels the feelings of another, achieves a kind of empathy, and grasps the meaning of another. There is the possibility of mutual prehension which is the expression of genuine love. Not only may we prehend each other, but God prehends us and we prehend God. God both influences us and is influenced by us. Not only does God share our enjoyment and suffering, but in a lesser way we can enjoy or suffer with God, and "we enjoy God's enjoyment of ourselves."[9]

God works for our reconciliation, for this is what it means for persuasive love to act. "In Christ God was reconciling the world to himself" (II Cor 5:19, RSV margin). When we are reconciled, we love each other. But the question always arises as to who is the other. If everyone has the right to be a person in relation to others, and this means lifting the burden of oppression, it is obvious that this is a vision that is far from being realized.

Love has an unconditional element about it. Its expression requires a recognition of equality, so that a precondition of love is some degree of liberation from previous conditions of second-rate humanity. This is what fouls up most attempts to overcome racial discrimination. Yet, if God, who is superior and unsurpassable, loves those who are creatures, and God's creatures who are finite can love God, how does this modify the claim of equality? Can love exist prior to liberation?

The hint here is that God's love is a way of establishing the worth of the one who is loved. Redemption, as promised through

9. Charles Hartshorne, *The Divine Relativity* (New Haven: Yale University Press, 1948), p. 141.

the work of Jesus Christ, leads both to reconciliation and liberation. So we are to treat other persons always as ends and never as means.

We cannot teach love. I suppose we can condition people to have tender feelings or to behave in a way that simulates love. We can provide opportunities for reconciliation through pastoral mediation. But chiefly what we do, quite properly, is to teach *about* love. That is what the gospel story is all about, and we can point to instances of love in action in many stories. So we tell stories about those who love, and help make distinctions between the various kinds of love.

There is nothing new about the emphasis on persuasive love, but we understand love better when the coercive element is minimized. It is clear that we show love of God by loving other human beings, and God's love is mediated to us by others. Whatever we do to "the least of these" we are doing to God (see I Jn 4:20-21, Mt 25:31-46). But this is not humanism even when interpreted in terms of interpersonal relations, for we understand that this is God's work as much as ours; the consequent nature of God is process and works among us. Thus we can talk meaningfully of being forgiven and reconciled.

Most of the time, our approaches to religious education do not make this clear, for it is not easy to do so. Yet it is the nature of God, as conceived by process thought, to bring things together, to work for harmony, and to restore relationships. If, then, we can experience God's presence as interpreted by process thought, we can be reconciled to each other and to God. The opportunity to experience this can come within the community of believers.

(6) *Sense of worth.* It is clear that all forms of discrimination destroy the sense of worth. That is the abiding result of years of slavery. To some degree all who are oppressed find it difficult to accept the fact that they are of value. Yet there is always a seed, even in the most oppressed person, of one's own importance. Even in some animals this may be observed. Morality is the result

of this human capacity to recognize one's significance in relation to others. This may lead, under even unfavorable circumstances, to faith in God.

Human beings are shaped by unrealized ideals. Most children develop ideals that guide them toward the future; sometimes the ideals are impossible and they need to be altered toward more realistic expectations. But dreams are shattered because society discriminates against its members, not on grounds of legitimate hopes but on the basis of barriers set up by one group against another. Getting into medical or law school has been difficult for women, blacks, native Americans, Spanish speaking Americans, and various others for no objective reason whatever.

Often estimates of worth are in terms of wealth, social class, race, or religion rather than in recognition of the worth of a human being as such. It is the sense of worth, suggests Schubert Ogden, that leads to belief in God; and correlative with this is the fact that belief in God strengthens the sense of worth. This is consistent not only with process thought but also with the basic teachings of Christianity and Judaism, although in certain forms Christianity has unduly emphasized unworthiness as an approach to God.

The church has not always treated children as equals in the sight of God or of the congregation. Certainly the churches have been class and race conscious either in terms of membership or of leadership within a congregation. They have asserted that God loves everyone, but make it clear in their actions that this is really so only when they are "like us." Educationally, this becomes a challenge, for the quality of life of the congregation is transmitted to its members and especially to children. When we teach that Jesus loved children, we should underscore this with the children's experience of being loved. Instead of God as a watchdog, we might well stress that God shares our actions, ideas, hopes, and fears, and that what we think and do lives on in the memory of God, who is able to transform our ways when they are evil into potentialities for good in the future.

(7) *Jesus Christ.* While process thinking is only beginning to work out a full Christology, enough has been done to suggest ways of thinking that are consistent with our modern view of the world. Instead of starting with Jesus as God, process thinkers begin with the consideration of Jesus as a human being in relation to God. They may say that Jesus prehended God more fully than others; or that God's subjective aim was more fully actualized in and through Jesus' subjective aim; or that the impact of Jesus in and on history is carried on in the life of the church; or that God had a particular subjective aim for Jesus that marked him off from other human beings; or that we prehend the living Christ today because what he stood for continues in the memory of God. Jesus is the "chief exemplification" of what it means fully to accept the leading of God's persuasive love in our lives.

There is an incarnational principle in process thought, so that we can speak of the everlasting Logos who is manifest in a particular way in Jesus Christ. The incarnation in the Christian tradition may be thought of as a novel event, an emerging novelty, in that it has not occurred before and had a unique revelatory significance. Yet its meaning depended on past events in the history of Israel, and it erupted in the fullness of time. It changed the structure of consciousness of a subculture within a surrounding culture, and the impact of this resulted in the emergence of the church as another novel event.

God's primordial nature was not made more loving or sensitive because of Jesus. However, if on the grounds of process thinking God's consequent nature is influenced by human events, God was changed by what happened to Jesus, sharing in both the suffering and the joy of his life and death. These happenings occurred within history, and Jesus became everlastingly part of the memory of God. This affected human history not only

through human memory but also through the possibilities released through God's grace, which includes the promise of
human redemption.

There are three levels of thinking about Jesus for educational
purposes as we move from history to the experience of the presence of Jesus as the Christ and to the formulation of a Christology. There is, first, the fact that Jesus is remembered. There are
stories about him. We can remember him as a historical figure
who had an impact on history. This is significant not only because it is the way children come to know of him but because this
is the raw material for our thinking about him. Second, Jesus is
known still in the continuing memory of the church, in its sacraments, and in his objective immortality in the memory of God.
There is an experience which Christians call the presence of the
living or risen Christ. Third, Jesus is interpreted. Throughout
Christian history a key question has been "What think ye of
Christ?" Theologians have played with all sorts of answers, and
now the process theologians are facing up to this question. Educationally, it may be suggested that a process Christology may
prove more suitable for today than many other interpretations.[10]

For process thought, Christology leads directly to consideration of the church, for it is through the church that what Jesus
was lives on. The church is conceived organismically, as the
body of Christ, the vine and the branches, or the fellowship of
the spirit. Christ is recognized as the head of the body, of which
we are members. The sacramental and the incarnational aspects
of God's nature are seen together in the dynamics of life in the
church. But the church as we know it does not measure up to
these norms, and therefore as a human institution it only points
in this direction. The church as portrayed is a projection of
human hope in the light of our knowledge of God. So we are
members who keep an ideal (the old invisible church?) before us,

10. See John Knox, *Christ the Lord* (Chicago: Willett, Clark, 1945).

and we seek to become a congregation of faithful people. The quality of life we reach as a congregation determines the level of our educational achievements.

A NEW WAY OF THINKING

This chapter has dealt with theological and educational theory. As we have examined the ways in which process theologians might look at various issues, we are introduced to what for some is a new way of thinking. The approach is radically empirical, pragmatic, and pluralistic, and yet it is not afraid of theory. Unless we come at empiricism with a theory, Whitehead reminds us, we are not likely to have a basis for the selection of data or for reflection on our experience. Unless there is a hypothesis, there is nothing to be verified by induction from the data. A world view begins to emerge from such thinking, and if Whitehead and his followers are right, that world view is very much like the one we have described. We will consider the use of method in theology in chapter four.[11]

To what extent does a theology derived from this kind of thinking speak to the conditions of modern life? We have taken a somewhat arbitrary sample of the questions asked by black theologians and other minority groups (which is where Christianity has historically found its strength) and have attempted to see the correlation between these issues and process thinking.

The human condition today is the cause of both despair and hope. As we move from the past to the future in the process of becoming and perishing, we live in a present that causes confusion. Christian education is challenged to deal with issues that illuminate the situation in which we live from a theological perspective, so that we may find meaning in our lives and in the

11. See my *The American Spirit in Theology* (Philadelphia: Pilgrim Press, 1974) for a historical approach to this position, beginning with William James.

world. We have looked briefly at six of these issues: evil, suffering, liberation, freedom, reconciliation, and human worth. As Christians, we focus on Jesus Christ as the key to what life means. These issues face all people as soon as they are capable of asking questions.

But we still have to resolve questions about the world itself. One helpful approach has been to start with a series of proposals based on nature's relation to God as an even more elementary approach to process thinking, theology, and education. To those proposals we now turn.

3

Nature and God

As modern science has provided a framework in which we view the world around us, the predominant perspective has been of the universe as a mechanism in which all operations are automatic, based on stimulus and response. There has been a long history of this kind of thinking, the most disastrous probably being the influence of Descartes with his two worlds, that of mechanistic activity and the superadded one of spirit and God. The latter could be ignored in any scientific endeavor and God became an unnecessary hypothesis. There have been many protests against mechanism by both scientists and theologians in the past centuries, but Charles Birch claims that "the average scientist is prepared to live with a concept of mechanism that is... three hundred years out of date."[1]

There has been a strong reaction against viewing the world as a mechanism and the participants as automata, beginning at least with Charles Darwin, who pointed to the elements of change and instability in the chance mutations that are the basis for the coming into being of novel emergents. Darwin saw chance variations as the building blocks of evolution, found in the mutations of genes. Most such mutations lead to disastrous results, as witness the extinction of so many forms of life. But the few mutations that aid in new developments over many eras are what count. There is in this evidence an escape from the scientific determinism of physics, chemistry, and biology.

Human beings have adapted to new conditions through gene-

1. Charles Birch, *Nature and God* (Philadelphia: Westminster, 1965), p. 32.

tic mutations and through human invention. The adaptations through genetic changes have usually been beneficial, but those coming as a result of human invention may in the final analysis prove to be more damaging than helpful. Human actions have led to the development of new cultures, which can be modified through education, influence, or force. What becomes clear is that although human beings can alter the process, the process goes on. Human beings are not separate from nature, they are part of it. Thus organism becomes the model for thinking rather than mechanism.

From this point of view, God is understood as active within the naturalistic order as the source of creative transformation. God's providence does not protect us from such evils as accidents, poverty, suffering, disease, or death, for God does not interfere. God keeps the rules, as Whitehead has said. God's providence, then, is that "nothing in all creation can separate us from the love of God."

Birch quotes Ecclesiastes 9:11 (KJV): "I returned, and saw under the sun, that the race is not to the swift, nor the battle to the strong, neither yet bread to the wise, nor yet riches to men of understanding, nor yet favour to men of skill; but time and chance happeneth to them all."[2] Of many things we say that they "just happened." We recognize that chance operates at the center of things, and that the behavior of the electron is unpredictable. But chance operates within limits or else it becomes chaos. God is for Whitehead the principle of limitation, that which keeps creativity from becoming chaos, as well as persuasive love operating in our midst.

RELIGIOUS NATURALISM

Naturalism in religious thought is contrasted with supernaturalism. Traditionally, naturalism and supernaturalism were

2. See Birch, *Nature and God*, p. 76.

two different arenas, the former a result of human reason and experience and the latter based on revelation. There is no way to demonstrate the truth of either position, except the pragmatic way of judging the results.

Naturalism has become a way of thinking with as few presuppositions as possible. As long as supernaturalism is not necessary adequately to account for all the data, and naturalism is broad enough to include all forms of experience, a simple metaphysics can provide the framework for theology's pictures.

Reality is to be conceived as a natural organism, interrelated in all its parts, so that all that exists is included in a vast set of connections. The history of this organism is described, as far as this world is concerned, by the theory of emergent evolution. The meaning of the natural world is understood in terms of emergents of meaning and value in temporal history. God is to be discovered by an examination of the data provided by observation of the natural world. Thus, natural theology is not only reinstated but becomes the final court of appeal for religious knowledge. An epistemology similar to that of the natural sciences is applied to the religious object, and the resulting concept of God represents a reality within the natural world.

This kind of naturalism has a vital religious outlook. Knowledge of God results from the impact of the environment upon the human organism. The organism reacts by a series of acts which organizes its behavior intelligently, and this leads to the discovery of patterns leading to predictable results. When these patterns have become sufficiently fixed to determine satisfactory outcomes, one has knowledge. This is the way all knowledge is obtained, including knowledge of God. Such knowledge is never merely subjective, whether it applies to God or an apple, because the only satisfactory conclusions must be related to the response of the environment to one's concepts.[3]

3. See Henry Nelson Wieman and Walter Marshall Horton, *The Growth of Religion* (Chicago: Willett, Clark, 1938), pp. 258–259.

The only knowledge we can have of anything comes from the relationship between organism and environment. The difference in degrees of knowledge among people is due to variations in natural capacities, opportunities, and ways of testing results. The discoverers in any field develop their natural capacities of observation, appreciation, imagination and experimental behavior far beyond those of their contemporaries, and this is what makes possible the discoveries. There is no distinction between the secular and religious genius, except that the latter is concerned with the impact of the *whole* of the environment upon the organism. Revelation, for the theistic naturalist, is possible anywhere and anytime there is the proper relation between event and appreciation. It is the same as any other knowledge, except for its superior value. It is found and tested in the same way.

God is to be found in the natural world. The naturalist believes that God can be discovered at work. By observation of what God *does,* we can infer that God *is.* Henry Nelson Wieman spoke of God as "the growth of meaning and value in the world" or as "creative interchange." Bernard Eugene Meland calls God the "creative order" of the universe. God is the principle, the process, the pattern of integration which is evident to all who observe the workings of nature, society, and the individual human organism. God is revealed as such to those who have eyes to see.

God is not identical with the natural world. There is no pantheism involved here. God is "wholly other" than the natural order and yet God pervades the natural order. God is not identical with humanity but works in and through human beings. God is superhuman and transcends all that humanity may do itself. As a "creative synthesis" God is the persuasive guide of all that is, and yet God is other without being beyond it. If the natural world is all that is, God cannot be supernatural, for the latter realm is nonexistent.

The naturalist is much less certain about the nature of God

than the more orthodox thinkers. The naturalist claims to know very little about the nature of God, claiming that the concept of God is only an "operational" idea which aids in fathoming the mystery of God's nature. As Wieman says, "God is always more than we can think." But the naturalist is equally sure that "God always is."

God is known primarily through God's relations with humanity. It is in the connections between God and humanity that one finds the data for developing a concept of God. If we use the model of "Father" for deity, as Wieman is willing to do, it means that God is the creator of personality, that all human beings belong in community, and that God's love falls on all people. God as "growth" brings forth human personality, fosters, sustains, transforms, and promotes it in a community of love. God's activities in the realm of human community are attested by the evidence of the ages.

This, in brief, is naturalistic theism. Its essence is that we must live in absolute commitment to the will of God, and God's will is discerned through a life of worship, sensitivity, and responsiveness which is always open to God's will in each unique situation. Prayer is simply commitment to God, and this is the heart of religious living.

TRADITIONAL CHRISTIANITY

Traditional Christianity has always been frankly supernatural. Christianity has included belief in both a natural and a supernatural realm, in a supernatural revelation of God's will and nature to a chosen few, and in religious living based upon the acceptance of supernaturally given beliefs. There have been many variations of this formula, some denying one or more aspects of the main stream of thought; but never has any number of Christians conceived their religion in naturalistic terms. There have been many types of theistic metaphysics forming the background for a Christian world view, but most have had room for the supernatural. Knowledge of God has centered in the Bible and the church, both of which have been conceived as supernaturally endowed. Individuals have also claimed to have revelations, but they have thought of them as supernatural in their source.

With the exception of a few neo-supernaturalists, however, the main stream of Christian thought has always made room for the natural knowledge of God. Faith and reason have usually supplemented each other, with faith being superior. God is the end of all knowledge, whether it be natural or supernatural. The completion of this knowledge, however, has always centered in the supernatural revelation found in the incarnation of Christ. For traditional Christianity this has always been conceived as the supreme and final revelation of God. Any other attempt to know God must, in the nature of the case, fall far short of the revelation that is in Christ.

Religious naturalism seems to be at odds with traditional Christianity from start to finish, for even when the naturalists accept the centrality of Christ they interpret his work on the basis of their naturalistic assumptions. The revelations of the historic Jesus are those of a supreme religious genius, and God was in Jesus reconciling the world to himself through the responses of the people and through the processes of natural, moral, and spiritual law. Historically and naturally considered, Jesus is central; but this leads to nontraditional interpretations of the elements in the life and death of Jesus which traditionalists call supernatural.

AS NATURALISM VIEWS CHRISTIANITY

True Christians, according to Wieman, are distinguished by three marks: first, they are unconsciously shaped by the historic past that centers in Jesus; second, they turn for guidance to that past in association with a fellowship that shares their views; third, they carry the total tradition and lore into the present without regard to its value for today.[4]

Wieman believes that Christian living is definitely grounded in the past. Christians are bound by traditions, helpful or otherwise. Yet Christians live in the present; they are part of the historic progress and they live "at the growing edge of the historic continuum." But, says Wieman, granting that the Christian heritage is important, a person may accept all the things that make up Christian belief and character and not be truly and uniquely religious, unless one follows the religious way.

The religious way, says Wieman, is the most precious thing in life, more precious even than any beliefs, traditions, or practices of Christianity. Thus, to be distinctively religious is "to live only 'for the will of God.' The will of God is the creative synthesis of each unique situation."[5] One is absolutely committed to God.

For the naturalist, the Christian heritage is an aid to the religious way, but the religious way strikes more deeply than any particular religion. It is centered at the heart of the human experience of God, in the crisis of each unique moment. No tradition, no beliefs, and no fellowship can guarantee that the essence of religious living will be found. The whole of the Christian heritage is instrumental to the doing of God's will.

This is not meant to be a condemnation of Christianity. Most of the naturalists have been reared in the Christian community, and they have not broken with that fellowship. This does not mean that those who call themselves Christian are not religious. It only points to the obvious fact that many conform to all the preachings, doctrines, and practices of the Christian community without ever becoming distinctively religious. They fail to make the final step of absolute commitment to God.

4. See Wieman and Horton, *Growth of Religion*, pp. 281–82.
5. Wieman and Horton, *Growth of Religion*, p. 283.

All naturalists do not agree with Wieman in his evaluation of Christianity. It is possible to accept Christianity naturalistically and empirically and still maintain that Christianity is the best expression of the religious way, provided its full implications are accepted. Christianity at its best involves the absolute commitment to a God of love, and whenever it fails to demand this it falls short of its primary purpose. Absolute commitment to God provides the norm for evaluating all Christian living.

CHRISTIANITY'S ATTITUDE TOWARD NATURALISM

Those who hold to the position of traditional Christianity may take one of three attitudes toward naturalism: (a) naturalism is the antithesis of Christianity; or (b) it is a temporary expedient for presenting essential Christian truths to this age; or (c) it is *logically prior* to Christianity, and serves as a philosophical foundation for the reinterpretation of Christian beliefs.

(a) Proponents of the first position insist on the supernatural origin of Christianity. They say that the revelation of God in the Bible, in Christ, and in the church is the heart of all true religion. By the use of reason we may test and communicate the supernatural truths of Christianity, but faith is superior to reason. Religious experience is valid only when it is the experience of the Christ of faith. The only salvation which Christianity teaches is the forgiveness of sins through the supernatural atonement of Christ on the cross, and this guarantees the saved eternal life. This is "foolishness" to all who do not have it.

Religious naturalism is of no help. It does not protect the centrality and finality of either the Bible or Christ. It has no place for the faith which supersedes reason. It stresses the religious values of all experiences, instead of emphasizing the centrality of the experience of the saving grace of Christ. It teaches that salvation is possible apart from faith in Jesus as the Christ and in the cross. It denies the heart of the Christian faith when it fails to interpret the death and resurrection of Christ as the hub of the universe, around which all meaning moves. It does not accept the concept of God clearly revealed in Jesus Christ as authoritative, but goes back to one's own experience and history as the final ground of truth.

There are also certain psychological reasons for the rejection of naturalism. Naturalism does not pretend to speak with the voice of authority, but admits that its concept of God is a tentative and instrumental one. It rejects the certainty which has been the bulwark of dogmatic Christianity. It is psychologically impossible for most religious people to combine the attitude of tentativeness of belief with absolute commitment to God. Also, in rejecting authority, the shadow of doubt is cast upon both Bible and church. Instead of two great immovable stones of authority and certainty, naturalism has only two helpful and relative reference points for religious living. Many Christians find this psychologically inadequate.

The whole approach to naturalism, then, is foreign to traditional Christianity, according to this line of reasoning. Naturalism rejects both certainty and authority, even in the Bible and the church. It puts its finger of doubt upon traditional interpretations of the atonement and incarnation. By its rejection of supernatural revelation, it seems to substitute mere human concepts for divinely given truths.

(b) Proponents of the second interpretation claim that naturalism is only to be understood in the light of the Christian position and tradition. Instead of being opposed to Christianity, naturalism is understood as a temporary expedient for adapting the Christian message to a new age. Although many errors are contained in its teaching, its chief purpose is to make clear the Christian message in the language and thoughts of today. Any study of the history of Christian thought indicates clearly that Christian theology has been forced to readapt itself to successive changes in culture in order to be intelligible.

People who hold this position insist on the central truths of traditional Christianity, but they conceive the essence of Christianity as a continuous growth, with Christ as the chief cornerstone. As the Christian message spread, it adapted itself to the new philosophies and sciences, to the Greek, Roman, and Teutonic minds. In recent times, no one would claim that the religious thought of a Kant, Schleiermacher, or Ritschl is final or even inclusive of the whole Christian message. Augustine, Aquinas, Calvin, and Luther gave particular interpretations to Christianity to insure its survival in new ages. Such theologies are not complete or total, but they are instrumental to the understanding and practice of the Christian way to salvation in a given culture.

The same thing can be claimed for religious naturalism. It is the attempt to present Christianity to an age which is able to think only in naturalistic terms, which sees life as an organic whole, and which cannot find meaning in many of the traditional and frankly supernatural concepts.

From this point of view, there is at least a charitable attitude toward naturalism. There are lingering doubts as to whether the naturalists are doing as able a job as Ritschl did for his age, because the naturalists claim so little about God that is hard to believe. Also, the naturalists use concepts which are difficult to correlate with traditional beliefs. The naturalists call themselves "theists." If "theism" means simply "belief in God," the words "naturalistic theism" have meaning. If, however, "theism" means belief in a transcendent, all powerful and all knowing, transcendent and immanent, creator God who is in charge of everything, then the naturalists have no right to the term.

So although the naturalists may be accepted by those who hold this position because they represent a temporary expedient in the communication of the essentially religious note of the Christian message for today's world, one must remain extremely critical of their conclusions—as they themselves are critical. It is a valuable and necessary effort, but it is merely a means to an end. It is limited to the natural truths of Christianity, and it fails to maintain its supernatural aspects.

(c) To evaluate naturalistic theism either as the antithesis or a temporary statement of Christian truth and leave it there is to miss the most important aspect of its contribution to modern thought. It may also be thought of as *logically prior to Christianity,* as philosophically necessary as natural theology has been to the thought of the most traditional Christians.

Naturalism is not specifically theology at all. It is a philosophical study of the phenomena of religious living. It is not specifically Christian because its scope is wide enough to include minute examinations of all types of religious living. For those who insist on the absoluteness of the Christian revelation, it may be thought of as a forerunner. At least, it serves as a philosophical basis upon which may be built the superstructure of Christian belief.

Naturalism is primarily empirical. All knowledge comes from the analysis of experience and the rational inferences which may be made. If this is the way knowledge works, then we have an invaluable tool by which to examine all the discoveries of religious thinkers throughout the ages. Revelation is no less a gift of God because it is also our insight into God's nature. God is no less present in our daily living because we observe that God arouses our latent energies.

This means that no matter what we claim for our Christianity, it may be analyzed by the instruments of naturalism. Even Barthianism, with its radical disjunction between natural and supernatural theology, may be understood as a natural phenomenon. A Barthian could not become reconciled to the concepts of the naturalists, but that does not prevent the naturalist from having a profound insight into the workings of the Barthian mind and religion. The naturalist is trying to get back of surface things and traditional concepts in order to discover what actual processes are at work.

There is no denial of the facts of religious living. The facts are obvious to any trained observer. But the naturalist has better tools and techniques for observing what happens and for analyzing the data. If a naturalistic interpretation accounts for all the data, there is no need for a supernatural rendering. Logically, the naturalist's approach is prior to that of the supernaturalist. Historically, as far as Christianity is concerned, the supernatural approach has been prior.

Religious naturalism, if it is true to itself, stops at this point. It gives a natural account of the religious phenomena of the world to the best of its ability. That is all it should be expected to do. If it does this adequately, it has provided us with the logically prior foundation for a theological superstructure, which should be consistent with the foundation but which may go far beyond it. This is the principle to which Roman Catholic theology has always adhered, however short it may have fallen in practice. Natural theology has fulfilled the place we are suggesting for naturalistic theism, which is probably no more than a modern refinement.

Naturalistic metaphysics and empirical method carefully combined provide the foundation stones for a new theology. This is what naturalism should attempt. In order to develop a new theology in any complete form, it is necessary to go beyond the rigorous empiricism of naturalism. By the use of analogical beliefs and rational superstructures, it is possible to work toward a theology which will be adequate for the world today. Such a development is badly needed. This may prove America's distinctive contribution to ecumenical Christianity.

Naturalistic theism as we have described it is derived primarily from the thought of Henry Nelson Wieman. Others have worked along parallel lines and we will be referring to them at other points in this book. The emphasis on empirical method, broadly interpreted, is found in the process theologians who have moved beyond the strict naturalism of Wieman's metaphysics. The process theologians are equally opposed to traditional supernaturalism, and in the case of Schubert Ogden distinguish between classical and neo-classical theism. Such thinkers as Bernard Eugene Meland, John B. Cobb, Jr., David Griffin, and others influenced by Charles Hartshorne and Alfred North Whitehead, are working on specifically Christian interpretations of empirical and process thinking.

Naturalism is opposed chiefly because it is not understood, but conservatives who understand it also oppose it. It is feared because devout people believe it is attempting to replace Christianity. But it is not attempting to replace anything essential to Christianity. It is not just a temporary means of communication. Naturalism may be legitimately opposed only by those who deny the validity of human knowledge of God and rely exclusively on supernatural sources of revelation. If any natural theology be acceptable, naturalism may be understood as one type of natural theology.

ON USING CHRISTIAN WORDS

If naturalistic theism serves as a natural theology which is the basis for any valid theology, if it is a legitimate interpretation of religious experience, and if it is fitted to test the truth claims of Christianity, there remains the question of the use of Christian words to point to and show those experiences which lead to Christian beliefs.

Henry Nelson Wieman suggested ways in which naturalistic theists might respond to the use of Christian words. One possibility is the repudiation of the vocabulary of Christians by seeking new words to express what happens in religious experience. A second solution is to select a few *religious* words which can be reinterpreted to fit the current experiences, but to oppose the use of traditional Christian symbols; specifically *Christian* words should be avoided except in rare exceptions. A third way is to borrow from the logical positivists and use Christian words for their *emotive* power alone. They are like "stop" and "go" signs.

None of these solutions satisfies the Christian who accepts naturalistic theism as the basic element in theology.[6]

If we reach our beliefs by a critical use of empirical method, we discover those realities which lie at the heart of religious living. We may assume that in their original meaning, traditional Christian words were used to point to realities of religious living not immensely different from what is experienced today. Although our basic understanding of these realities is different, these words designate the reality upon which we depend for a meaningful existence. The use of Christian words keeps alive the tradition that contains within it previous experience of human history and assists us in seeing the continuity of the work of God. The words come alive not only as a report of experience, but as symbols they awaken our responsiveness and shape our conduct. Symbols acquire emotive power within a community of worshipers who share the same symbol system.

Christians may interpret the world in terms of naturalism and may use it as a metaphysical system that helps our understanding of nature and God. In many cases, it is proper to use the words of naturalistic theism to help those outside the Christian tradition understand Christian experience and concepts. But we who are educators must be able to translate back and forth and thus indicate how traditional words and symbols continue to have meaning today. The vocabulary of the naturalistic theists is that of the modern world, and for many the educational process includes the movement from that vocabulary to the Christian words which express the Christian heritage in worship.

A clue to the way in which we may use Wieman's vocabulary for clarity and traditional words for their emotive power is found in the suggestion that metaphor is the primary means of religious expression. Image thinking, story thinking, poetic expressions

6. See Henry Nelson Wieman, "On Using Christian Words," *Journal of Religion* (July 1940), pp. 260–262.

are found throughout religious literature. "No animal ever understood a metaphor: that belongs to intelligence."[7] The images of
God, Jesus, church, and many other aspects of Christian belief
are expressed through metaphors that must never be taken literally. The prophets loaded the Hebrew mind with rich images and
metaphors that carry over into the New Testament and traditional Christian symbols and creeds. The early Christians, trying to understand Jesus' death and the atonement, found in their
own Jewish tradition the lamb, the fire, the blood as metaphor.
The parables may be thought of as drawn-out metaphors. The
disciples are called living epistles. Many metaphorical phrases are
rich in imagery, as in "For *of* him and *through* him, and *to* him,"
or "One God and Father of all, who is *above* all, and *through* all,
and *in* you all."[8] Such concepts have a richness that analytic
procedures cannot match, yet they are open to interpretation in
terms of process thinking.

The educator moves back and forth among such languages. It
is not an easy task. We need the expertness of grasping the
technical vocabulary of theological analysis, we must be accurate
in our use of traditional language for the purpose of pointing to
and illuminating experience, and we need the richness of
metaphor for communication that will reach the motivating
functions of a person. The variety of language categories comes
into play at this point in the educational process. The development of such categories has assisted in understanding the rich
metaphors in the Christian tradition, and by helping learners to
identify these categories we have enabled them to move away
from the literalism that is deadly in the direction of the rich,
imaginative, pictorial image thinking of the gospel.[9]

7. Horace Bushnell, "Our Gospel a Gift to the Imagination," *Building Eras*
(New York: Charles Scribner's Sons, 1881), p. 252.
8. Bushnell, "Our Gospel a Gift," p. 265. See my "God's Gift to the Imagination," *Perkins Journal* (Spring 1979), p. 10.
9. See my *The Language Gap and God* (Philadelphia: Pilgrim Press, 1970).

Naturalistic theism provides thought forms and a vocabulary that help relate Christian beliefs to the world of empirical study. Empirical method is basic to this approach to theology, and the movement from one language category to another is properly a problem in translation as well as a movement from empirical findings to overbeliefs that are consistent with the empirically based concepts with which we begin. We will look at this empirical method in the next chapter.[10]

---

10. Wieman's position is summarized in my *The American Spirit in Theology*, chapter 5, pp. 75–99, and in *The Empirical Theology of Henry Nelson Wieman*, ed. Robert W. Bretall (Carbondale, IL: Southern Illinois University Press, 1963), esp. pp. 19–115.

4

Empirical Method in Theology

In the first three chapters, we have considered the way in which our view of revelation determines our theological and educational outlooks. We then looked at the developments in American theology coming from the view of revelation as a coincidence of particularly revealing events and particularly appreciative minds and the empirical and process thinking that leads to fresh theological categories. This led to a brief summary of process thinking and its implications related to key queries coming from theologies developed by minorities. Process thought, we claimed, has ways of dealing both theologically and educationally with such issues. We then turned to religious naturalism as a kind of restricted empirical study that is logically prior to doing theology itself but which provides a solid basis for theological speculation. We concluded by looking at the problem of using Christian words in a naturalistic framework and came to the conclusion that this can be done with care provided we understand the metaphorical nature of the theological language.

What has been assumed throughout these early chapters has been the use of empirical method as basic to the larger inquiry that is still to come. Empiricism in theology not only assists in establishing foundations for theological claims, but also contributes to our understanding of religious education in theory and practice.

Empirical method in theology is similar to its use in other fields of knowledge. It means that a concept can be verified by an appeal to further experience. In the sciences, this use of experience is controllable and repeatable, but in theology there is no opportunity for such control and any repetition is never exact. Empirical knowledge is always tentative and inductive, depending on how we select and interpret the data.

Experience is, however, an ambiguous term and is often vague in its references. It is sometimes limited to sense experience or to the use of words that refer to a process of verification through the senses. Sometimes it is used to describe purely impersonal objects. It may be only a subjective element in the consciousness. It may be the observation of both subject and object from a vantage point outside of both. It may be considered primarily in terms of interpersonal relationships. It may be a vague sensuousness referring to a total bodily experience in which particulars are abstracted from the whole. The interpretation may become so broad that the question becomes, "What is not based on experience?"

REALITY AND EXPERIENCE

Paul Tillich interpreted empiricism in American theology in three categories: ontological, scientific, and mystical. The ontological, arising from philosophical positivism, assumes that "reality is identical with experience." Nothing is transcendent. For Tillich this means that "an immediate participation in religious reality" precedes theological analysis, and that "religious objects are not objects among others but that they are expressions of a quality or dimension of our general experience." The question is one of phenomenology rather than existence.[1]

Edwin R. Walker, however, describes empiricism at this level as "a method of getting knowledge by developing a hypothetical

1. Paul Tillich, *Systematic Theology* (Chicago: University of Chicago Press, 1951), I, 42–43.

proposition to explain a body of observed facts, then deducing the implications of the hypothesis, and then testing these implied propositions by means of further observation."[2] This knowledge is derived from sense data; otherwise the concept (whether of God or anything else) will have only pragmatic or formal meaning. As Henry Nelson Wieman wrote in his first book, "Either God is an object of sensuous experience, or else he is purely a system of concepts and nothing more. . . . There can be no question about the reality of religious experience; and all experience is the experience of something."[3] God, then, is something that affects our senses, although not in the same way as when we touch a tree. The medium of all knowledge is sense experience.

The empirical is always related to the rational. There is no dualism between the empirical and the rational. Experience is not knowledge; it is merely direct acquaintance. As Richard I. Aaron has pointed out, traditional philosophical empiricism, from which the more recent empirical theology was derived, emphasized the impact of sensation on the perceiver, but soon it was necessary to add introspection as part of experience, and in the end it has been necessary to include the activity of the participant, so that "it seems obviously more hopeful to think of sense perception in terms of a prepared mind widening its horizons rather than of an empty mind receiving impressions."[4] We bring habits, skills, techniques, and expectations to our experiences; perceptions become recognition and discovery, but the discovery comes to the sensitive and trained mind and is akin to revelation or disclosure. From this point of view, the rational

2. Edwin R. Walker, "Can Philosophy of Religion Be Empirical?" *Journal of Religion* XIX (October 1939), p. 316.
3. Henry Nelson Wieman, *Religious Experience and Scientific Method* (New York: Macmillan, 1926), pp. 28, 29.
4. Richard I. Aaron, in *Contemporary British Philosophy*, 3rd series, ed. H. D. Lewis (New York: Macmillan, 1956), p. 15.

element is a portion of sense perception rather than something either added or opposed. Although knowledge based on empirical verification and knowledge derived from rational propositions are different and need not be confused, an empiricism which does not contain the rational element does not lead to knowledge.

William James combined radical empiricism, realism in epistemology, pragmatism, and pluralism. His analysis of knowledge includes several important distinctions: knowledge *by acquaintance* is based on first hand direct experience, knowledge *about* is second hand but consistent with experience. An epistemological realism means that the object is real apart from experience of it. We have direct experience not only of things but of conjunctive and disjunctive relations between things. "The parts of experience hold together from next to next by relations that are themselves parts of experience."[5] Reality is an "experience-continuum."[6] However, James is careful to qualify this statement by saying that the ultimate object may lie outside the direct experience of the knower, as long as it exists as part of the total universe of experience, with cognition in it. It is in this context that James' oftquoted statement should be understood: "Let empiricism once become associated with religion, as hitherto, through some strange misunderstanding, it has been associated with irreligion, and I believe that a new era of religion as well as philosophy will be ready to begin."[7] For James, this method led him to postulate a divine "More" at work in a pluralistic universe, a deity that was working for good in an environment not completely controlled by God.

Experience is often used in a broader sense. We are aware of

5. William James, *The Meaning of Truth* (New York: Longmans, Green, 1909), p. xii.
6. James, *Meaning of Truth*, p. 152.
7. William James, *A Pluralistic Universe* (New York: Longmans, Green, 1909), p. 314.

events, objects, ideas, values, so that Douglas Clyde Macintosh speaks of "perception in a complex" or "perceptual intuition." This may be rational, appreciative, imaginal, and perceptual. "The first two have to do with the apprehension of axiomatic truth and intrinsic value, respectively. Imaginal and perceptual intuition differ from each other in that the latter is certitude of reality as present, whereas the former is certitude of truth about reality not presented sufficiently for perception." Self-knowledge, introspection, remembering, desiring, thinking, and willing are open to perceptual intuition.[8] Such a broad use of empiricism leaves the restriction to sense data far behind. How empirical is such a broad-based intuition?

Empiricism is frequently restricted by some thinkers to observations that omit the observer, as in some empirical sciences. John Macmurray, on the other hand, places religious experience in the field of personal relations. "The field of religion is the whole field of common experience organized in relation to the central fact of personal relationship. . . . The datum from which religious reflection starts is the reciprocity or mutuality of these. . . . Religion is about fellowship and community, which are facts of direct, universal human experience."[9] This opens up the approach of Martin Buber and others who stress the I-Thou relationship as central, both at the human level and toward God. At this point, we may find significant data for theological reflection.

Empiricism may also be looked at from the standpoint of social studies and the place of the participant. When the model of persons in relation is used, the links with observable fact are not predictive, but they may provide for articulation. What is disclosed is ultimately a mystery, but with experience there is pro-

8. See Douglas Clyde Macintosh, "Empirical Theology and Some of Its Misunderstanders," *Review of Religion* III, May 1939, p. 396.
9. John Macmurray, *The Structure of Religious Experience* (New Haven: Yale University Press, 1936), p. 23.

gressive partial understanding. Ian T. Ramsey writes that a purely scientific model, which leaves out the participant, can never lead to religious knowledge or even to adequate articulation, but when such models are replaced by social models which include the participant, a disclosure may result. Ramsey sees quite clearly that mystery is at the heart of all religious experience or beliefs and that the language we use about God must be "logically odd," but in the end he comes down hard on the significance of the experiences of worship, wonder, and awe. Ramsey writes, "Without such an empirical anchorage all our theological thinking is in vain, and where there is controversy and argument we are to look for their resolution where they are fulfilled: in worship."[10]

SCIENTIFIC EMPIRICISM

Tillich speaks of a second kind of empiricism, which he calls "scientific."[11] But the religious object, he continues, cannot be understood as a scientific object and cannot be verified on scientific terms. It can be verified only through participation, but this task is never finished and therefore no verification is possible. However, empirical theologians such as Macintosh and Wieman have made claims that are opposed to Tillich's position. Macintosh was always careful to qualify his claims, but in his *Theology as an Empirical Science* he spoke of empirically based laws of religious experience which lead to knowledge of God; such knowledge is incomplete, but it is essentially scientific in the certainty it provides. The divine does operate dependably in human experience. Macintosh distinguished between "a scientific empirical theology" which provides the data for examining the existence of God and the other disciplines of theology which

10. Ian T. Ramsey, *Religious Language* (London: SCM, 1957), p. 89.
11. Tillich, *Systematic Theology*, I, 44.

spell out the concepts. In his first book, Wieman made a similar claim, but he believed that "the datum of religious experience is so exceedingly complex that no method has yet been devised which is fit to treat it scientifically." Yet he said that "mystical experience... must be scientifically interpreted if we are to know what God is."[12]

Wieman later moved away from this position, especially from dependence on the analysis of the religious consciousness. He also made fewer claims about the scientific basis of religious knowledge, preferring to place the emphasis on reason "defined as the method of analysis, observation, inference, prediction, experiment, and logical coherence."[13] But, he added, insofar as religious knowledge "depends upon the emergence of a new theory by way of creativity and the critical examination of the theory by reason, . . . it is the same as scientific knowledge about anything."[14]

Whereas observation and reason are essential for the interpretation of any experience, scientific verification usually involves control and prediction of a kind not possible in the interpretation of general experience or religious experience. This has led some writers to speak of the scientific "spirit" rather than method. Ian T. Ramsey has developed what he calls "the method of empirical fit," by which he means that out of models which are both scientific and personal and which are born of insight there is a capacity to match a wide range of phenomena and a variety of human needs. It is "an overall characterization of a complex, multivaried pattern of behaviour which it is impossible in a particular case to specify deductively beforehand."[15] This is why we

12. Henry Nelson Wieman, *Religious Experience and Scientific Method* (New York: Macmillan, 1926), pp. 23, 29.
13. Henry Nelson Wieman, *Man's Ultimate Commitment* (Carbondale: Southern Illinois University Press, 1958), p. 138.
14. Wieman, *Man's Ultimate Commitment*, p. 150.
15. Ian T. Ramsey, *Models and Mystery* (London: Oxford University Press, 1964), pp. 17, 38.

cannot talk of God in straightforward language, for we always need to qualify our statements in strange and logically odd ways. The danger of any theology is that it may speak as if it has "privileged access to the diaries of God's private life."[16]

MYSTICAL EMPIRICISM

Tillich's third form of empirical theology is designated as "mystical." It is "secretly presupposed by the ontological as well as by the scientific concept of experience." It can take the Christian theologian beyond the limits of Christian experience.[17] The emphasis on religious experience or consciousness, which has been presupposed by many theologians, was isolated by Schleiermacher: "to feel absolutely dependent and to be conscious of being in relation with God are one and the same thing."[18] This is a continuing experience throughout life. It is not empirical, however, because for Schleiermacher empiricism cannot make the necessary distinction between what is essential and what is contingent.[19] Schleiermacher may be said to have pointed to one interpretation of religious experience as a forerunner of empirical theology, but later thinkers refined his approach and developed a method that was empirical.

William James made a careful examination of the varieties of religious experience the source of his primary data, but his methodology was already established for verifying on empirical and pragmatic grounds a concept of God. Macintosh, likewise, stayed within the realm of religious experience, but he did not believe that all religious experience was equally helpful, and he

16. Ramsey, *Religious Language*, p. 91.
17. Tillich, *Systematic Theology*, I, 44–45.
18. Friedrich Schleiermacher, *The Christian Faith* (Edinburgh: T & T Clark, 1928), p. 16.
19. Schleiermacher, *Christian Faith*, p. 4.

worked on the criteria that helped one to discriminate in identifying the distinctively divine elements. There is need for the
expert who can properly interpret the significance of the data of
experience.

There is a broader view of empiricism which interprets all of
experience as a source for all knowledge, including religious
knowledge. There may be special occasions of insight or disclosure, but they result from the ongoing stream of experience.
There may be a religious dimension in general experience. The
quest for God is located in human experience generally, and
therefore to restrict religious knowledge to a base of a narrowly
religious consciousness or experience or mysticism is to isolate it
from the knowledge derived from normal living. William Temple
put it clearly when he criticized William James for using isolated
experiences only: "The phrase 'religious experience' may also
mean the constant experience of life and the world that comes to
the religious [person]—an experience which is pervaded and
permeated by religion. Now it is this, and not the former, to
which any religious person attaches importance."[20]

Whitehead broadened the empirical base by describing what
might be called "bodily" or "nonsensuous" experience. Schubert
Ogden calls this "an intuitive awareness of our own past mental
and bodily states and of the wider world as they compel con-
formation to themselves in the present."[21] One's initial experience is of the whole, and then one abstracts from the whole to
select the particulars. This can be illustrated by the experience of
a painting, the Grand Canyon, or simply by entering a room.

20. William Temple, "Some Implications of Theism," *Contemporary British
Philosophy*, 1st series, ed. J. H. Muirhead (New York: Macmillan, 1924), p.
424.
21. Schubert M. Ogden, "Present Prospects for Empirical Theology," *The
Future of Empirical Theology*, ed. Bernard E. Meland (Chicago: University of
Chicago Press, 1969), pp. 81–82.

One is aware of the total impact before one begins to select particulars. This is what Whitehead calls nonsensuous awareness as distinct from the concrete particulars of sense experience.

William James was right in the claim that we experience relations as well as objects, facts as well as values; therefore, some experiences are more significant than others. We have what Bernard E. Meland calls "an appreciative consciousness," or we are aware of the "thickness" of some experiences that takes us beyond the immediate moment. There is a rich fullness of experience that points to the reality of God. There is an intuition of holiness, an experience of creative transformation, that stands at the center of experiences that have religious significance.

We begin to understand how the words empiricism and experience are used. Empiricism may be an appeal to evidence based on sense data, but it may be expanded to include pragmatic tests and various kinds of intuition; it may be restricted to subject-object impersonal relations, or it may be expanded to include the participant as part of the process, or it may focus on interpersonal experiences. The testing of such experiences may be restricted to controlled experiments or it may include observation on a broader basis, or it may be in terms of what Ian Ramsey calls "empirical fit." The experiences appealed to may be mystical, more broadly religious, or experience as a whole—or some combination of these. Some kind of clarification is called for if we are to deal adequately with the varieties of empirical method.

There have been many criticisms of empiricism as a method, but it is hard to establish any concepts that are not derived from experience. The basic assumption underlying empiricism is a realistic epistemology that claims that what we experience actually exists separate from the knower. Once the data are established and interpreted, it is then possible to move into over-beliefs that are consistent with the empirically tested concepts but which are due to speculation or imagination as one brings to bear on these beliefs the value judgments or traditional ways of thinking.[22]

WHAT EMPIRICISM DOES

To approach beliefs on the basis of empirical method gives one a start in educational procedures. Little children learn about their world by touching, smelling, hearing, and seeing. They revel in museums that have "please touch" signs on important statues or sculptures or artifacts. They are excited by what they learn on field trips, especially where there are the smelling of flowers or animals, the hearing of unusual sounds, and the seeing of new sights. The natural world provides many instances which call for responses in terms of wonder, curiosity, awe, and dread. Small children experience entities that adults ignore. The more senses they use, the more they will learn and the better they will learn it. Soon they learn to express their learning through drawing pictures or through the development of their vocabulary. The use of art provides a new level of learning. We know much more today about how to appeal to the senses through the audio-visual techniques. We seek to accompany the learning process with enough of a "warm glow" to make the experience a pleasant one.[23]

It is important to keep this kind of learning alive. High school students are likely to move into the area of formal operations, concerned more with concepts and propositions than with the data that make them alive. Perhaps they have moved away from

22. See my chapter, "Empirical Method and Its Critics," in *The American Spirit in Theology* (Philadelphia: Pilgrim Press, 1974), pp. 119–139; see my chapter, "How to Test Our Beliefs," in *This We Can Believe* (New York: Hawthorn-Seabury, 1976), pp. 21–38.
23. See Kathrene M. Tobey, *Learning and Teaching Through the Senses* (Philadelphia: Westminster Press, 1970).

learning through interpreting data to a level of thinking on the basis of data provided by others. Such formal operations are necessary, but not at the expense of the aesthetic and sensuous elements of life.

All data cannot be first-hand without limiting what the human mind can accomplish. Scientists seek to replicate the data of previous experiences. In the field of religion this is not possible. Too many of the data are derived from historic events which have their own unique meaning. One does not replicate the crucifixion of Jesus, although murderers may seek to kill others by means of crucifixion. So we turn to the record of history, seek to establish the data derived from historic events in the light of our own perspective, and move toward a new formulation of beliefs for today. Empiricism and a process view of reality play an important part in this process, but it demands also a careful scrutiny of the evidence coming from historic sources.

At the center of this historic tradition is the Bible, and its authority has been interpreted in a variety of ways. We will examine some of the claims in the next chapter.

5

Varieties of Biblical Authority

The Bible is considered generally as the primary source for Christian beliefs, although it is related in various ways to tradition as an interpreter. Thus, the Bible is said to have authority over believers. In some cases, this authority is claimed to be absolute, but this may be a matter of influence in relation to other sources, such as tradition and current theological systems. Authority may be grounded in a theory of origins, of inspiration, or of infallibility. Or it may be grounded in the ultimate authority of God. Thus, a theory that is not verifiable becomes the ground for the claim of authority.

The distinction may be made between a hard and a soft authority. The hard type is based on a kind of inerrancy that claims the subjection of the believer, or it may be derived from an emphasis on the church as the correct interpreter. Such a view is usually acquired within a Christian community that shares this outlook, and thus its theology is likely to be equally authoritative. The soft authority approach has arisen from the development of ecumenical dialogue and the pluralism of recent theology, with the emphasis on the right of the individual to think out one's own theological system. The Bible, as James Barr suggests, is authoritative because it "is built upon *cumulative experience*" and therefore it has "spoken to us with authority."[1] In this way of thinking about authority, we can understand the response of

1. James Barr, *The Bible and the Modern World* (New York: Harper & Row, 1973), p. 29.

those who reported that Jesus spoke as "one having authority." It is a matter of rightful or persuasive power as against coercion. One remains free to decide which authority to accept, and then one submits to that authority. This leads to pluralism, because authority differs for different people. But this is not the whole story. As long as authority is persuasive rather than coercive, persons remain free because they are not faced by an arbitrary external power.

Most people share the view of authority of the community in which they grew up or to which they belong, and this means that they start with a theological bias by which they interpret scripture and tradition. However, they remain free to reject that view of authority in favor of another one. Even those who hold a hard view of authority find that they must account for the freedom of others whose interpretation of authority is different.

It may help if we examine some specific views of several communions, making some generalizations about a variety of opinions about authority. We will look at the Eastern Orthodox who place scripture and tradition on the same level, the Roman Catholics who hold tradition to be superior to the scriptures, the fundamentalists who assert the verbal infallibility of the Bible, the left-wing groups who believe reason to be superior to any historical revelation, and classical Protestants as represented by Anglicans or Episcopalians who accept a soft view of the authority of scripture and treat tradition with great respect.

EASTERN ORTHODOX VIEWS

The approach of the Eastern Orthodox is a dual one: there are two sources embedded in Orthodox theology, the scriptures and tradition. The Orthodox Church is held to be the unerring bearer and teacher of all truth. To the Orthodox there is no Bible or tradition without the church, so that the church is actually prior to its authorities.

God himself has revealed what human beings should believe, so that they may believe in God and honor God. This process helps humanity to respond in such a way that they will be saved as they worthily turn to God. Knowledge of God is possible through natural means, by the use of reason and the interpretation of history and experience, but this knowledge is of value only as it serves to prepare for faith. The dogma of the church stems directly from a sphere of revelation centering in the Bible, the early ecumenical councils, and the Nicean-Constantinopolitan creed. This creed in summary form contains a full and complete confession of faith. The Orthodox Church claims that its faith has not been changed and that it reflects the dogma of the primitive church through the first eight centuries. There have been more explicit formulations of doctrine since then, but no real changes have taken place.

The Bible is not conceived by the Orthodox as explicitly containing all things necessary to salvation. "The Holy Scriptures, from their avowed purpose, neither were written nor purported to be a full and systematic presentation of the Father first imparted by a living voice."[2] Much has come down from the secret apostolic teaching and from the practices and the customs of the true Catholic church.

The Orthodox Church treats the Septuagint (the early Greek translation of the Old Testament) with the same reverence that Rome gives to the Vulgate. Although emendations are accepted on the basis of the Hebrew text, the Greek Septuagint has canonical standing and no new translations into modern Greek are accepted.

The scriptures are said to be "inspired" but not to be "literal" in their authority. No modern scholarship or criticism can destroy this inspiration, for it depends on the energizing power of

2. Quoted by Frank Gavin, *Some Aspects of Contemporary Greek Orthodox Thought* (New York: Morehouse-Gorham, 1923), p. 17.

the Holy Spirit in the writers and in the church. The rule of interpretation is "the mind of the church," as Hippolytus has said. No single person, even a patriarch, is recognized as having final authority on these matters. The hierarchy, meeting in ecumenical councils, becomes the voice of the church and therefore is infallible when their decisions are accepted by the church as a whole.

The form of the Bible is human, but the essence is divine. Different degrees or levels of inspiration may be distinguished. These degrees are "related to (a) the gradual progress of the divine revelation, (b) the differences of manner of outpouring and energy of the Holy Spirit, and (c) the more or less abundant showing forth of the spiritual gift of inspiration, in proportion to the receptiveness of the inspired writer."[3]

Although the scriptures are concerned with supernatural revelation, there is a place for natural theology. A supernatural revelation needs a natural theology and revelation as a base. Through the external cosmos, the human conscience, and natural history there can be human knowledge of God, but when achieved it points to the inadequacy of the human spirit and the corresponding hunger for revealed theology. But even supernatural revelation is limited by the finite capacities of those who receive it, and only at the end of time will there be a complete revelation.

The church is the guardian of all revelation, and therefore the interpretation of scripture by individuals is always suspect. It is here that the oral tradition comes to the fore. The New Testament arose from this oral tradition, and the latter remained more detailed than what was reduced to writing. Thus the tradition, "written not with pen and ink upon parchment, but in the hearts of the faithful by the Holy Spirit, may more properly be called the first canon of Faith."[4] Oral tradition is the original instru-

3. Panayotis I. Bratsiotis, in *Biblical Authority for Today*, ed. Alan Richardson and Wolfgang Schweitzer (Philadelphia: Westminster, 1951), p. 24.
4. Quoted by Gavin, *Greek Orthodox Thought*, p. 26.

ment. Nothing was written until Moses' time. Jesus wrote nothing. Tradition speaks to everyone, while books are available only to the few. The Holy Spirit is the author of both scripture and tradition. Heretics have always cast tradition aside, because anything can be proved by scripture, but people are bound to the truth by tradition.

There is some question among Orthodox theologians as to which elements in the tradition are binding, although even here there are two elements to be noted: if the findings of a later council or synod add nothing new to the original tradition, they are valid; and if the seal of acceptance of one synod through "the mind of the church" is given to new findings by subsequent synods, they also become valid and binding. This provides for flexibility and development in doctrine, although not for the evolution of entirely new concepts.

This line of reasoning is made abundantly clear in a statement by St. Basil the Great, as quoted in one of the catechisms: "For were we to dare to reject unwritten customs, as if they had no great importance, we should insensibly mutilate the Gospel, even in the most essential points, or rather, for the teaching of the Apostles leave but an empty name. For instance: let us mention before all else the very first and commonest act of Christians; that they who trust in the name of our Lord Jesus Christ, should sign themselves with the sign of the cross; who hath taught this by writing? To turn to the east in prayer; what Scripture have we for this? The words of invocation in the change of the Eucharistic bread and the cup of blessing; by which of the saints have they been left to us in writing? For we are not content with those words which the Apostle or the Gospel records, but both before and after them we pronounce others also, which we hold to be of great force for the Sacrament, though we have received them for unwritten teaching. By what Scripture is it in like manner that we bless the water of Baptism, the oil of unction, and the person himself who is baptized? Is it not by a silent and secret tradition? What more? The very practice of anointing with oil; what written word do we have for it? Whence is the rule of trine immersion: and the rest of the ceremonies at Baptism, the renunciation of Satan and his angels? from what Scripture are they taken? Are they not all from this unpublished and private teaching, which our Fathers kept under a reserve inaccessible to curiosity and profane disquisition, having been taught as a first principle to guard by silence the sanctity of the mysteries? For how were it fit to publish in writing the doctrine of those things, on which the unbaptized may not so much as look?"[5]

While to the Protestant this fascinating argument may seem to stand the truth on its head, the Orthodox writers contrast their position with those held by Protestants and Roman Catholics. Rhôsse writes that Protestants "are incapable of having the Faith which was taught throughout the years, for they deny in principle the equal validity of Tradition as a source of Christian Truth, and reject the Church as the supreme interpreter of Holy Scripture."[6] Homyakov shows in brilliant fashion how the Protestant view is inadequate from the Orthodox perspective: "Protestants call the Bible Holy Scriptures, but with what justification? Why do they ascribe such an absolute authenticity and authority to a book which is nothing more than a collection of separate writings, ascribed to different authors of whose very names we are not always certain? Does the authenticity come from the historic authenticity of the content? But such an authenticity, even if exactly proved by criticism, which is not at all the case, could have significance only for the historical part, which is only a small portion of the Scriptures, and would be no guarantee for the dogmatic, by far the most important section. Or is it the names which give this guarantee? But those names are very often unknown or doubtful, and there is no shadow of foundation for believing the names of St. Mark or St. Luke or St. Apollos to be

5. *Catechism of the Orthodox, Catholic, Eastern Church*, p. 8.
6. Quoted by Gavin, *Greek Orthodox Thought*, p. 43 note.

more reliable than Papias or St. Clement or St. Polycarp. Yet the writings of these latter are not recognized as having Biblical authority. Does the authenticity arise from the pure doctrine expressed in the Book? But then there must exist a norm for this doctrine, which is before the Bible and stands as a standard of its sanctity. The Canon, and only the Canon, confirms the Bible as Holy Scriptures, and here not even the finest logic can undertake to separate the Canon from the Church. The Canon rests on the confidence of the Church. To accept the Holy Scriptures is to accept the irrefutable authority of the Church."[7]

Although the Protestant view of scriptures is rejected, Zankov believes that there is a closer affinity between Orthodoxy and classical Protestantism, especially as illustrated in Lutheranism and Anglicanism, than between Orthodoxy and Rome, primarily because he believes that Rome has rejected the authority of the Bible while Protestants take seriously both the Bible and the early councils and writings of the Fathers. He does not minimize the differences, but he thinks there is no hope of reunion with Rome, while there is hope in the Ecumenical Movement, where Orthodoxy is now a participant. Liberalism and nationalism are suspect; it is conservative, classical Protestantism in which he has some confidence. He believes that Rome has a proper theory of development, but distorts it in practice by promulgating novel doctrines without regard to either scripture or tradition. In the last analysis, only the Orthodox Church has kept both the full tradition and the full teaching of scripture, backed by the supreme authority of the true Church.

ROMAN CATHOLICS AND AUTHORITY

We have used the position of the Eastern Orthodox Church as a frame of reference for evaluating and comparing other positions. We turn now to the Roman Catholic Church. A group of

7. Quoted in Stefan Zankov, *The Eastern Orthodox Church* (New York:

English Roman Catholic bishops once referred to Tyndale's translation as "a certain heretical and damnable book called the New Testament."[8] They were probably more incensed by Tyndale's anti-Catholic marginal notes, but it is true that the Bible seems at times to be treated as having little doctrinal significance and its reading by lay people was not encouraged. Technically, the Catholic Church accepts a literal interpretation of scripture, but it is careful to keep the interpretation subject to the church's authority. It is stated this way in Vatican II:

"Those divinely revealed realities which are contained and presented in sacred Scripture have been committed in writing under the inspiration of the Holy Spirit. Holy Mother Church, relying on the belief of the apostles, holds that the books of both the Old and New Testament in their entirety, with all their parts, are sacred and canonical because, having been written under the inspiration of the Holy Spirit... they have God as their author and have been handed on as such to the Church herself. In composing the sacred books, God chose men and while employed by Him they made use of their powers and abilities, so that with Him acting in them and through them, they, as true authors, consigned to writing everything and only those things which He wanted."[9]

The line of argument is much the same as that proposed by the Orthodox, who agree that Rome has a proper theory of development. The Roman view, however, goes beyond that of the Orthodox emphasis on "the mind of the church" to a hierarchical view of authority of the church which centers in the pope, as the

---

Morehouse-Gorham, 1930), pp. 76–77. See Panayotis I. Bratsiotis, in *Biblical Theology for Today,* ed. Alan Richardson and Wolfgang Schweitzer, p. 21.
8. C. Anderson Scott, *Romanism and the Gospel* (Philadelphia: Presbyterian Board, 1946), p. 159.
9. *The Documents of Vatican II,* ed. Walter M. Abbott, S.J. (New York: America Press, 1966), pp. 118–119.

successor to Peter. "Hence, by divine institution he enjoys supreme, full, immediate, and universal authority over the care of souls."[10] The church, says Rome, existed before the New Testament, wrote the New Testament, and decided the canon of the New Testament, which means that the church already had a standard of faith and an authority superior to the New Testament in order to accomplish this. It also implies that the unwritten, secret tradition exists in the teachings and the liturgy and the councils of the church.

Both the Orthodox and Roman Catholic churches agree that it is not obvious, as Protestants are supposed to believe, that the scriptures are inspired or inerrant, save in a divine testimony, not being contained in the Bible with sufficient clearness. Even a sound Christian scholar cannot recognize any necessary warrant and must rely on the living tradition of the whole church. Vatican II reasserts that "the Scriptures are not self-explanatory" and "they require the Church's magisterium or teaching authority to explain what the more substantive passages mean and how they are to be lived out by the faithful . . . under the guidance of the successors of the apostles united with Peter's successor, the Bishop of Rome."[11]

Tradition comes into the picture not only to assist in understanding scripture but also as a separate stream dating back to the apostles. "Sacred tradition and sacred Scripture form one sacred deposit of the word of God, which is committed to the Church."[12] Tradition is carried on by the church through its preaching and liturgy, and tradition leads into the whole concept of development.

When Cardinal Newman attempted to justify dogmas such as the Immaculate Conception and the infallibility of the pope,

10. *Documents of Vatican II,* p. 397.
11. John A. Hardon, S.J., *The Catholic Catechism* (New York: Doubleday, 1975), p. 23.
12. *Documents of Vatican II,* p. 117.

both admittedly nonscriptural, he wrote, "It is a first strong point
that, in an idea such as Christianity, developments cannot but
be, and those surely divine, because it is divine; a second that, if
so, they are the very ones which exist, because there are no
others; and a third point is the fact that they are found just there,
where true developments ought to be found—namely, in the
historic seat of Apostolical teachings and in the authorized home
of immemorial tradition."[13] It is clear that once we grant the
possibility of development of Christian doctrine, on terms either
of Orthodoxy or of Rome, we run into almost unsurmountable
difficulties in refuting their claims. Why should we stop with
one, or five, or seven, or seventy councils?

Development, however, is an empirical fact of history, not
only in Orthodoxy and Rome who have theories about it, but
also in Protestantism, which has no adequate theory to explain
it. The challenge is clear. Traditions continue to develop in all
parts of the Christian churches today, most obviously in many
developing countries where Christian doctrine, liturgy, and practice are being adapted to local cultures. But Protestants do not
find a whit of evidence for "the survival of an oral, unwritten
doctrinal tradition after the Scriptures have appeared and have
begun to circulate."[14] There are sources of information other
than the scriptures about the early church in the writings of the
Apologists and Fathers, and much of value may be found there;
the Apocryphal New Testament also enlightens some aspects of
biblical understanding, as do the Dead Sea Scrolls, but these are
written sources.

There is more a tendency since Vatican II to let the scriptures
speak for themselves, but the emphasis is still on the authority of
the church to provide correct teaching.[15] Within this tradition,

13. John Henry Newman, *The Development of Christian Doctrine* (London:
Longmans, Green, 1949 ed., Cap. III), p. 120.
14. Hanson and Fuller, *The Church of Rome* (London: SCM, 1949), p. 69.
15. Berard L. Marthaler, O.F.M. Conv., *Catechetics in Context* (Huntington:
Our Sunday Visitor, 1973), pp. 42, 86.

it is possible for Hans Küng to make the following points:

"The Bible is not simply God's word: it is first of all and in its whole extent man's word, the word of quite definite individuals.

"The Bible does not simply contain God's word: there are not certain propositions which are God's word, while the rest are man's.

"The Bible becomes God's word: it becomes God's word for anyone who submits trustfully and in faith to its testimony and so to the God revealed in it and to Jesus Christ." [16]

If this sounds more like Karl Barth, it is not surprising. For there has been a great deal of dialogue between Protestant and Catholic theologians and biblical scholars, and as a result there has been a meeting of minds on many issues. But the official position has not changed in any radical way, which is why Küng has been in trouble.

The Protestant rejects the Orthodox and Catholic claims for the authority of an oral tradition because the Protestant does not believe that such a tradition exists. There are many customs, rituals, and practices coming down from earliest times, arising out of the life together of the Christians, especially in their worship. There is much that is good in the customs listed by St. Basil, such as the sign of the cross and anointing with oil, but the Protestant would at least place such practices at the periphery of belief and ritual. Furthermore, the Protestant rejects both the Orthodox and Roman views of the authority of the church, although this leaves the difficulty of defining heresy or providing for a sound theory of development, unless one asserts a freedom of the believer to move beyond the confines of both scripture and tradition.

THE FUNDAMENTALISTS

We turn now to three Protestant views, those of the fundamentalists, the left-wing liberals, and classical Protestants.

16. Hans Küng, *On Being a Christian* (New York: Doubleday, 1976), p. 467; see Karl Barth, *Church Dogmatics*, I, 2, sec. 19–21.

The fundamentalists agree in theory with the Orthodox and Roman Catholic positions that the scriptures are infallible and without error, but move on to an insistence on verbal inerrancy and the exclusive authority of the Bible without conscious recourse to tradition. In 1923, the Presbyterian Assembly passed a resolution which affirmed the infallibility of the Bible, belief in the virgin birth of Jesus, in the substitutionary atonement on the cross, in the bodily and physical resurrection and ascension of Jesus, and in his mighty miracles. Frequently there is added to this list belief in the imminent second coming, with a thousand years of Christ's leadership, followed by a final state of bliss under the direct supervision of God himself.[17]

The fundamentalists insist on the verbal inspiration of the writers and on the Old and New Testaments as the only infallible rule of faith and practice. No principle of interpretation is assumed. Biblical scholarship is restricted to textual criticism, where scholars such as J. Gresham Machen have made genuine contributions, for most fundamentalists insist that only the documents in their original languages are infallible. The King James Version is held in the highest regard, although other translations are now being used.

This position fails to provide a procedure whereby the Bible can come to terms with modern knowledge, especially in the field of science. There is no principle of development, as in the Orthodox and Roman communions, whereby traditions may illuminate biblical passages and new knowledge may make the Word of God more relevant.

Furthermore, the strict biblicism of the fundamentalists was not consistent. There is a principle of interpretation which seems to other Christians to provide the means of selecting certain

17. See Edwin H. Dian, *The Presbyterian Conflict* (Grand Rapids: Eerdmans, 1940), p. 34; J. G. Machen, *The Christian Faith and the Modern World* (New York: Macmillan, 1936), pp. 32–86.

doctrines to the exclusion of others equally or more significant. They insist on the virgin birth as a biological fact, which means that belief in the incarnation turns on one historical question. They interpret the atonement in terms of satisfaction and substitution and do not allow for other theories which have existed throughout the history of the church. They insist on a bodily resurrection and ascension as the only interpretation of the biblical evidence. They affirm that the miracles of Jesus were acts that defied the laws of nature, thus eliminating God's actions within the natural order. Their interpretation of the creation stories disregards what scientists know about evolutionary theory.

So the biblical literalism of the fundamentalists may be seen as colored by theological presuppositions. The Orthodox and Roman query of where these prior assumptions come from is impossible for them to answer on their own grounds. It would seem that there is an unwritten and hidden tradition within Protestantism that guides the fundamentalists in their interpretations of the scriptures.

The extreme literalism of the fundamentalists has placed them outside the mainstream of ecumenical Christianity. Although churches containing fundamentalists are within the ecumenical movement, the sectarian groups which are officially fundamentalist do not seek the ecumenical fellowship on either the local or international level, and often they stand in opposition to the work of the ecumenical bodies.

LEFT-WING CHRISTIANS

The opposite extreme from the position of biblical inerrancy is held by certain left-wing Christians. Some liberals in mainline churches and some Unitarians and Quakers can be classified in this category. Normally, they are not organized and they often disagree among themselves, so that no statement of their position may be considered definitive. The position is not a new one and antedates the fundamentalists by at least a century. The attitude toward the Bible was expressed by W. E. Channing in 1819: "Our leading principle in interpreting Scripture is this— that the Bible is a book written for [human beings], in [human] language, and that its meaning is to be sought in the same manner as that of any other book. . . . We indeed grant that the use of reason in religion is accompanied with danger. But we ask any honest [person] to look back at the history of the Church, and say, whether the renunciation of it be not still more dangerous."[18]

Using the canons of philosophical reasoning as a basis for interpreting scripture, it was natural that the presuppositions of a liberal culture should color the meaning of the gospel. The optimism of liberalism's doctrine of the goodness of humanity and of the love of God became a subjective element in the interpretation of both scripture and history. Biblical scholarship often reflected the assumptions of modern anthropology and of the philosophy of inevitable progress. This left-wing type of liberalism, significant as it was in opening humanity's eyes to knowledge of new facts and interpretations, was often incapable of letting the facts speak for themselves. When Albert Schweitzer flashed across the horizon with his theory of Jesus' consistent eschatology, Dean Inge of London rejected such a view because no English gentleman would believe such a thing. Later on, however, Schweitzer became a darling of the liberals because they admired not only his scholarship but also his theology.

What happened to left-wing liberalism was what had happened to the Orthodox, Roman, and fundamentalist approaches: a foreign element became more dominant as a basis for interpretation than the internal meaning of scripture itself. In each case a theory of development overwhelmed the basic authority, and

---

18. Quoted in Vergilius Ferm, ed., *Encyclopedia of Religion* (New York: Philosophical Library, 1945), p. 443.

scripture was forced into the straight-jacket of prior and often unstated assumptions. But whereas the other positions we have considered were held by official groups and churches, the left-wing view was expressed only by a few small churches such as the Unitarians and among individuals who maintained membership in other churches or in no church. In some cases, such as the modernist movement of the Roman Church, individuals such as Alfred Loisy were condemned. Even Teilhard de Chardin was not allowed to publish his writings during his lifetime. Some who sought ordination in various churches were denied, and they changed to more liberal denominations.

This left-wing movement was significant because it forced other Protestants to face certain facts which otherwise might have been obscured, and therefore many of the developments among the liberals have found a place in the current thinking of classical Protestantism. Other movements have become offshoots of the earlier developments and are now affecting both Catholic and Protestant theology, especially in the development of process thought.

MAINLINE PROTESTANTS

Somewhere between these two extremes of Protestant thinking and also showing a contrast to Orthodox and Roman Catholic views is the attitude maintained by a large majority in the major Protestant denominations. Deriving their position from Luther, Calvin, Hooker, and others, this point of view has been attained through slow growth and at great effort. It is a position that has come to terms with biblical scholarship, modern science, and current cultural values without losing the insights and convictions of evangelical Christianity. As an example of mainline Protestantism which is still aware of its Catholic heritage, the position of the Protestant Episcopal Church may be taken as representative.

The reformation in England was a declaration of independence from arbitrary authority and the replacement of it with a persuasive moral authority which rested on the acceptance of obligations by the individual. The *Book of Common Prayer* was strictly scriptural in its interpretations, and what was considered scriptural in the inherited Catholicism was retained along with the newly discovered Protestant insights. The genius of Thomas Cranmer in the first two editions of the Prayer Book, showing a swing toward a more Protestant base in the second edition, was typical of Anglicanism.

The Episcopal Church agrees with the Lutherans and Calvinist communions that "Holy Scripture containeth all things necessary to salvation," but this is not an acceptance of any kind of infallibility or inerrancy. In 1795, some portions of scripture were deleted from the lectionary with the reason, quaintly put, that they "were inexpedient to be read in mixt assemblies."

Within the Bible, however, is to be found the unique, true, final, and saving revelation of the one true God. This is the claim made by all Protestant Christians. The Bible *contains*, that is, has within it as an essential and discoverable element, what is *necessary* for salvation, for it is the record of the mighty acts of God in history. It tells the story of God's relation to humanity in a drama of redemption through the creation of the universe, the covenant with Israel, the coming of Christ, the establishment of the church, and the promise of a consummation in history of God's aims, with the demand that humanity respond with commitment.[19]

This conclusion is drawn from the character of the books of the Bible. In spite of the Orthodox and Roman claims that the authority of the Bible must be buttressed by the church, "the Bible possesses authority for Christians on the ground that it is the classical literature of that progressive revelation of God in

19. See my *Biblical Theology and Christian Education* (New York: Scribner, 1956).

history which culminated in Jesus Christ," say the competent English theologians who wrote *Doctrine in the Church of England*. [20]

These same writers claim that only a broad principle of interpretation guides us. The authority of scripture does not preclude any findings of biblical scholarship, historical study, modern scientific views of the world, levels of spiritual and moral values, or new thought forms. The standard is clear. It is "the Mind of Christ as unfolded in the experience of the Church and appropriated by the individual Christian through His Spirit."[21] Allowances must be made for discovering the actual words of Jesus in the gospels, and yet "it remains true that the religious and moral teachings of the gospels convey faithfully the impress made upon the Apostolic Church by the mind and personality of Jesus, and thus possess supreme authority."[22] The use of the term "mind of Christ" as a means of judgment lacks the clarity of legal and literal renderings of authority, but it provides a perspective in terms of basic attitudes by which the remainder of the Bible can be understood. The emphasis on "the mind of Christ" has the objectivity of the teachings of Jesus as recorded in the synoptic gospels, but it also includes the insights provided by history and by the subjective elements of the individual's own choice. It is a question of appropriating an attitude or disposition or spirit of Jesus rather than a rigid command. This solution does not provide a hard or absolute authority, but it makes room for the principle of development based on scripture which is more reliable than the other theories we have considered.

20. William Temple, ed., *Doctrine in the Church of England* (New York: Macmillan, 1938), p. 31; see pp. 27-31.
21. Temple, *Doctrine in the Church of England*, p. 32.
22. Temple, *Doctrine in the Church of England*, p. 33. See my *A Symphony of the Christian Year* (New York: Seabury, 1954), pp. 213-219; Robert Dentan, *The Holy Scriptures* (New York: Seabury, 1949), pp. 5-24; Robert A. Bennett and O. C. Edwards, *The Bible for Today's Church* (New York: Seabury, 1979), pp. 282-285.

The scriptures are part of the tradition. There is always a developing tradition within the life of the church. The sound test of this development is always scripture, and thus tradition is subservient to scripture. The authority of the church, therefore, is always inferior to that of scripture. There is a suspicion even of the general councils, for errors crept in at least within the first three centuries.

The claim of the Orthodox and Roman Catholic churches that because the church created the scriptures primary authority resides in the church is exploded by the classical Protestant view, for the true foundation of both scripture and church is Jesus Christ. Insofar as the church may be said to have written the New Testament, it made itself subservient to the revelation recorded in the total Jewish-Christian tradition, including the Jewish Bible or Old Testament. Thus, the church is subject to the Word of God, or else we could not say that the Holy Spirit influences the church; but the church is not limited to the scripture, and there are other sources of knowledge which must be considered.

In controversies of faith, according to the Articles of Religion of several Protestant communions, the church has authority to declare positions heretical. This is primarily a matter of jurisdiction or discipline, but it leads to the restriction of doctrinal anarchy. The test is always in terms of scripture. "Although the Church be a witness and keeper of Holy Writ, yet, as it ought not to decree anything against the same, so besides the same ought it not to enforce anything to be believed of necessity of Salvation," say the Anglican Articles of Religion. Yet it has become more difficult to define heresy, and in the trial of Bishop James Pike it was deemed that heresy could not be a useful concept. The famous statement of Erasmus is relevant: "By identifying the new learning with heresy, you make orthodoxy synonymous with ignorance."[23]

23. This appeared on the masthead of the British *Modern Churchman* for many years as a slogan of Anglican Modernism.

It should be made clear that this does not do away with tradition. The warnings of the Orthodox and Catholic theologians
against the excesses of biblicism or bibliolatry need to be noted.
"Once tradition is repudiated, it is necessary to manipulate Biblical texts in order to regulate the details of social life and church
life; this leads to a newfangled Biblicism and to novel absurdities
of all kinds. The Biblical teaching is always to be interpreted by
reason and tradition; apart from reason and tradition the Bible
can be manipulated to support any kind of nonsense or heresy."[24]

Those communions which maintain creeds or credal affirma-
tions see the creeds to be of value as clarifying or representing
scriptural truths. There is a remarkable passage on the use of
symbolic language in *Doctrine in the Church of England:* Statements in the creeds which cannot be accepted literally may
"have value as pictorial statements of spiritual truths, even
though the supposed facts themselves did not actually happen. . . . It is not therefore illegitimate to accept and affirm particular clauses in the creeds in this symbolic fashion." This
statement is immediately qualified: "It is, however, in any case
essential to hold that the facts underlying the Gospel story—
which story the creeds summarize and interpret—were such as to
justify the Gospel itself." In the historical figure of Jesus of
Nazareth we believe that "the Word was made flesh and dwelt
among us."[25]

Classical Protestantism, with its faith based on scripture,
allows for the right of private judgment. Individuals in the
church are to use their reason and work out their own faith. They
ought to test out their theories in practice, so far as their abilities
and training qualify them, to think out their own beliefs, and to
distinguish between what they have accepted on authority only
and what they have appropriated in thought and experience. But
they must recognize that it is only in the fellowship and worship

24. Alan Richardson, in *Biblical Authority for Today* ed. Richardson and
Schweitzer, pp. 118–119.
25. Temple, *Doctrine in the Church of England*, pp. 27–28.

of the community that they can come fully to appreciate and accept.[26] Lest this seem too liberal, coming from the leadership of William Temple, a quotation from the Catholic wing of Anglicanism is significant: "The final appeal is to the spiritual, intellectual, and historical content of divine revelation, *as verifiable at the threefold bar of history, reason, and spiritual experience.*"[27]

We have interpreted classical Protestantism according to Anglican formularies. Anglicanism partakes deeply of the Catholic and Renaissance traditions, moreso than other Protestant communions, but all of Protestantism shares to some degree in this approach. Both freedom and authority are subsumed under the concept of loyalty to God and to the Christian community. Freedom exists as a fact, because no one else can do our believing for us, no matter what the degree of coercion. All persons approach the Bible from specific perspectives, and therefore there will be a variety of interpretations. What the church expects is that where there is commitment to the God revealed in Jesus Christ, a consecrated reason may safely examine the inherited doctrines of the church and the historical foundations of faith. Thus authority and freedom are blended together in the worshiping community which has its roots in the historical revelation of God in Christ.

FREEDOM AND PERSUASIVE AUTHORITY

It can be shown that all communities of believers and all individuals approach the Bible with particular perspectives, assumptions, and theological convictions, and therefore they find in the Bible what they are looking for. At the worst, this is proof-texting out of context, and we are reminded that the Devil

26. Temple, *Doctrine in the Church of England*, p. 36.
27. A.E.J. Rawlinson, in *Essays Catholic and Critical*, ed. Edwin Gordon Selwyn (London: SPCK, 1926), 95, italics in original.

can cite scripture for his purpose. Usually, however, the "threefold bar of history, reason, and spiritual experience" operates within a community, and as a member of the community one seeks support for those beliefs from the data of scripture. This process remains highly selective. The centering on "the mind of Christ" is a subjective and selective process that provides a normative basis for interpretation. When Whitehead, for example, refers to "the brief Galilean vision," it becomes a basis for his view of God's persuasive love.

Believers are shaped by the Bible. David Kelsey suggests that "God 'uses' the church's various uses of scripture in [its] common life to nurture and reform the self-identity both of the community and of the individual persons who comprise it. Theological proposals are to elucidate what that identity is and ought to be, and what reforms are called for and why."[28] The response is an imaginative act. This leads to a second proposal: that theology is in some way controlled by scripture, but this is a broad concept that becomes intelligible only after a "root metaphor" ("the mind of Christ"?) is established. This leads on to the possibility of genuine disclosures to the believer exposed to this process, what Kelsey calls "the work of God the Holy Spirit." "No 'theological position' would presume to tell us how to use scripture so as to 'guarantee' that God will be present to illumine and correct us."[29] There is an openness to the leading of God and to the future of such a position. Thus no rigid and hard authority can be accepted, but only the soft and persuasive authority that allows for human freedom and imagination and for the continuing influence of God's persuasive love on humanity.

This leads to a more open and liberal interpretation of biblical authority than that found in many Christian communions, but it does not go so far as the position of the left-wing liberals. Free-

28. David H. Kelsey, *The Uses of Scripture in Theology* (Philadelphia: Fortress, 1975), p. 214.
29. Kelsey, *Uses of Scripture in Theology*, p. 215.

dom under authority, with the historical revelation of God in Christ interpreted according to the "root metaphor" of "the mind of Christ," and with an understanding of the development of Christian doctrine over the years, supplies a sane and balanced view of the place of scripture among Christians today. It is in this sense, with a proper appeal to history, reason, and spiritual experience, that Christians in their God-given freedom may believe that "the Holy Scriptures contain all doctrine required as necessary to salvation through faith in Jesus Christ."

Those who hold to an empirical and process theology find this approach congenial. It provides for the interpretation of revelation in Temple's terms as "the coincidence of a particularly revealing event and a particularly appreciative mind." It places the Bible within the framework of speaking of God within a metaphysics that reflects a modern picture of the world.

When interpreted in this way, the Bible is particularly suited for educational endeavors. In chapter thirteen we deal specifically with the use of the Bible in education, but here it needs to be noted that we are asking students to use their secularly developed skills to analyze, criticize, compare, and evaluate material from the Bible for the purpose of understanding how God is revealed through such study. The appreciation of the content of the Bible is not an end in itself but is a tool for the coming into faith in God and for responding to God's aim in the world.

6

Being Human
in the United States

The Christian has specific beliefs about what it means to be human. These are stated in theological terms by saying that we are children of God or that we are made in God's image or that we are sinners. But this relation to God by which we identify our humanity is affected strongly by the historical situation. It is not likely that a middle class suburban black person, for example, thinks of being human in the same terms as a slave ancestor did. What happens to a person in the process of growing up affects one's estimate of self worth. There needs to be some criterion by which one establishes a sense of worth if one is to be productive as a person.

In this chapter, we will look briefly at what it means to be human in the United States, thus bringing together some insights from critical observers of the social and personal scene in the United States with inherited Christian interpretations.

A MIXED BAG

In 1930, Halford Luccock of Yale wrote *Jesus and the American Mind.* Some of the chapter headings indicate clearly that the misgivings of 1930 are similar to those a half century later. The scene today is a mixed bag which leads to a great deal of confusion. Luccock pointed to the dual heritage of the United States, the legacy of Puritan and frontier inheritance, and in these two basic forces of American life he saw many of the contradictions as well as the paradoxes which make up the image of what it means to be human in the United States today. He described other factors; one of these he identified as "externalism," by which he meant "preoccupation with the material surface and instruments of life, which comes partly from the emphasis on the practical which is part of the primary inheritance, partly from the lavish production of the machine, from the drive of capitalism and the multiplication of wants which at the present time is unquestionably the greatest of American industries."[1] Side by side with this concern with externals, Luccock found "the religion of prosperity," which has its roots in covetousness and the worship of money, in which

> "All the world's a market place,
> And all the men and women merely buyers.
> They have their purchases and deferred payments,
> And one man in his time supports many salesmen."[2]

This materialism, as described by Luccock, was accompanied by "the mental lock step." There was a "herd mentality" long before it was called "other directedness" or "socio-biological conditioning." It was a pugnacious spirit of conformity which made genuine freedom of thought difficult. But Luccock thought that something could be done about all of this, providing these traits of American character did not infect the religious institutions.

No one is likely to deny the main points made by Luccock. They have become more obvious in the years since he wrote, and they are not peculiar to Americans. The conditions of American life have magnified certain emphases, partly because of the conditions of American prosperity and expansion which made expression of such urges easy.

1. Halford E. Luccock, *Jesus and the American Mind* (New York: Abingdon, 1930), p. 101.
2. Luccock, *Jesus and the American Mind*, p. 154.

However, this portrait is hardly adequate, and Luccock did not claim that it was. Jacques Maritain, in his delightful "love letter to America," claimed that "the American people are the least materialist among the modern peoples which have attained the industrialist stage."[3] It is true that Americans share with the rest of humanity the desire for material things, but there are also certain qualifying factors which are peculiarly American, and these are the key to understanding the American mind.

The chief attitude toward money that impressed Maritain was its use in works of mercy. Not only through foundations and government aid, which are impersonal, but through private gifts to charities, colleges, churches and synagogues, is this attitude expressed. Organized charity has become one of the largest financial operations in America, and this materialistic fact points beyond materialism!

Other factors in life in the United States point to the "good" side of the human image. Maritain's list is not different at many points from the ideals commonly held by adherents of the American way: the possibility of free discussion on all issues in American life, the concern for moral and religious values in politics and education as well as in churches and synagogues, the development of the humanities in education, the possibility of education for every resident of this nation, the yearning for the spiritual life both within and outside of organized religion.

The religious revival in the years following World War II is pointed to by some people as evidence of America's spiritual soundness, but although the facts support the opinion that a revival in terms of numbers took place until about 1964, there is serious question whether there was a genuine religious change. Attendance figures dropped rapidly in the years 1965–1970 and there is not much recovery evident in recent years. However, as

3. Jacques Maritain, *Reflections on America* (New York: Scribners, 1958), p. 29.

Will Herberg saw as early as 1955, there was an increasing religiousness within a framework of secularism, both of which need to be "seen against the background of certain deep-going sociological processes that have transformed the face of the American people in the course of the past generation."[4] This movement was later identified by Robert Bellah and others as a civil religion, which at its best had a transcendental dimension but which grew from the values of American life.[5] At the same time there was a growth of what has been called the "new religious consciousness" that met the needs of many people who were no longer satisfied by traditional religion or civil religion.

Mixed with these religious developments were devastating experiences that destroyed for many people any confidence in the culture or its leaders. The Viet Nam war challenged people's confidence on many fronts: at an early date it was understood as immoral by a minority; confidence in the military leadership was eroded as events contradicted predictions and moral claims, and ultimately there was such revulsion that United States forces were withdrawn. It is hard to estimate the damage that Watergate did, but there is a continuing distrust of almost any kind of leadership. If we listen to some of the more dismal prophecies, we may believe that our technology will bring about our ruin, and this will be combined with periodic starvation and other devastating effects on both the developed and the developing countries.

The hopelessness of our age is often described in terms of misspelling "God." *Waiting for Godot* has this theme. Two hoboes are hoping for some kind of fulfillment to their hopeless lives and are certain that Godot will appear. But every time that they make an appointment, they are told that they will have to wait. Nothing can break down the barriers. This is seen not only

4. Will Herberg, *Protestant - Catholic - Jew* (New York: Doubleday, 1955), p. 15.
5. See *American Civil Religion*, ed. Russell E. Richey and Donald G. Jones (New York: Harper & Row, 1974).

religiously but also in secular lives, especially in the bureaucracy of totalitarian states. In the opera by Gian Carlo Menotti, *The Consul*, Magda tries to obtain permission to join her husband, who has fled the country. She cannot get beyond the secretary to the consul:

> MAGDA: I must see my John, and only you, only you, can help me. May I speak to the Consul?
>
> SECRETARY: I give you these papers, that is how to begin. Your name is a number, your story is a case, your need a request, your hopes will be filed. Come back next week.
>
> MAGDA: And will you explain to the Consul?
>
> SECRETARY: But what is there to explain?
>
> MAGDA: Explain that John is a hero. . . . Explain that the web of my life has worn down to one single thread, that the hands of the clock glitter like knives. Explain to the Consul, explain!
>
> SECRETARY: But what is there to explain?
>
> MAGDA: Explain that John is a hero, explain that he's *my* John! Explain to the Consul, explain! Tell him my name, tell him my story, tell him my need!
>
> SECRETARY: Fill in these pages, that is how to begin. Your name is a number, your story is a case, your need is a request, your hopes will be filed. Come back next week.[6]

The breakdown in morality in today's society is not different from what Paul described in his letter to the Romans. He began by reminding the people that "it is not that they do not know the truth about God: indeed he has made it quite plain to them. For since the beginning of the world the invisible attributes of God, for example, his eternal power and divinity, have been plainly discernible through things which he has made and which are commonly seen and known, thus leaving these men without a

6. *The Consul*, by Gian Carlo Menotti. © 1950 by G. Schirmer, Inc. Reprinted by permission.

rag of excuse. They knew all the time that there is a God, yet they refused to acknowledge him as such, or to thank him for what he is or does" (Rom 1:19–21, P). There is a natural knowledge of God which has always been available. But people tend to ignore such knowledge and "God therefore handed them over to disgraceful passions. Their women exchanged the normal practices of sexual intercourse for something which is abnormal and unnatural. Similarly the men, turning from natural intercourse with women, were swept into lustful passions for one another.... Moreover, since they considered themselves too high and mighty to acknowledge God, he allowed them to become the slaves of their degenerate minds, and to perform unmentionable deeds. They became filled with wickedness, rottenness, greed, and malice: their minds became steeped in envy, murder, quarrelsomeness, deceitfulness and spite. They became whisperers-behind-doors, stabbers-in-the-back, God-haters; they overflowed with insolent pride and boastfulness, and their minds teemed with diabolical invention. They scoffed at duty to parents; they mocked at learning, recognized no obligations of honor, lost all natural affection, and had no use for mercy. More than this—being well aware of God's pronouncement that all who do these things deserve to die, they not only continued in their own practices, but did not hesitate to give their thorough approval to others who did the same" (Rom 1:26–32, P).

These are some of the specific ways in which Paul understands the condition of sin by which human beings are separated from God. The good news of Christianity is that those in this condition can be reconciled to God and be renewed by the power of the Holy Spirit. Instead of waiting for Godot, we are asked to do more than fill out a form and come back next week. We are to "seek the Lord where he may be found," and the Lord, who in Whitehead's words is a "fellow sufferer who understands," will provide the creative energy by which we can be restored to our full humanity.

There is a common condition which humanity shares. We are made in the image of God and we turn to other images, including those described by Paul. But the culture in which we live provides a variety of ways in which we see both our worth and our worthlessness.

MANY IMAGES

As we seek an image of what it means to be human in American culture, we discover that there are many such images, some of which have been due to the constant immigration during many years and others which have developed within the cultural matrix which is distinctively American. There is a cultural pluralism reflected in ethnic customs and practices, in mores in sections of the country, and in religious rootages. It has been said that there are many customs in the United States, most of which are restricted to large or small areas, and that the only universal custom is "the seventh inning stretch." This is something of an overstatement, but we know that manners, accents, cooking procedures, and even the image of a successful person are geographically oriented.

At the same time, we can speak of "the American way" and know what we mean. It is a vague concept in a pluralistic society, and yet it stands at the center in such a way that ethnic and religious customs are seen as variants within this democratic way of living. It has its roots in history, so that Will Herberg can say that the American self-image is an "Anglo-Saxon" model, with "the *Mayflower*, John Smith, Davy Crockett, George Washington, and Abraham Lincoln as symbols for all."[7] Newcomers to America are expected to change almost everything except their religion. As long as one is a Catholic, Protestant, or Jew, one can be counted as an American if one accepts the

7. Herberg, *Protestant - Catholic - Jew*, p. 33–34.

American way. This is still true to a great extent, but since 1955 there have been developments leading to pride in ethnic backgrounds and new heroes have emerged who break the stereotype, such as Martin Luther King, Jr. The liberation movements have altered the American consciousness, especially for blacks and women, and to some degree for other minorities, so that the Anglo-Saxon model no longer holds, and yet segregation and discrimination continue as part of life.

The American ideal and the facts of existence do not always merge. It is claimed that the nucleus of Americanism is Christianity, and certainly the American way is based on religious presuppositions. But it helps to understand how the secular and the sacred are related if we realize which religious convictions are at the center of the Declaration of Independence and the Bill of Rights. The faith of the Puritans or the convictions of the Anglicans in Virginia did not dominate the human image reflected in these documents, although people of Puritan and Anglican persuasion were involved in the writing of them; a secularized natural theology akin to Deism was reflected there, something both acceptable and unacceptable to Jews, Catholics, and Protestants. Because there is a benevolent creator, who created human beings in God's image, we recognize that God has endowed them with certain "inalienable rights," including "life, liberty, and the pursuit of happiness." There is nothing here of the glorification of God, and the pursuit of happiness is not equated with enjoying God forever. Furthermore, it was not clear that blacks and perhaps women had these rights.[8]

The American way combines the religious and the secular images of what it means to be human, but the application outside the Anglo-Saxon framework has been difficult to achieve. Immigrants discover that they can pass the barrier by means of educa-

8. See my *This We Can Believe* (New York: Hawthorn-Seabury, 1976), pp. 5–7.

tion and the use of the English language, provided that they are not highly visible. Black and Oriental Americans, because they are so easily identified, do not receive equal treatment. A Jew from central Europe or a Protestant from France or a Catholic from Italy has little trouble appearing in the "image" of an American, but the black or red or yellow skinned person has to plead, "I want to be treated as a human being." This is a far cry from Paul's statement that "there is neither Jew nor Greek, there is neither slave nor free, there is neither male nor female; for you are all one in Christ Jesus" (Gal 3:28, RSV).

There needs to be recognition of what it means to be human in a pluralistic culture, and yet there needs to be a priority of images if we are to do justice both to our heritage and our future. The image of humanity preached in church and synagogue stands in judgment on those who hear and do not believe as well as on those who believe and do nothing about it. There are some people who reach a higher level of behavior by reflecting on a secular image. The racial problem, for example, we faced more openly on the sports field than in the churches, although we may assume that Branch Rickey's Christian faith had something to do with hiring Jackie Robinson. Blacks were playing baseball on integrated teams in Georgia long before they were allowed in some Georgia churches. The distance between our claims for the value of being human in the Jewish and Christian traditions and the practices of Americans in the same traditions leave much to be desired.

For some people, going to church is "a kind of moral life insurance policy." It is a centering on feeling good about oneself, avoiding the discomfort of comparing one's own values with the social and ethical imperatives of the gospel, and of being with the right kind of people. The emphasis in some parishes is on making friends and engaging a spiritual force that will make one a more effective person. The important emphasis is on harmony and peace whatever the real situation may be.

Such religion lacks the insight and the imperatives that make Christianity radical. Often it means identifying oneself with the governing class. As was the case during the rise of Adolf Hitler, this can be dangerous. There were many good Christians who refused to associate themselves with Hitler, but they also refused to take a stand, and when the time of obvious crisis came, they were not ready or able to take a stand. There were other Christians who identified their faith with the welfare of the German state and who accepted Hitler from the beginning as a savior. Only a minority of Christians saw Hitler as an enemy, as what Karl Barth called an agent of the anti-Christ, and they offered firm resistance. If one is an American first and a Christian or a Jew only when it is convenient, there is little chance of the civil disobedience that is essential to a healthy faith and a healthy citizenship.

The central problem is this: If there is an image of humanity, with some variations, which is common to the Jewish and Christian traditions, and if this image is competing with other images derived from other sources, what can we do about it? Or are there images in our secular culture which provide support for the basic religious image, and if so how can we bring these together in an effective manner?

EDUCATIONAL TASKS

This points to the educational tasks of churches and synagogues. The children and adults who come to the churches already have an image of what it means to be human derived from their total educational background, chiefly from home and school. We have become aware, more than ever before, of the significance of the early years in the development of a self-image. Small children already have a pretty good picture of themselves as loved or unloved, accepted or unaccepted, important or unimportant. They have responded with anxiety or with a sense of security, with guilt or with confidence, as the parents have inculcated these evaluations. Their motivations for behavior are pretty well established, and the roots of materialism or selfishness or altruism have found fertile soil.

Their continuing education includes the school, and the church or synagogue, but the home still remains the primary influence. They now have new opportunities to overcome their anxieties or to grow in their security, but they may fail at any point. Their images of themselves may go through various stages, and certainly they are gaining a more generalized image of their value as they meet more people. Probably the only people who are likely to affect them are those who are significant to them, except in the case of dramatic or traumatic experiences with occasional acquaintances or strangers. This growth in self-understanding and self-worth continues, with changing emphasis, throughout their teenage years, and more and more those of their own age make an impression on their scale of values and their sense of worth.

In this process, we can see both secular and sacred forces at work. Theologically, we may find God at work in both areas, and the total image may be sufficiently unified to transcend the secular-sacred distinction. It is likely that they think of themselves as whole persons, acting in the American way, whether they are Catholic, Protestant, Jewish or unrelated to a religious institution.

The goal in this process is to understand human beings as created in the "image" of God. We reflect to some extent the nature of God, for we believe that God is present in us and we in God. We are creatures of God, and we seek to behave as those committed to God's aims, although often we choose not to align our aims with God's and therefore we count ourselves as sinners; usually we are a combination of obedient servant and rebellious opponent at the same time. The measure of our relation to God is found in our faithfulness.

"The righteous lives by reason of his faithfulness" (Hab 2:4b,G).
"For by grace you have been saved through faith; and this is not your own doing, it is a gift of God—not because of works, lest any [one] should boast" (Eph 2:8-9, RSV).

It is this emphasis on grace and faith, based on the redemptive love of God, that stands at the center. Because we are created in the "image" of God, and because God acts as persuasive love, we have freedom to respond by aligning our aims with what we conceive to be God's general aims for us, so that we do those works which are worthy of our calling. This is the logic of biblical faith. This involves us in a confrontation with God before we can discover what our self-image is.

This view of humanity is a balanced one, and yet it is paradoxical. It sees a human being as a child of God and still a sinner; as able to achieve goodness in freedom and yet only by the grace of God; as seeking God's kingdom on earth and yet seeing the kingdom as God's act; as in a tragic human situation and yet living the abundant life now; as saved through the redemptive love of God and yet needing to be saved through repentance and commitment; as an individual and yet finding sanctuary in the religious community; as loved of God and yet suffering God's judgment. This is the paradox of our human predicament.[9]

The church's educational task is to make relevant such an image of humanity in the contemporary scene, so that it speaks to the secular images. The persons being educated are facing the pressures on the consumer, they are up against the demands of acceptance on the basis of conformity, and they are seeking for meaning with or without reference to the dimension of religious faith. What they need is a framework of biblical faith, so that they may be enabled to evaluate competing images, appropriat-

9. See Randolph C. Miller, ed., *The Church and Organized Movements* (New York: Harper & Row, 1946), p. 6.

ing those which provide resources within the secular realm for a more comprehensive and effective image and rejecting those which contradict their biblical insights. This is a complicated task, for often they have to separate the wheat from the chaff in order to make a sound judgment. There is much, for example, in the various schools of psychiatry which contributes to our understanding of the Christian image, and yet distinctions must be made if we are to see persons as ends in themselves.

The focal point in such an educational process is the concept of God, for only as one has an adequate concept of God can one understand what it means to be created in God's image. This moves us into the realm of theology, where, if the organism model of the body is used, we can discover great similarity between the interrelations of the human body and God's interrelations with the world. If we can think of the subjective aims of God moving from the potential to the actual in terms of persuasive love, we may gain an insight into how as human beings we reflect God's "image" by seeking to bring those potentialities for good which we can envision into actuality through the means open to us. H. Richard Niebuhr wrote, "By revelation in our history, then, we mean that special occasion which provides us with an image by means of which all the occasions of personal and common life become intelligible."[10] There may be moments of insight or disclosure when we fit together our sense of worth with God's aims for us.

This leads to the need for sensing the presence of God, and this takes place primarily in the worshiping community, where the story of God's relationships with human beings is heard within the context of lesson, proclamation, prayer and sacrament, and where the response to this presence is shared within the community of believers. This is the source of the content of religious education, which is made practical through what occurs

10. H. Richard Niebuhr, *The Meaning of Revelation* (New York: Macmillan, 1941), p. 109.

in classrooms, informal relations in the home, school, and community, as we face the problems of everyday living. From this background we come to an understanding not only of what it means to be human but of what is expected of human beings in terms of moral and social activity. Thus we see both the continuity and the conflict with the secular community and come to a deeper understanding of our relationship to God and our neighbors.

The job which the church and the synagogue can do, it seems to me, is reasonably clear. Under no restrictions from any theory of the relationship of church and state, they are free to teach, nurture, guide, and even indoctrinate according to their own inclinations. When church and synagogue are oriented in terms of a dynamic theology, they can deal with the "becoming" and "perishing" of persons as they seek the "image" promised them by God, and which they already possess even if they do not know it. Because church and synagogue are also related to the world, they can provide meaning in religious terms for the whole person in all relationships. This, as I see it, is one of the challenges facing religious educators today.

There are many views of what it means to be human. "We are more simply human than otherwise," as Harry Stack Sullivan said. To be an American and also a Christian or a Jew is a dual image, forcing us to seek a combination that allows us to live fully in the world that is ours. On both sides of this image is the emphasis on the sense of worth, both as a citizen with rights and as a creature of a God who relates to us as persuasive love. But both Christians and Jews have been uneasy with this solution, for the secular world has always made them uneasy. Israel was *chosen as a nation* to a unique relationship and task. Christians also experienced the attraction of a new covenant, so that their primary allegiance to God got them into trouble with the world. The problem, then, in the light of more recent theologies, is how to be a loyal child of God in the world God is ruler of. If God is in the world and the world is in God, our alignment with God should make us at home in the world. But this is not the way it works out, for human beings remain free to develop their own cultures, their own empires, and their own world organized apart from God. So the Christian or Jew is never completely at home in the world.

Whitehead writes that basic to our existence is the sense of worth. This presupposes that reality has within it that which is worthy. "Our enjoyment of actuality is a realization of worth, good or bad. It is a value-experience. Its basic expression is— Have a care, here is something that matters! . . . My importance is my emotional worth now."[11] Each individual is important, has worth. This is an essential note in the gospel. We have value in ourselves and are of value in the sight of God. Human beings have importance. They can become joint-heirs with Christ. Therefore we seek to align our aims with God's aims for humanity. But we know that we fall short and seek a way to express our potentiality for goodness. In *All the King's Men* two men talk about goodness:

"'Goodness. Yeah, just plain, simple goodness. Well, you can't inherit it from anybody. You got to make it, Doc. If you want it. And you got to make it out of badness, Badness. And you know why, doc?' 'Because there isn't anything else to make it out of.'"[12] No matter how far we stray from the paths of living according to the will of God, there is hope that we may turn and be saved.

A CHRISTIAN MODEL

A third century document, *The Address to Diognetus*, provides a model of what it means to be a Christian. It reflects the culture

11. Alfred North Whitehead, *Modes of Thought* (New York: Macmillan, 1938, renewed 1966 by T. North Whitehead), pp. 159, 160.
12. Robert Penn Warren, *All the King's Men* (New York: Harcourt, Brace, and World, 1946), pp. 272-273.

and politics of the times, and it tells us what a Christian was like according to the almost impossible ideal held up by the author. It also corrects a number of false impressions.

"Christians are not distinguished from the rest," he writes, "in country or speech or customs. For they do not live somewhere in cities of their own or use some distinctive language or practice a peculiar manner of life."

It is clear that Christians do not go out of their way to be different. They do not plan to be conformists, as we shall see, but such matters are unimportant.

"They have no learning discovered by the thought and reflection of inquisitive [people], nor are they the authors of any human doctrine. . . . Though they live in Greek and barbarian cities, as each [one's] lot is cast, and follow the local customs in dress and food and the rest of their living, their own way of life which they display is wonderful and admittedly strange."

The author is telling us that Christians are like everyone else, *but*. . . ! That little word, *but*, runs through the remainder of the description. They look like any other bankers or housewives or ditch diggers or plumbers, *but*. . . ! The author continues:

"They live in their native lands, but like foreigners. They take part in everything like citizens, and endure everything like aliens. Every foreign country is their native land, and every native land a foreign country." In our modern parlance, they do not seem to be subject to outside influence or to be other-directed; they are not conformists; they have a sense of inner-direction. Look at this description of family life:

"Like everyone else they marry, they have children, but they do not expose their infants. They set a common table, but not a common bed. They find themselves in the flesh, but they do not live after the flesh." Here the author recognizes that sex and marriage and children are a normal part of life. In those days it was common to expose unwanted children, especially girls, but the Christian did not do so. For the Christian, hospitality meant sharing one's food but not one's spouse. Christians see the flesh as a basis for pleasure but not for license.

The author by implication is defending Christians against the charge of being odd-balls. They are not pious, holier-than-thou types, but participate in the affairs of the world. At the same time, "they remain on earth, but they are citizens of heaven." This dual citizenship makes one a better neighbor, a better worker, a better citizen, so much so that the fate of the world hangs on these citizens of heaven. What annoyed the pagans was that Christians would "obey the established laws, and in their own lives they [would] surpass the laws."

The author then runs through a series of paradoxes: "They love all [people], and are persecuted by all. . . . They are unknown, and they are condemned; they are put to death, and they are made alive. They are poor, and they make many rich. They are in need of all things, and they abound in all things. They are dishonored, and in their dishonor they are glorified. They are abused, and they are vindicated. They are reviled, and they bless. . . . Those who hate them cannot give a reason for their hostility."

This may seem far-fetched in a nation where Christianity is respectable. But Christians were put to death along with Jews in Hitler's Germany. Ministers have lost their pulpits for interpreting the gospel to include minorities. Lay people have cut off their gifts to church agencies when policies displease them. There are always strong pressures to conform.

Throughout history, the story has been the same. The prophets were stoned by respected members of the community. Jesus was crucified at the instigation of respectable members of the religious community by the legal guardians of the law. The Salem witches were destroyed by righteous and often self-righteous Puritans. The temptation to join the crucifiers is always strong.

The author sees the vocation of Christians in a clear light: "To put it briefly, what the soul is to the body, Christians are to the world." Christians hold the world together. They hold the community together. They do this because of their remarkable sense of loyalty that rises above loyalties to family or partisans or nation.

The capacity to be a Christian is not based on human wisdom alone. Our author knows a bit about the Greek philosophers and writes with satire: "Do you accept the empty, silly accounts of the recognized philosophers, some of whom said that God was fire (they call that God to which they will go!), and others, water, and others some other one of the elements created by God? . . . For God, the master and creator of the universe . . . formed a great marvelous plan and communicated it to his child alone." He sent Christ "as [one] seeking to save, as persuading, not compelling, for compulsion is not the way of God."[13]

Christians have power to become more fully human, because God's gift of grace is active within them. It is not supposed to be easy, but the rewards are great. There is much pressure from those who are unsympathetic both in and out of the churches. The stress is on God's love:

> Christ came to win us by good will,
> For force is not of God.
> Not to oppress, but summon us
> Our truest life to find,
> In love God sent his Son to save,
> Not to condemn our kind.[14]

---

13. "The Address to Diognetus," 5:1–15, 17; 6:1; 8:2, 7, 9; 7:4c. *The Apostolic Fathers,* translated by Edgar J. Goodspeed. (New York: Harper & Row, 1950), pp. 278, 280.
14. Hymn 298, by F. Bland Tucker. *The Hymnal 1940* (New York: Church Hymnal Corporation, 1940, 1943, 1961). Text altered.

7

Values and Appreciation

We have considered the understanding of the concept of God through the interpretation of experience, the adoption of an organismic or process world view, the place of God in nature, the use of scripture, and the meaning of being human. Another way of understanding our idea of God is through the study of values. The concept of value may seem to be abstract to some people, but we will see that it is a concrete way of determining the basic elements of Christian living.

Value is a relatively new term in philosophy. It is normally taken to be the equivalent of the good. It is a study of the worth of things and persons. It is characteristic of objects and therefore value is thought of as "out there" rather than the product of subjective decisions. What happens in the world is understood as a mixture of pattern and activity. "The notion of the importance of pattern is as old as civilization," wrote Whitehead. "Every art is founded on the study of pattern. Also the cohesion of social systems depends on the maintenance of patterns of behavior; and advances in civilization depend on the fortunate modification of such behaviour patterns. Thus the infusion of pattern into natural occurrences, and the stability of such patterns, and the modification of such patterns, is the necessary condition for the realization of the Good."[1]

---

1. "Mathematics and the Good," in Paul Arthur Schilpp, ed., *The Philosophy of Alfred North Whitehead* (Evanston: Northwestern University Press, 1941), pp. 677–678.

Any infusion is an element of novelty, so that there are emerging values. The stability is a guarantee that in the process there are certain guidelines that reflect the everlasting nature of God as a principle of limitation that keeps creativity under some control. The modification is essential so that there may be an accounting for the growth of value which we experience and ascribe to the working of God in our midst. In the balance of stability, modification, and growth, we find the emerging novelty to which we ascribe the "good." These modifications are described as "fortunate" and therefore due to some kind of purpose or chance that works for the welfare of increasing values.

We "feel" values, but this is more than simply an emotional response, although it includes that. There are feelings which indicate levels of appreciation, so that we can speak of appreciable activities which carry with them a sense of obligation. Others *ought* to feel the way we do about the beauty of a symphony or the heroism of a Mother Teresa. We have feelings of satisfaction or dissatisfaction which we can share. We feel very deeply about some realities and much less so about others. Some appreciations are more intense than others, and thus some values are considered higher or more obligatory than others.

The good may be understood under the categories of beauty and harmony. The aesthetic view of harmony and unity is the dominating factor in understanding values. This can be demonstrated with the uses of harmony, no matter how complex, in music as compared with discord. Evil is portrayed as aesthetic destruction; well-being is communicated through the use of various harmonies. Music may express harmony as such, or a mixture of harmony and discord, or sheer discord. It may also tell a story and lead toward a conclusion or end. There will be satisfaction and therefore value.

Goodness and truth are values to be subsumed under the overall category of beauty. It is one thing to describe a person as good or truth-telling, and quite another to speak of a person as beautiful. The latter indicates a well-roundedness that is missing in mere goodness or a teller of bare truths. We "feel" the difference.

This approach to values leads to a concept of God as a creative entity which creates values and provides for the creative transformation of whatever comes into contact with the divine. There is a coming into existence of values without human help. There is a factor or entity in the universe which produces values. When we get in tune with this process, we become the creators of value in our own lives.

Human beings are the arbiters of value. They only can decide what is satisfactory or appreciable; they only can feel and respond to the intrinsic reality of value in an event or entity in their experience. The response is in terms of purpose. Thus the future opens up to the person as valuer in a new way and emerging novelty becomes a possibility for new appreciations.

PARTICULAR VALUES

Let us turn now to specific experiences of value. There is value in the simple act of eating. We get hungry and we eat. By this act the body is restored to its proper equilibrium and its energy is raised to a level for facing the future. The food has value because through the process of ingestion it eliminates the primary feeling of hunger and provides resources for further activity and for the building of the human organism. Basic to the act of keeping alive, itself a value, is the value of food.

Eating has a secondary value. Although we all can subsist on a rigid and tasteless diet, there are added values in the pleasure of eating a variety of well-cooked foods. When we eat alone, we may prepare monotonous meals for ourselves, but if we can afford it we will from time to time seek out a famous restaurant in order to enjoy a delicious repast. We can eat alone and like it.

The act of eating may also be an occasion for fellowship. There is no hospitality quite as intimate or satisfying as sharing a meal with friends. The hospitality of some desert tribes, according to reports, illustrates this sense of fellowship: a traveler who shares the tent of a desert dweller for the night as likely as not may have one's throat slit, but if the guest partakes of food, he or she comes under the rule of hospitality which means that the host will protect his guest even at the cost of his own life. In every culture, a meal together enhances the sense of community, especially when a meal occurs at a time of special significance, as at Christmas or on an anniversary.

In the Christian tradition, looking back to that most meaningful of meals, the Last Supper, there is the celebration of the Lord's Supper under various conditions and by different names throughout Christendom. It is here, in partaking of the foods which are the staff of life, bread and wine, that the Christian fellowship feels most definitely in the presence of the living Christ; and it is important to remember that there can be no communion except where two or more are gathered together. In recent years we have recaptured both the table fellowship and the passing of the peace that expresses the basic meaning of community.

The act of eating has value in itself and in its potential relations to other events. Behind the act of eating, however, there are complex series of relations which contribute to the value. Coffee is raised in Brazil and is brought by ship to this country; the beans are roasted, ground properly, blended for taste, placed in vacuum-sealed cans or airtight jars, and distributed to the stores. Then the coffee has to be carefully prepared to give it the proper aroma. At any point in this interrelated series of events, an error would destroy the final value of the coffee for us. This series of relations is external to us, and yet they contain the potentiality of good for us.

This coffee, or any other food, may not have value. If an error has been made, the coffee may have a disvalue for us; it may be just a matter of unpleasant taste or it may be poisoned. If coffee keeps one awake, it may be good when one needs extra energy and bad when one needs sleep. If coffee leads to jangled nerves, it may always be bad for such a person, in spite of its perfect preparation. In like manner, food that is a value for some people may set up allergic reactions or cause great distress for others.

Values, then, include both outer and inner relations and the reaction of the individual to the final result. In the case of food, this result comes from the satisfaction given by the food and its related enhancements through fellowship or worship. In other cases, we need a longer perspective. Ministers discover that they can do a better job of pastoral counseling a week after a funeral than at the funeral. The emotional charge dies down in a week and the evaluation is more accurate. Values depend on the place they occupy on our time schedule. Death may or may not have disvalue in a particular situation; but the fact of death is a blessing when it comes at the close of a long life. Our negative evaluation of death always applies to the deaths of others whose loss we feel deeply, while the one who dies may welcome it. Life and death always involve tragedy as well as the sense of well being and abundance, and the feelings of value and disvalue are inevitably mixed. [2]

The potentiality of value lies in the external relations, the outward events. Good comes to us from the event. Values are appreciable activities, events that can be appreciated when someone comes into contact with them. There are feelings of satisfaction or dissatisfaction. The Grand Canyon becomes beautiful *for us* when we see it, but the potentiality of beauty is always there. The world is full of possible values, and if we live for values we will find some of them. A symphony is beautiful when it is broadcast whether anyone is listening or not. This

2. See my *Live Until You Die* (Philadelphia: Pilgrim Press, 1973), pp. 133–148.

objectivity of value applies to beauty, goodness, truth, and all other values. They are all appreciable activities whether they are being appreciated or not.

Values are the connections between events, linking us at one end of the series. The values are real, but do not become significant for us until we make the move to assimilate them into our consciousness. Most people would agree, for example, that color is real and sometimes beautiful, but those who are color blind have no basis for agreeing or disagreeing with us. Similarly, because some people are tone deaf, we do not deny the beauty of music. It is the same for those who have no sense of taste; a meal is still pleasant for those whose taste is unimpaired.

There is no separation of fact and value, but our sense of value or disvalue is determined by the degree of creativity exhibited in every event. "There is nothing in the real world which is merely an inert fact. Every reality is there for feeling; it promotes feeling; and it is felt."[3] We are drawn by our feelings to experience value in every entity from the human spirit to an electron. At the upper end is the human person and the practice of ethics. "Personality is the extreme example of the sustained realization of a type of Value."[4] When the self-identity of one's past is brought to bear on the meaning of the present moment, there is personal identity, which is the basis for valuing and decision. Our relation to God is to deity as "the measure of the aesthetic consistency of the world."[5] This world is many layered, and the "binding cement is value."[6]

3. Alfred North Whitehead, *Process and Reality* (New York: Macmillan, corrected edition, 1978), pp. 310 (472).
4. Schilpp, ed., *The Philosophy of Alfred North Whitehead*, p. 690.
5. Alfred North Whitehead, *Religion in the Making* (New York: Macmillan, 1926), p. 86.
6. Brian V. Hill, *Education and the Endangered Individual* (New York: Teachers College Press, 1973), p. 170.

HABITS

Frequently we lose our appreciation of values because our habits are hardened and we cease to be sensitive to certain experiences. Many of us have been in the habit of driving at high speeds, watching the traffic and failing to see the scenery. Because of the shortage of petroleum, some of us have been forced to drive at 55 miles per hour, which gives us the opportunity to see more; or perhaps we travel by bus and are freed to watch the scenery throughout the trip. Others may focus on what they habitually see and thus they fail to respond to the wonder of children at play, or the beauty of falling leaves, or the music of the spheres. Out habits, which can be convenient shortcuts for getting things done, may also prove to be blinders, keeping us from the fullest experiences of values.

We can develop the habit of seeking values. One church featured this slogan: "Put habit on the side of religion." It is not difficult to get into the habit of going to church, but the persons who stop each Sunday and think about going to church will inevitably get into competition with the comic strips or sports pages or mowing the lawn, or decide that they have worked too hard this week to put forth the minimum effort necessary to get to church. All habits that lead to growth involve conscious effort in developing them, and then higher values are sought almost automatically. If one is in a rut, it is because one has lost sight of the potentialities of value which inhere in every event.

One habit that is essential is *the habit of developing new habits.* This keeps us from being satisfied with routine existence. William Lyon Phelps used to tell how he became a lover of symphony music. He had insight enough to know that others found great beauty in symphonic music, but when he went to a concert he was bored. He kept on going because he had been told some value was there. By constant exposure to the beauty of the symphony, he finally came to an appreciation of the great beauty and meaning that was there to be discovered. He persevered in developing a new habit.

We are not going to live for values until we sensitize ourselves to them. One aspect of our awareness of reality is the work of what Bernard Meland calls the appreciative consciousness. It is a level of awareness which we can consciously develop, a depth of sensitivity that we may not realize we are capable of, an aesthetic aspect of experience that we sometimes submerge. By exposing ourselves to values we believe to be there, as was the case for Professor Phelps, we find the values that are there. The higher the value, the more effort we must expend.

DEVOTION TO VALUE

Religion can be understood in terms of devotion to value. When we understand the universe as containing within it vast potentialities for the development of actual values and see God's aim as the achievement of value in the world, then we know that when we seek the highest and best that we can conceive, we are at least approximating God's will for us.

Our judgments of value do not depend upon the individual's appreciation. Although nothing is of value to the individual until one learns appreciation, it is essential to remember that we are also judged by the values to which we respond. To be sure of our individual preferences, we must test our value judgments against the experience of history. History records the value judgments of humanity, of nations and civilizations, and we do well to discover the values of the past found in those experiences. Also, we rely on the judgments of the experts (although our choice of experts depends on our prior criteria of value). A woman strolling through the Louvre, looking at the pictures with a hypercritical air, expressed disappointment in one of the paintings by a great master, and the guard reminded her: "Madame, these pictures are not on trial; you are."

Our appreciation of values grows by participation in the value experiences of others. We agree to eat a disagreeable food because someone whose judgment we trust says it is good, and by experiment we discover in time that it is good. Those who do not participate fully at a dancing party become "wall flowers," but when they are drawn into the activity they soon discover the values that are there by giving themselves wholeheartedly to a new experience. Value experiences may be moments of insight or even of conversion. Our patterns of thinking and appreciation are radically changed by a suggestion from without, so that we arrange our data of experience in new forms that provide a feeling of harmony. It takes perseverence as well as openness to achieve deeper appreciation.

THE MULTIPLICITY OF VALUES

There are many types of value. When we consider them, we can put them into some kind of order, so that one will seem higher than another. When we speak of "lower" values, we usually refer to bodily, economic, or recreational values. Without normal satisfaction of these basic values, it is difficult to appreciate the higher ones. An exception might be the religious ascetic who starves and mistreats the body in order to have a specialized religious experience, but most people need physical well-being in order to move on to the appreciation of beauty. The lower values are always stronger than the higher ones, for the higher depend on the lower for their existence. This leads to a strange paradox: those who are the most grievous transgressors are those who offend against the lower values, while those who are the most worthy are those who achieve the higher values.

There is no punishment for turning off a symphony broadcast, but there is for robbery. There is no punishment for avoiding a lecture on sex, but there is for rape. All those acts for which we place people in jail are transgressions against the body, property, or money, and only rarely for failures in interpersonal relations, except perjury. White collar crimes are not punished as severely as crimes against material and bodily rights. The acts for which people are praised are in the realm of intellectual, aesthetic, or religious values. Society is satisfied to protect its people from the evils in the lower part of the scale of values.

Some people live only for the lower values. They are satisfied if the stomach is filled, the sexual urges are satisfied, and their physical well-being is protected by adequate warmth and comfort. They are satisfied to keep outside the clutches of the law. They live in terms of law and order and try to keep the "thou shalt not" attitude of the Ten Commandments. These are strong values, and genuine morality builds on them. Their strength does not establish their superiority but only their elementariness, their priority as a condition for living for the fuller and richer and weaker values.

Most people move to a higher level than this. Their approach to values is positive, and they live for such values as bravery, wisdom, fullness of life, fidelity, love, and moral greatness. The emphasis is on the achievement of goodness rather than the avoidance of and release from sin. It is the "thou shalt" attitude of Jesus' summary of the law.

Living for values involves us in a synthesis of these two orders. We need the protection of the law; we need to know what we cannot do and what disvalues to avoid. The process of growing in appreciation of values moves through stages, and each one builds on the prior step. This is particularly true for moral values, but there is similar development of the appreciation of all values. As we move upward in the scale of values and of appreciation, we begin to have a sense of positive achievement. We need the attitude of Jesus' teaching: "I came to fulfill the law and the prophets—not to destroy them." We move beyond that colorless and automatic description of virtue as it appeared in the little girl's prayer: "Dear God, please make the bad people good and the good people nice." The positive response of the person who is sincere, who shows a radiant and captivating virtue, who seeks the fullness of good for its own sake, is evident in the persuasion of Christian living at its best.

We have to choose between values. There are so many potential values offered to us that we cannot have all of them at once, and the choice of one eliminates many others. When we begin to list the possible values, the number is likely to confuse us unless we have some general categories by which to classify them. Nicolai Hartmann, the great writer on ethics, begins by pointing to the foundations of value which are found in the individual person. We have life, consciousness, activity, suffering, strength, freedom of will, foresight, and effective purpose. These are the resources in each of us that enable us to bring values into our experience.

The fundamental values, says Hartmann, are the good, the noble, richness of experience, and purity. There are three classes of special moral values. The first grouping comes from Greek thought: justice, wisdom, self-control, and Aristotle's doctrine of "the golden mean," which is "nothing too much." The second group finds its source in our Christian heritage: steadfast love, truthfulness and uprightness, trust and faith, modesty, humility, aloofness, and sociability. The third group has four qualities: love of the remote, radiant virtue, personality and personal love.[7]

Most of us are inclined to take one of these values as supreme and devote ourselves to it. But we make exclusive judgments, for these values stand in tension with each other. We achieve justice at the expense of mercy and love, purity at the cost of richness of

7. See Nicolai Hartmann, *Ethics* (New York: Macmillan, 1932), Vol. II, pp. 125-381.

experience, humility at the risk of not asserting our values, sympathy at the expense of honesty. Sometimes these choices are irreversible, as when one give up the negative values of virginity, celibacy or purity for the positive values of fullness of experience and the richness of sexual relations; the virginity cannot be regained. We need constantly to remind ourselves that *living for values is never living for one value alone.* We must not make a god of any single value, even of love. God is not a value, but the primordial nature of God includes the possibility of all values. We come nearest to a single goal when we speak of *wisdom,* which is something different from other forms of knowledge. Wisdom in Latin is *sapientia.* It is described by Hartmann as "moral taste, and indeed fine, discriminating, cultivated taste, the refinement of moral capacity, in so far as this capacity, directed towards the fullness of life, signifies appreciation of everything and an affirming, evaluating attitude toward whatever is of value."[8] This kind of appreciative consciousness includes moral discrimination based on careful analysis, but it goes beyond this level of the ought to a recognition of the richness and fullness and plurality of life.

FAITH IN THE SUPREME VALUE

The supreme value cannot itself be a value, else other values would be distorted. God is the energizing factor and the source of values. The potentiality for value lies in the primordial nature of God, so that we can say that God brings values into existence. God works immanently in the consequent nature through the growth of values as they come into existence. God includes all potentialities for all values in the primordial nature, even the contradictions between values. Only the "mind" of God can contain the contradictions between such values as love and jus-

8. Hartman, *Ethics,* Vol. II, p. 239.

tice. In our devotion to God, we are also devoted to the achievement and appreciation of values in the world and seek to become agents who can create values.

Our task is to be aware of the possibilities of value in each situation, so that we can align our aims with those of God, as far as we can comprehend them. Our failure is that we do not see the hidden values reigning in our daily experiences. In times of crisis, we see the darkness and not the light; and yet the light shines in every period of darkness. People bemoaning the world situation do not see that we are at one of those crossroads of civilization when the world can become a shambles or become more valuable than before. The potentiality is there, and so are the risks. God seeks to turn the world in a positive direction, and it depends on us whether this will occur.

If, in living for values, we see through the particular values to the work of God in the world, our devotion to value becomes our devotion to God. The religious person lives for the will of God, which means that we seek to align our moral choices and our selection of values with what our wisdom (*sapientia*) tells us are God's aims. We make all our preconceived goals and values secondary, and we are not blinded by them because we are sensitive to the emerging riches which God gives us in every event. We are constantly getting into predicaments which are different from what we expected. We commit ourselves to the reality or process for which the word "God" stands rather than to our previous evaluations, and thus we are open to novel values which were unexpected.

In the family, for example, we discover that when we meet the conditions of mutual love, the values which emerge are out of all proportion to our effort. The wife who says, "I did not know I ever could love anyone so much," has simply widened the horizons of her appreciation. She and her husband have grown together more than they have grown in themselves. It is hard work and requires not only effort but increased sensitivity. There are new values when wife and husband can send messages unconsciously by facial or bodily expression. What has happened is that love grows when God's conditions are met, and the emerging novelty leads to deeper love and understanding.

The opposite is equally true. When a marriage is beset with pettiness, lack of complete trust, and failure to show insight and sensitivity, the marriage suddenly falls apart out of all proportion to the meanness shown. If we fail to meet the conditions of living for values and in commitment to God, the work of disvalue sets in.

The gifts of God are the most generous in human experience, and when we meet God's conditions the results are beyond any values we may have hoped for. There is a growth of meaning and value working not only in marriage but in all living, in fellowship and friendship, in business and international relations, and throughout the realms of organic and inorganic life.

We live for values, but that is not enough. We live for God and commit our wills in freedom to God's will, for God is the source and giver of all good things. It is this faith which is essential to our philosophy of life.

We have been thinking of all kinds of values, in which the appreciation of events and relations is central. We can appreciate values of goodness as seen in others or as imagined, just as we can appreciate beauty in others or in events and relationships, as well as in imagination. And there is increase in the levels of appreciation. We speak of our improved taste or discrimination in aesthetic activities. We recognize our new capacity to enjoy foods that formerly were considered unfit for us. There is the same kind of increase in the discriminations that we make in moral judgments. Children may think in terms of punishment or of satisfying their own needs. They may develop a kind of behavior that is pleasing to others or recognize the place of law in doing one's duty. It may be that this is as much development as we may expect, but it does not take us beyond a kind of authoritarian or even totalitarian government. Much religious ethical thinking stops at this point, where doing one's duty is sufficient. But some persons see duty in terms of contract rather than law, with recognition of the rights of others as basic.

MORAL AUTONOMY

At none of these levels do we find genuine moral autonomy. We are close to it when we make contractual agreements, but there is still an element of imposed conformity. If we are to be free to align our aims with God's aims, to live for values as they promise to become actual in our experience, to share the risk and adventure of living meaningfully, we need to reach a higher level of moral judgment where we are governed by our own consciences. One does not live at this level with great consistency, nor is there a need to if what we have said previously about habits is true. But there comes a time when we may drink the hemlock with Socrates, or be shot with Martin Luther King, Jr., or say with Luther, "Here I stand! I can do no other!" It leads to persecution for some conscientious objectors, to escape to Canada or Sweden for others, and death on the battle field for still others. This level of moral autonomy, derived from the functioning of one's conscience, draws upon values that are deeper than those of the law, and they may lead to the authorization of individual acts that are good for one person and would not be for another. The recognition of this diversity of values is what makes possible a move toward a higher level of moral insight, with the attendant risk that a personal moral judgment may be entirely wrong.

When ethics has a religious base, such a conclusion becomes a possibility. God's aims for human beings are understood in general terms, and in this sense are universal, but as these aims become concrete in human experience and are particularized, they may differ in their expression. Love may have universal validity as a value, but it is expressed differently by a nine-year-old girl and a nineteen-year-old woman, or by a celibate priest and a married father of two. As values become specific, they become relative and relevant. Yet there is safety in the herd instinct of relying on external authority, on law and order, on the rigid application of moral principles without exception. It is a good way to control sporting games, but not the best way to run a family. It is necessary in the army, but hardly suitable in a church.

Most of us most of the time, and some of us all of the time, need external controls; we are passive before authorities, or take orders even when our own consciences are bothered, and live according to socially accepted values without questioning them. Only occasionally do we have experiences that break through the routine responses, so that the appreciative consciousness is set free to take in a wondrous experience of one kind or another. In and through worship we may find that our sense of wonder is enriched and deepened, or our appreciation of beauty rises to a new level. Our task, it seems to me, is to keep ourselves open to such possibilities which are all around us. For this openness to values can be enriching, provided that we direct our attention to potentialities of emerging novelty.

The hidden abilities of human beings is often wasted, Whitehead said that "very few people are adequately drawn out—some are never drawn out at all, and remain, to all purposes, idiotic; though no one knows what their latent powers might have been. Others are about half drawn out; some happy encounter, some favoring condition elicits their peculiar abilities, but the waste of undeveloped faculties must be tremendous. For the powers of the individual are unique and unpredictable. This has been one of the great discoveries of the human race and it is still proceeding very slowly."[9]

9. Lucien Price, *Dialogues of Alfred North Whitehead* (Boston: Little, Brown and Co., 1954). p. 152.

The educational implications of this quotation are obvious. Good education will tap the potentialities in each learner. Teachers will seek to discover the direction in which a student should be led, and provide the stimulation to unleash the opportunities for development. Values will be presented as a way of stirring the imagination and of inspiring new aspirations.

This approach to values is realistic and provides a basis for hope. We believe that values become actual due to human and cosmic activity and also due to God's structure of the dynamics of life. Thus, values are real and not the figment of the imagination or the construct of the human mind, and they are evidence of God at work in the world. However, God's work depends on human decisions and actions, and therefore as human beings align their aims with what they understand to be God's aims, we will move toward a more desirable kind of society. We are likely to lose our faith in human endeavor, and a reading of history is not encouraging, but if God works to bring about the growth of meaning and value in the world, then there is a basis for the hope that God's persuasive love will lure human beings into the orbit of love as a basis for their lives. The basis for hope is written into the nature of reality, so that no matter how dark with foreboding our view of the future may be, we believe that God is able to take what perishes and make it the basis for a new becoming, and thus God makes all things new.

This turns our attention from the nature of values to the relevance of Christian ethics as a form of human decision and behavior, which we will examine in the next chapter.

8

The Ethical Fruits
of the Tree of Faith

Christian ethics lie in the dimension of faith and works. Jesus spoke of the tree which bears good fruit, and the letter of James says that faith without works is dead. If we are saved by grace through faith, the response is in terms of vocation, of living a life worthy of our calling. There is a tree of faith, and the fruits are ethical in the broad sense of living for value. The umbrella value is beauty, and the good and the true are understood within the category of the aesthetic. Thus faith issues in beauty of character.

One's ethics are derived from either a conscious or unconscious view of the nature of values and the degree of obligation derived from it. If, as we have proposed, values are appreciable activities about which we have strong feelings, and if they adhere to facts so that facts and values are always experienced together, so that values are objective, and if God is the source of values whereby they are brought into the world, we have an obligation to align our aims with what we conceive to be God's aim for us. If these values are primarily aesthetic, so that the good is subsumed under the harmony and unity of the beautiful, we have a base for aesthetic as well as moral and knowledge judgments. This broadens the horizon of religious response beyond the limitations of "mere morality." Love, said Whitehead is "a little oblivious as to morals."[1] But not to values.

The problem of Christian ethics is primarily the discovery of

1. Alfred North Whitehead, *Process and Reality*, (New York: Macmillan, corrected edition, 1978), p. 343 (521).

God's subjective aims for human beings and our autonomous response to it. Unfortunately, it is not so simple as it seems. No one is sure what God's will is, although it is related to persuasive love. God's will is not limited to human systems, and therefore it is difficult to predict what God's will may be tomorrow. But God's general aim is part of God's everlasting nature, and the problem is to know what specific values are to be sought in a given situation. But even if one is convinced that one knows God's will, it is still difficult if not impossible to carry it out. Reinhold Niebuhr spoke of it as an "impossible possibility."

The dual problem of Christian ethics, of discerning God's subjective aim for humanity and then aligning ourselves with God's aims, is full of complexity. It involves a study of anthropology and sociology against the background of what it means to be human. It includes the study of sources, authority, and response in Christian behavior. It leads to an exercise in the interpretation of the general aims of God in relation to the prudential human situation.

SOURCES

Christian ethics are grounded in the New Testament. The ethics reflected in the agreed teachings of Jesus are distinctly religious, finding the author in God, and yet such ethics have profound social effects. The relation between human beings and God is essentially moral, and the change demanded by repentance means a change in one's moral character. The main test of a person is the inner check, of whether one's attitude toward other persons and God is right. Jesus' ethics are inward in the insistence that we are no better than our thoughts. The basic attitude is essential, assuming of course an organic relation between attitude and action. If our attitude is right, to that extent will we seek to do God's will as we understand it.

This emphasis of Jesus is not profoundly altered by the rest of the New Testament. Paul puts more stress on our sinfulness and the need of grace, but the same moral relationship between God and human beings is central. God's will is ethical, and while no specific ideal can summarize God's will for us in a particular situation, there are certain norms which are general guides for all situations. There are no concrete instructions for particular problems.

The insights of Christians since the New Testament times have added to the sum of particular advice for human problems, but they have given no new guidance for the discernment of the will of God. New situations have evoked answers which cannot be paralleled in scriptural experiences, and thus many details have been added to the ideals of Christian living, but the general principles have remained the same. The revelation of God found in Jesus Christ, with its teaching that in the attitude of complete commitment and willingness to search out the hidden values of each situation according to the basic attitudes of the teachings of Jesus, is the primary source of Christian ethics.

AUTHORITY IN ETHICS

Because Christians have not been able to make this commitment and search unaided, in their ethical dilemmas they have relied upon three authorities: the church, the Bible, and human conscience.

Some churches have handed down ethical rulings, but in almost every case such rulings have been outworn and outgrown in a short time. The restrictions of the Puritan sabbath ran counter to Jesus' teaching that the sabbath was made for human beings. The ceremonial laws of the Roman church, especially the petty rulings concerning penance and indulgences, helped cause the Protestant reformation. The rulings against contraception have caused untold misery among the faithful. Christian groups differ concerning the ethics of war, patriotism, saluting the flag, family planning, abortion, and various economic and social problems.

However, there is authority in the churches, especially in the area of general principles. The ecumenical councils of old carried an authority which lasted as long as the solutions proffered were relevant to the situations in which people found themselves. Modern ecumenical councils have the authority of the keenest minds, and the World Council of Churches, with its combination of ecumenical theology in its variety and ethical insight, offers guidance for the world today. Between the conflicting statements of various churches and councils, the individual is forced to choose, and in choosing one must rely on an authority other than the churches themselves. We are thus forced back to the authority of either the Bible or our own consciences.

The Bible as an authority has always presented a problem. It has always been the authority of the Bible as interpreted by groups of individuals, using theological presuppositions as a basis for selection of texts and interpretations. In itself, the Bible is as confusing as any sixty-six (or eighty) books by authors holding different points of view. Excerpts from the Bible can be selected to encourage any kind of behavior.

We have suggested in a previous chapter that some biblical interpreters have turned to the "root metaphor" of "the mind of Christ" as a guide. The remainder of the Bible acquires a focus in the spirit or attitude that Jesus showed, and even the remainder of the New Testament is understood as deriving its authority from the teachings of Jesus, especially as found in the synoptic gospels.

The appeal to "the attitude or spirit of Jesus" or "the mind of Christ" has the objectivity of relying on what we believe Jesus said and did, but it also includes the subjective elements of the individual's choice. We cannot escape the necessity of interpreting Jesus in the light of our own experience. God's aims are always conceived in terms of our own highest values, although we recognize that God is more than and different from our highest human ideals. Jesus through my eyes hardly provides a dependable authority for ethical behavior, and yet it is our only means for interpreting the ethical authority of the Bible for these times.

Thus, we are forced back of the church and the Bible to the individual conscience. But the conscience by itself is no more than the ability to choose between right and wrong, without any definition of the content. It can be conditioned always to choose wrong. Environment, heredity, education, and other elements of experience enter into every value judgment. Conscience by itself does not guarantee ethical action, even if it chooses the right path. The contents of the selections of conscience come from another source.

Conscience, which is far from infallible, must rely on the insights of others, especially the church and the Bible, which are not infallible either. Thus devoted, sincere, and seeking Christians are caught in a vicious circle of relativity. If we lack the courage to attempt to stand on our own feet before God, we fall back on church and Bible, and thus we are guilty of absolutizing views which can be shown to be relative. This is simply idolatry, however noble it may be, for it substitutes something less than deity for God. But if we insist on remaining individualists, we lose the resources of the group and tradition, and are in danger of absolutizing our own ideas, which are even more relative than those of the groups we have rejected.

Then there is the danger of admitting the relativity that is present. Supposing that we have the insight to avoid the absolutizing of either the authority of the church or the Bible, and we remain humble enough not to absolutize our own value judgments, this leaves us without an ethical center of gravity at all, and we can be swayed by the opinions, pressures, and propaganda of the environment, by our own wishes and hunches, and by our hidden wills to power. This becomes a form of self-deception. This is where many of us find ourselves if we reject the authorities of church and Bible.

THE NATURE OF CHRISTIAN ETHICS

The trouble with all of these positions is that they have failed to grasp the nature of Christian ethics or of the relation of God's will to human wills. Reinhold Niebuhr's reminder that Christian ethics are an "impossible possibility," which is absolute and thus beyond the scope of prudential ethics, points to an absolute which lies in the aims of the primordial nature of God and is thus everlasting. Church, Bible, and conscience when properly blended can be a relative guide for prudential ethics, if we see that there is a relationship between human ethics and God's absolute will. Whenever God's will is translated into human and finite terms and becomes concrete, it ceases to be absolute and becomes permeated with the relativities of human experience.

The will of God is thus beyond all human wills, and God's thoughts are higher than human thoughts. In God reside the potentialities for all finite goods and values which come into the world. But only the potentialities are infinite and transcendent and abstract; the moment they enter history they become finite and partial and immanent as God's work of growth of value in the world.

The point of reference for all human living is this abstract and absolute will of God, which cannot be known in any satisfactory way through any human agency. We find hints pointing to it in church, Bible, and conscience, and in the teachings of Jesus we find the great command which is also the height of religious irony: "Be ye therefore perfect, even as your Father which is in heaven is perfect" (Mt 5:48,KJ). This is true, but it must be kept in a state of tension by Jesus' other admission: "Why do you call me good? No one is good except God alone" (Lk 18:19, NEB).

If the will of God is hidden in God's primordial nature and if we must live among the relativities of a finite world, we are faced with a dilemma, but this does not destroy our assurance or our hope. On the one hand, we cannot simply talk about the relevance of an impossible ideal; and, on the other hand, we dare not claim that our prudential ethics can be called the will of God for us and thus eliminate the tension. We are called to resolve this tension in terms of hope.

THE RELATION OF CHRISTIAN ETHICS TO LIFE

Christians historically have found four possible solutions to the problem of the relation of God's will to social living.

The first solution, offered by many leaders in Christian ethics, is that the answer is found simply in doing the best one can in each situation. This means building up a system of ideals, perhaps in terms of altruism or humanitarianism or utilitarianism, and then equating that system with the will of God. Translated into social realms, there have been Utopian dreams such as Christian socialism, the social gospel in many forms, and paternalistic capitalism. Provided these dreams are kept purified, we may be assured that we are on the way to the kingdom of God on earth.

This leads to identifying prudential ends with the absolute will of God. It ignores the dilemma between the relative and the absolute. If the ends achieved continue to be absolutized, effort ceases and pride enters the picture. It is this type of thinking that identifies God with democracy, church, or some other human institution. It confuses the absolute, abstract, potential will of God with some social or political or military strategy, such as prohibition, pacifism, blue laws, antiabortion stance, or other platform of suggested behavior.

In spite of its error, this type of thinking has been prevalent among all groups of Christians. It is the error of the Roman church in identifying itself with the kingdom of God on earth. It is the error of those Protestants who have identified the will of God with capitalism and industrialism. It is the error of smaller groups who have identified God's will with various Utopian schemes. It is the error of those liberals who insist that if we only play the game we can "build" the kingdom of God on earth.

In all of these cases, the result has been to banish the tension between absolute and relative values. No matter how verbose the representatives of these positions may be on the subject of sin, they fail to see that their sin lies in making their relative ethical ideals identical with the absolute will of God. Even when their ideals are good, as they usually are, they are only partial and relative.

To these criticisms, adherents of this view answer that we must have prudential ethics, and of course that is true. These prudential ethics must be grounded in the Christian tradition and in the will of God, and that also is true. The absolute must be made relevant to the human situation, and that is true. What they fail to recognize is that this cannot be done by the substitution of any prudential or situational ethics (no matter how well disguised or piously phrased) for the commitment of the self to the reality of God.

A second solution is the claim that the ethics of Jesus are absolute ethics, and therefore his sayings are irrelevant to the present situation. They say that no one could follow Jesus literally and live. Even he could not stand against the world. His teachings, therefore, are applicable only to the coming kingdom. The kingdom, so holders of this view claim, will come by a divine act, and when the kingdom comes the absolute commands of Jesus will be met.

A variation on this theme which is equally disastrous is the claim that Jesus taught interim ethics. This means that all of

Jesus' teachings applied to the brief period before the coming of the kingdom. Paul, they say, also taught interim ethics, and many of his sayings only make sense in that perspective.

Now there can be no doubt that both Jesus and Paul thought that the end of the world was coming soon, and some of their sayings can best be understood in this light, as, for example, Paul's advice about refraining from marriage. But it would not apply to Jesus' teachings about divorce. It would not apply to many sayings of Jesus about the fulfillment of the law and the prophets.

Scholars have listed many arguments against this theory, but its main weakness is that it fails to make Christian ethics relevant to our historical situation. We are faced with ethical decisions now, and if Christian ethics apply only to an eschatological kingdom, or to the brief interim before the coming of the kingdom (which has not come), then we had better look elsewhere for ethics which will help us in this world.

This is the kind of solution reached by Albert Schweitzer, and it means either retreating to the first position of prudential ethics or of deriving ethics on other grounds from the teachings of Jesus.

A third solution begins with the emphasis on the impossibility of love as a workable ethic, unless it is interpreted in terms of justice. This position is associated with Reinhold Niebuhr. He builds up a sense of tension which is essential to Christian living (a tension which is destroyed by the extreme forms of both prudential and eschatological views). He makes the sense of tension real, vital, and inescapable.

The relevance of an impossible ideal, however, is never made quite clear. It is relevant only to prove the impossibility of getting away from failure in any ethical endeavor. The tension is one-sided because in the end it paralyzes moral effort at the source. The ideal is so absolute that we lose sight of it in our prudential living. When we do good, we know that it is still evil.

Instead of being an approximation of the will of God and there-fore worthy, it is a failure to reach the impossible and therefore not so clearly worthy.

In the second place, by making the "law of love" the substance of the impossible possibility, Niebuhr falls into the same moral idealism as the purely prudential thinkers. Although he has not fallen into the trap of identifying prudential ends with the will of God, he has assumed that the will of God can be known in terms of love. Thus, the will of God, which is absolute, is brought to terms with our ethical ideals and identified with our highest insight. Niebuhr includes justice as a secondary category of love; but if the term love is to have meaning, it cannot include all the other categories by which we live. If love is an impossible possi-bility, justice as a possibility is to be contrasted with love, not subsumed under it. Love does not stand simply in a state of tension beyond our strivings, as Niebuhr contends; it stands also in contradiction to some of our endeavors which might also point toward God's aims for us.

The will of God transcends human moral categories, including love, in order for it to be absolute and relevant at the same time. Any ideal must be thrown over if we see that the aim of God opposes it. Although God is primarily persuasive love, this does not exhaust God's nature. God includes love and all other ulti-mate values in the primordial nature, for God is the potential for all values. Thus we must seek for a solution other than Niebuhr's in order to avoid either a paralyzing tension or a God limited to love which is an impossibility for humanity.

The fourth view, and the thesis of this book, is that we can have *approximation* in Christian ethics. The insights contained in the three previous theories must be accounted for. The will of God in the primordial nature is absolute and not achievable by creatures. But that is only part of the story. God's will is also expressed in time, for God is Lord of history. The Holy Spirit is God immanent, at work in the world and in us. Thus God's will becomes relevant to history and to us through the consequent nature.

People, living in the finite perspective of history, can align themselves with the processes which God has set in action, and in so doing they can *approximate* God's will. They do not achieve God's absolute will, which remains as pure potentiality in God's everlasting nature, but they become sensitive to the *possibilities of value* in each concrete situation, and thus they can act as channels through which God's aims for humanity may be achieved.

Those who are committed to God's will seek to discover through every tool at their command the potentialities for value which are really present, and then to decide how best they can open themselves to the creative and transforming power of God. These decisions are of many kinds. Sometimes, there is a conflict between two courses of action, both of which seem to the rational mind to be good. Perhaps it makes no difference to God which way we turn. However, if we are really sensitive to God's will, we may see, in some cases, that only one of two seemingly good courses of action can fulfill God's aims. Sometimes the contrast is abundantly clear, and there is no doubt that one choice is the better. There still remains the tension, for there is the realization that even our best in human terms is less than the full potential offered by God. Finally, there are those terrifying experiences where the choice is between evils. No alternative is right, and yet there are no other possibilities. This is the hardest problem for Christian ethics. It is particularly true in cases of social action. Simply by being in an immoral society, the possibilities for us are relatively evil. This is obvious in the case of war, where the pacifist fails to defend one's country and stop the aggressor, while the nonpacifist must take part in war which is evil in itself.

Furthermore, in making any of these choices, there is the danger of pride. Even where the choice is good, there is tension between the human concept of the highest good and God's will.

This tension can be relieved sufficiently to allow for consecrated action by the realization that the highest course of action for us is an *approximation* of God's will. It is not God's absolute will, but it points in that direction. This position is similar to John Bennett's understanding of compromise, and perhaps the difference is purely verbal, but approximation seems to carry with it a motive that is dynamic and positive. In any case, we are protected against making the prudential an ultimate guide.

This last position avoids the dangers of a prudential ethic by seeing that the highest prudential and relative ethic is never more than the approximation of God's will, and it also removes the stalemate of an impossibility. It does not suffer from the limitations of moral idealism, and its reliance on the ethics of Jesus is self-validated in the present, despite the worldview of eschatology dominating the New Testament. It is flexible enough to take account of the approach through situation ethics but has more tension between the relative and the absolute, and it is not restricted to love as the only value to be considered.

The question then arises whether anyone can achieve God's absolute will. In individual action, there may be some cases where an act is so final and complete as to be perfect obedience to God's will. It may be some act of heroism, whether it be martyrdom or a mother's sacrifice for her child. It can come in a split second which may alter one's life completely. Unless such an act ends in death, however, the next act may make one a sinner again. Even Jesus asked, "Why do you call me good?" Yet we account Jesus sinless because his intention was in terms of complete commitment.

The Christian ethic is directed to the will of God, for it is a religious ethic. The mature Christian achieves a high degree of moral autonomy, for the connection between intention and action is located in the arena of human freedom. This is why living by grace is considered higher than living according to law, for human beings have access to the transforming and energizing presence of God as a means for achieving values. It is possible to achieve high levels of moral action without religious beliefs, but Christians are concerned with the resources of Christianity for ethical living, and this leads to the emphasis on discernment of God's will and commitment to it. Thus the religious dimension is prior to the ethical.

Although the will of God is absolute in the primordial nature, it becomes relative and relevant within the human and finite sphere. The tension between the absolute and the relative is lessened by the fact that those who are committed to God's will seek to approximate that will in their human choices and actions, in complete freedom and yet by the grace of God. Thus a prudential ethic stands under the judgment of God and is related to the will of God at the same time, without being identical with the will of God.

CHURCH AND INDIVIDUAL IN ETHICAL AND SOCIAL PROBLEMS

The authority of the church lies in its traditions which are born of experience and in the cumulative expression of the opinions of particularly devoted Christians among the leaders of the church.

The church's domain is the world of human experience. Its main job is not ethical or social legislation, but in its role as the central institution of the Christian religion one of its chief concerns is the formulating of ethical ideals which are approximations of the will of God for specific situations. It stating these ideals, the church hopes to inspire social legislation, to influence leaders among statesmen, to encourage citizens to support good leaders and laws, and to stimulate actions which will bring about conditions which are closer to God's aims for the world.

It is proper for the church to make statements concerning child labor, planned parenthood, abortion, race relations, women's liberation, concern for the oppressed, industrial relations, the use of narcotics and liquor, war and peace; these are moral issues which the church is competent to make decisions about and this may influence legislation, but the church's task is not to dictate legislation. It seeks to work through its members to persuade those with power to bring about the elimination of social and moral evils and to make possible the liberation of all people to be fully human. The church by itself may never stop war, but it can and does inspire people and nations to work for peace and for international cooperation. Although a greater United Nations may be necessary to set up the machinery of peace, the World Council of Churches may do more to inspire it.

Although the church has no business legislating about major or minor matters, and should make only the most general guidelines for its members, it should be deeply concerned with the personal and social ethics of its culture. Such statements as the official pronouncements of denominational leaders, the policy statements of the National and World Councils of Churches, the official statements of the Church of Rome, and the influence of many smaller and specialized groups of religious people carry with them a profound and guiding authority. It is conceivable that the group opinions of church leaders may be wrong (and occasionally they have been shown to be wrong, even reversing previous decisions), but they have a more persuasive authority than the conscience of the individual.[2]

If the church should enter directly into politics, it would cease to be a persuasive and inspiring force. It would turn it into a political institution with power. When it failed or was proved wrong, it would lose prestige at the level of specific political decisions and thus lose its future persuasive and inspiring force.

2. See John C. Bennett, *The Radical Imperative* (Philadelphia: Westminster Press, 1975), pp. 52–80, for illustrations of the churches and councils of churches in dealing with corporate and political situations.

When it succeeded, it would become captive to the power it had used, and thus would serve other ends than the will of God. Furthermore, only an authoritative church can afford the luxury of unanimity on social and ethical problems, and therefore there is the issue of the rights of the individual's conscience.

Individual Christians (even the clergy), simply because their authority is less, have the right to be more direct and demanding than the church in seeking to influence social change. The church, for example, can support population control in principle, but individuals, *as Christians,* may demand a certain type of legislation to control the obvious evils of uncontrolled births. The church can make statements concerning the justice of a particular war, and still allow freedom among individuals to choose between participation and conscientious objection. Also, on many issues Christians and churches may differ, as in the case of abortion, and each group will feel bound to support opposite sides. This does not mean that God's will is divided, but that human beings, as usual, have an inadequate or partial grasp of God's aims.

There is also an ethical demand within the life of the church. Some of the worst abuses were summarized when Liston Pope called "eleven o'clock on Sunday morning the most segregated hour of the week." Although many church people made strong efforts in the area of race relations, the churches themselves had a sorry record. The church has been legalistic rather than moral in its handling of divorce and remarriage, so that its divorced members could find no mercy. Local parishes have failed to pay their lay workers, especially those in maintenance work, a decent salary. Yet an understanding of the nature of the church, theologically considered as the people of God or the community of the faithful, points to profound personal relations between members based on mutual trust and love. The church seeks to be a community in which the unaccepted are accepted, status symbols are forgotten, and each person's sense of worth is recognized.

This ethical demand within the congregation is an end in itself, and also it is the basis for an ethical witness to those outside the church.

The problem of Christian ethics is the discernment of the will of God and doing it. The discovery is difficult in itself. We need to call on all our resources—of reason, observation, imagination, and will—in order to reach even an approximation in our mind, and then we need to call forth all our energy, sense of direction, and faith in order to achieve even this approximation which we have sensed. It is no wonder that ethical idealism fails; for without the strength that comes from the grace of God none of us can approximate the will of God, and then we will sin again. The sin of pride will result from achievement and spoil what God's grace has made possible; or we will fail in our intention from the beginning. In either case, God's forgiveness must accompany God's grace if we are to have any sanity at all. The Christian is a citizen of two worlds, and the tensions between those realms are never completely resolved. But both worlds are bearable because God is equally present in both, and we are always children of God as well as sinners, in the sight of both worlds and of God.

THE SETTING FOR EDUCATION

Good religious education is not concerned primarily with morality. As Whitehead reminds us, "Morality, in the petty negative sense of the term, is the deadly enemy of religion."[3] We need to stress the priority of religious commitment and the grace of God before we can place human behavior in its proper context. Because one has been reconciled or saved or redeemed or

3. Alfred North Whitehead, *The Aims of Education* (New York: The Free Press, 1929, 1957), p. 39.

restored by an act of divine grace, *therefore* one is to respond to such graciousness by seeking to align one's will with God's will. Because of what God has done, "Therefore I appeal to you. . . . to present your bodies as a living sacrifice, holy and acceptable to God, which is your spiritual worship. Do not be conformed to this world but be transformed by the renewal of your mind, that you may prove what is the will of God, which is good and acceptable and perfect" (Rom 12:1-2, RSV). "For by grace you have been saved through faith; and this is not your own doing, it is the gift of God—not because of works, lest any one should boast. . . . I therefore, a prisoner for the Lord, beg you to live a life worthy of the calling to which you have been called" (Eph 2:8-9, 4:1,RSV).

This leads to one more "therefore." "Therefore, my beloved, as you have always obeyed, so now, not only in my presence but much more in my absence, work out your own salvation with fear and trembling; for God is at work in you, both to will and to work for his good pleasure" (Php 2:12,RSV). The response to grace is to fulfill one's human nature, to reach a degree of maturity, to achieve a Christian style of life. This style of life places human freedom and moral autonomy within the framework of the larger beauty of the wholeness of being at one with other human beings in genuine community.

The beginning of education for ethics, from one standpoint of theology, is with God's action in accepting human beings as they are, offering them the opportunity to be at one with the divine in terms of purpose, and bringing them into community with God and with other human beings, with the church as one channel by which this *may* occur. There are no guarantees, because God's grace is the product of persuasive love and not coercive overruling.

The style of life that emerges from this grace-faith-vocation process is what Paul describes as being "worthy of your vocation." Francis O. Ayres, in his *The Ministry of the Laity,* described this style of life under five categories that would normally follow from "therefore."[4]

First is the stress on the affirmation of life. Life is meant to be enjoyed, and a Christian style of life finds all levels of enjoyment—what Alexander Miller called "a lip-smacking, exuberant delight in the ingenious beauty and variety of the created world; in wine and milk, oil and honey. It is a world whose paths drop fatness, where the little hills rejoice on every side."[5] The fruit of the spirit is expressed in daily life as "love, joy, peace, patience, kindness, goodness, faithfulness, gentleness, self-control" (Gal 5:22–23, RSV). This immediately takes one beyond a limited moralism to the broader values associated with the fullness of life.

A second element in a Christian style of life is awareness, sensitivity, discernment, appreciation. It has something of the freshness and the keenness of the senses which makes one sensitive to what is going on inside and outside of a person. It includes a kind of self-knowledge, but it does not dwell on the existential questions. It can be self-forgetful as it focuses on the needs of others. Ayres gives us a slogan: "Think straight, see it straight, *so that when you act* it will fit in."[6] When we are fully aware and able to think with a degree of maturity, we will act in responsible ways. It is a complex situation and we cannot know all the complications, but we try to fit in.

A third element is responsibility. This includes responsibility for those who stand in need of justice and of freedom from oppression, for those who are malnourished or economically deprived, for the political and social decisions that will help our

4. Francis O. Ayres, *The Ministry of the Laity* (Philadelphia: Westminster Press, 1962), pp. 79–126.
5. Ayres, *Ministry of the Laity*, p. 82.
6. Ayres, *Ministry of the Laity*, p. 95.

neighbors. These social concerns are inseparable from more individual and personal ones. Problems move from the private to the public domain and back again as we deal with them. We are responsible for the whole of the human condition, which takes us beyond morality and social concern to the total view of the whole from an aesthetic viewpoint. If we are to align ourselves responsibly with God's aims, we need to remind ourselves of Isaiah's words:

> Wash yourselves; make yourselves clean;
>> remove the evil of your doings
>> from before my eyes;
> cease to do evil,
>> learn to do good;
> seek justice,
>> correct oppression;
> defend the fatherless,
>> plead for the widow   (Is 1:16-17,RSV).

Ayres suggests that the fourth element is the sharing of Christ's sufferings. This is a more difficult concept to grasp, for it is drawn specifically from a religious tradition. The insight of process thought that God is a tender, patient, and suffering deity lends weight to our understanding of the suffering of Jesus. God is thought of as "the poet of the world, with tender patience leading it by his vision of truth, beauty, and goodness."[7] A suffering deity bears the joys and sorrows of human life. Human life, likewise, can share in the suffering of God, and can share in God's enjoyment of our human enjoyments. This mutual sharing leads us to understand what it means to share in Christ's suffering.

Jesus came into a world that was full of suffering. The people were oppressed. There was little hope of liberation. There were

7. Whitehead, *Process and Reality*, p. 346 (525).

factions within the household of faith. The opportunities to help those who were dispossessed of their dignity as well as their livelihoods were slight. Jesus was aware of their situation, and he recognized that the leaders were doing nothing for the downtrodden. Jesus said: "You know that those who are supposed to rule the heathen lord it over them, and their great men tyrannize over them; but it is not to be so among you. Whoever wants to be great among you must be your servant, and whoever wants to hold the first place among you must be everybody's slave. For the Son of Man has not come to be waited on, but to wait on other people, and to give his life to free many others" (Mk 10:42–45,G). This radical concept of leadership as servanthood lies at the center of understanding and sharing Christ's suffering.

The final element in response to the "therefore" that runs through understanding the religious response to God's grace is a secret discipline or a structure to one's life that limits and directs one's creativity. Jesus was no ascetic in the sense of withdrawing from food and drink or from society, but he did believe in providing a structure of prayer to accompany his strenuous labors on behalf of others. There are times of solitariness when we find ways to correct and strengthen out attempts to align our aims with those of God, or simply to come into a better understanding of what our Christian style of life should be like.

There is value in secrecy in relation to one's endeavors to be in communion with God. The emphasis on corporateness sometimes hides from us the need for a secret integrity known only to God. We don't need to sound a trumpet when we give alms, or advertise the fact that we are fasting or praying. We are to keep some gifts a secret even from ourselves. This goes beyond our charity to our own secrets. There may be times when confession that betrays our privacy may be necessary for our mental health, but simply to blurt out family secrets and hidden sins in a group process experience is not likely to further one's spiritual or mental health although it may be titilating for others.

Can we develop a theory and practice of education that starts with an understanding of the religious base for ethics? If there is a proper understanding of grace and faith in relation to works, so that we have a eucharistic ethic that goes beyond mere morality in action and finds its roots in God's grace, we may be on the right track.[8]

8. For an earlier treatment of the topic of this chapter, see my *The Clue to Christian Education* (New York: Scribners, 1950), pp. 138–169.

9

Christian Education
as a Theological Discipline
and Method

This chapter is a centerpiece of the book. It is a statement of my basic educational theory as expressed in my *The Clue to Christian Education*. In 1952, when I came to Yale, I had an opportunity to express my views in a lecture at the opening convocation. The major idea was that theology had deep implications for the kind of religious educational theory being espoused, and that a good theology would lead to a good educational philosophy. There was no attempt to deny the obvious successes of secular educational theory and its significance for religious educators. But it was an argument for a certain kind of sophistication among religious educators. In the years since 1952, a number of educators have worked with this concept, not by agreement with my theology, but by working on the relation of theology to education. My address first appeared in *Religious Education*, Vol. XLVIII, No. 6, November–December 1953, pp. 409–414. It was reprinted in *Who Are We?* edited by John H. Westerhoff III (Birmingham: Religious Education Press, 1978), which contains articles dating from 1903 to the present seeking to identify the nature of religious or Christian education.

It seems to me that the thesis expressed in 1952 needs to be reiterated within the framework of the argument of this book. Except for the updating of the language and a few references, this is the address as it appeared in 1952–3.

THE BACKGROUND IN 1952

Christian education is coming of age as a theological discipline and method. It is asserting a new autonomy as a theory of learning the Christian faith, it is indicating new developments of Christian growth in the family, it is drawing upon the learning process as well as on the Christian revelation as a source of a relevant theology, and it is expressing itself through the dynamic Christian life of the local parish.

In one sense, all of these so-called new developments are as old as the Christian religion and can be found in certain aspects of Hebrew religion. But in another sense, religious education began with the rise of the Sunday school in the early part of the nineteenth century and reached its highest level with the insights of Horace Bushnell who in 1847 wrote the first two chapters of the epoch-making *Christian Nurture.* But Bushnell was not taken seriously for another fifty years and during this time most religious education was ungraded and Bible-centered, with little concern for the capacities or the growing edges of the pupils. When finally Bushnell's insights were considered, they were for the most part misunderstood or divorced from the basic presupposition of the part that parents must play in the religious development of the child. Progressive education began its influential career among the leaders of secular education, and the church educators followed the lead of John Dewey and his cohorts. Mixed with sound educational theory was a secular metaphysics or even perhaps a simple naturalism among the secularists, and a type of liberal Christianity among the church leaders which lacked much of the profundity and depth of biblical Christianity. These leaders knew their educational theory, and they made use of all the findings of science in biblical study and theology as well as in educational processes, but their system crashed against the rocks of a resurgent orthodoxy.

It took a theological analysis to put Christian education back on the right track. This was resented among some educators who had not kept abreast of theological developments or who were not theologians in any real sense. A few of the most able among them were religious naturalists who knew more about Henry Nelson Wieman than about the classical theologians of the church, and it was hard for them to relate their teachings to any historic theology. Many others were hard-working technicians who were excited about developing new methods and techniques for stimulating interest in many areas of subject matter. They saw education as a social process within the context of a classroom situation, and often they saw clearly the relation of religious attitudes to the community, but they lacked precisely the insight upon which Christianity insists: the social process of Christian education is provided by the church which is the body of Christ. A sociology of education is not sufficient to provide a social theology of Christian education.

With this background in mind, we need also to note briefly three trends in Christian education before we look at it as theological discipline and method.

The first trend is the rediscovery of the function of the family as a primary agent of Christian education. From the days of Deuteronomy to the organic unity of the family stressed by Horace Bushnell to the experiments being made today, there is recognition of the effective priesthood of parents which has theological significance for the interpretation of baptism, confirmation, and other equivalent rites in the various churches.

The second trend is the rediscovery of the function of the total parish in a comprehensive educational program. At first, this was a sociological discovery involving the cooperation of all individuals and organizations in the parish educational program, but it led to theological implications. One crucial insight was that parish life could be a means of redemption, of that process whereby persons are taken from their status of alienation and restored to fellowship within the community.

The third trend which has been with us since at least the time of G. Stanley Hall at the turn of the century, is that children are not little adults but are developing organisms with growing edges which must be stimulated and directed. Graded vocabularies, projects adapted to age levels, use of concepts within the capacities of growing minds, and other secular discoveries are important. But there is one crucial question: *What is the religious readiness of the child?* This is primarily a theological question, for it involves the relevance of theology as a guide to a child's development.

THE PLACE OF THEOLOGY IN EDUCATIONAL THEORY

These three trends indicate the significance of our basic problem, which is to find out how Christian education is to be a theological discipline and method. This means that Christian education must be defined theologically.

The purpose of Christian education is to place God at the center and to bring the individual into the right *relationship* with God and one's fellows within the perspective of the fundamental truths about all of life. The major task for Christian education is to discover and impart the *relevance* of Christian truth. The key words are *relationship* and *relevance*.

Theology is a description of relationships. We may define theology as "the truth-about-God-in-relation-to-humanity." Our Jewish-Christian tradition arises from human experience, especially as recorded in the Bible and interpreted as the record of God's mighty acts in nature and in history. The Bible is the story of these relationships, in terms of covenants, judgments, and redemption. The focal point of such a theology is the story of Jesus of Nazareth, who through his life, death, and resurrection changed our understanding of the relationship between humanity and deity. "In Christ, God was reconciling the world to himself." Theology emerges as persons reflect on the story of this relationship.

Ultimately this comes to the fore in our own experience in what Martin Buber calls the "I-Thou" relationship. This "divine-human" encounter takes place in our lives within the framework of the Christian community. In this relationship, we are not simply related to a concept or idea or idol; we are in relationship with an entity or process which we call God. A little child is not integrated in the home by the child's *idea* of the parents but by the child's *relationship* with them in personal encounters. So it is with Christian faith; there is a personal relationship between the creature and the creator which becomes the source of redemption.

There is a slogan to describe this approach to Christian education: "*Theology in the background: grace and faith in the foreground.*"[1] Christian nurture takes place when the believer trusts in God and in turn God's gracious favor is experienced, for that grace was there everlastingly awaiting the human act of faith. Therefore, the application of theology to education leads to a dynamic personal relationship of grace and faith, and the concepts arising from the relationships of humanity to God are the theological guides to greater and deeper experiences of God.

The theology which is in the background must always be *relevant.* Sometimes theology is so abstract as to be irrelevant. Yet significant experiences are going on around us at all times. The rhythm of rejection and acceptance in the home, the sense of frustration and the maturity of accepting one's self as one is, the conviction of sin and the assurance of God's forgiveness, the feelings of separation from God and then of being in communion with God—these occur in the smallest children and in the most mature adults. It is a matter of relationships, not of vocabulary or of abstract concepts.

The significance of this for religious education is not always

1. I have developed this slogan in various ways: In *The Clue to Christian Education* (New York: Scribner, 1950), p. 7f.; in *Christian Nurture and the Church* (New York: Scribner, 1961), pp. 33–34; in *Education for Christian Living* (Englewood Cliffs, NJ: Prentice Hall, 2nd ed., 1963), p. 54.

obvious. It means that we may teach the glory of the redemptive life on every level of communication and that theology is relevant to every age group. Religious readiness is developed far beyond technical theological capacity. It also means that teachers of younger Christians must have a theology relevant to their own capacities and then be able to translate these insights into terms of relationships for the younger ones.

Theology also contributes to our understanding of the learners. Theology gives us insights into what it means to be human in terms different from a strictly scientific view. Theology begins with the assertion that persons are creatures of God and become children of God through baptism, and that they grow in grace in the life and fellowship of the church. Human destiny is to live in harmony with God, and this relationship is everlasting. But human beings are sinners; they are so disobedient, selfish, and traitorous to the nature which God implanted that they have crucified the best that God can do in sending God's unique son. Thus human beings are capable of crucifying the best person that God has made and at the same time are capable of being the Christ. One historic incident reveals to the full both the glory and the misery of being human.

But Christian theology does not stop with analysis. It turns to the cure immediately. The *reconciliation* which comes through Christ is the central issue. God has acted so that persons will be saved if they turn to God. The relationship of grace and faith is the heart of Christian nurture.

All learners fit into this pattern. Whether it be a child just entering church school, a person in the morning congregation, or an adult in a Bible class, the same fundamental understanding applies. The gospel is good news for all ages. Theology's task is to provide self-understanding in relation to God which is relevant to a particular age and specific needs. Christian education's task is to draw persons into the redemptive life of the community of the faithful.

The curriculum of Christian education has been described as a three-legged stool. Just as a stool is no good unless all legs are of equal length and strength, so Christian education is balanced when there are three equal emphases: knowledge of the data, development of Christian character, and life within the fellowship of the church.

This leads to one more conclusion about the significance of theology for Christian education. There is no Christian education which does not involve evangelism. Evangelism and education come together within the overall purpose of Christian education, for to evangelize is to confront persons with Jesus Christ, so that they will put their trust in God through him, and by the power of the Holy Spirit live as Christ's disciples in the fellowship of the church. This is to be distinguished from indoctrination, where the answers to all questions are prejudged. Evangelism within the bounds of education provides for confrontation with the challenge of Christianity, but avoids the pitfalls of manipulation and pressure associated with indoctrination and authoritarian educational procedures.

It should be clear that Christian education is in itself a theological discipline. Because its teaching builds on the relationships which the learners actually have, and because its teaching must be relevant to the every day lives of the learners, much that is taught arises from experiences in the teaching situation. This is both necessary and desirable, for if education is to lead to nurture and evangelism it must be in terms of meaningful experiences. But it is also dangerous, as is demonstrated by the amount of bad, irrelevant, and inert theological concepts which have appeared. There is a responsibility for the truth of the concepts being taught, so that we can say that we have a theological responsibility to *impart truth.*

There is, then, a theological requirement which Christian educators must face. There have been too few competent theologians among the educators, and often the professional theologians have provided little help to the educators. We will return to this point when we examine the place of Christian education in the curricula of theological schools.

EDUCATIONAL METHOD

We turn now to another problem: that of method. It seems to me that a number of current theologies, ranging all the way from neo-orthodoxy to reconstructed liberalism and including both existentialist and process categories, are capable of describing the "I-Thou" relationship within the context of the redemptive fellowship. My old professor, Douglas Clyde Macintosh, called it "the right religious adjustment." A theology based on the mighty acts of God as recorded in the scriptures and on the human response to those acts may be relevant for educational purposes. A barrier is placed in the way of Christian development when grace and faith are relegated to the background and a fixed vocabulary of theology is placed in the foreground.

The problem of method is technical. If we once develop a relationship theology which has the possibility of relevance at every level of human experience, the educational problem becomes that of finding methods which will bring this relevance into focus. This is not the problem of a false antithesis between content-centered and life-centered teaching. Any good teacher uses both kinds of methods and keeps a proper balance between the two. The crucial point for Christian education is the experiential or existential one: *no education is religious unless it is God-centered.* We teach within the framework of relationships between humanity and God and between persons and persons. Of course, this forces us back to the theological question: To what reality does the word God point? The techniques will pretty much take care of themselves once we grasp the fundamental theological significance of what we are doing.

James Bradley Thayer wrote: "While good teaching will differ widely in its methods, there is at least one thing in which all good teaching will be alike; no teaching is good which does not arouse and 'dephlegmatize' the students, which does not engage as allies their awakened, sympathetic, and cooperating faculties."[2] Unless the students are aware of the relevance of what they are learning, we cannot expect an enthusiastic response. Too often we can say of the students what Thomson said about the linnets who

"... sit
On the dead tree, a dull despondent flock."

The problem of relevance shows up at every level. In the 1950s, many lessons were shaded toward neo-orthodoxy. On the kindergarten level, there was help for parents and teachers in terms of neo-orthodox theology, some of which was relevant, but there were theological presuppositions lying behind the descriptions of children's thinking and behavior which were consistent with child development studies and liberal theology! This was due, I think, to the failure to work out a theological understanding of children from this point of view.[3] The significance of neo-orthodoxy was that it could not serve as a footnote to secular insights, although in less extreme forms it was able to utilize scientific data as footnotes for its theological interpretation of children and adults. Theology and educational theory can be in dialogue, with insights from both fields commingled in an overall educational theory suitable for Christian education.

The goal of Christian education has been discussed in terms of maturity. We are to put away our childishness and immaturity. The marks of maturity are poise, originality, and disinterestedness, whereby we attain balance, power to bear fruit, and free-

2. Quoted by Houston Peterson, *Great Teachers* (New Brunswick: Rutgers University Press, 1946), p. 341.
3. See Edith Hunter, "Neo-Orthodoxy Goes to Kindergarten," *Religion in Life* (Winter 1950–51), pp. 3–14.

dom from selfish motives. It is the full growth which is described in the letter to the Ephesians: "Reaching maturity, reaching the full measure of development which belongs to the fullness of Christ, instead of remaining immature, blown from our course by every passing wind of doctrine, by the adroitness of [those] who are dexterous in devising error; we are to hold by the truth, and by our love to grow up wholly unto [Christ]" (Eph 4:13b–15, M). Certainly this is a description of the goal of Christian education, showing the relevance of truth to the process of growing into the right relationship with God.

Christian growth is a process of increased integration centered on the living God in our midst. This process cannot be guaranteed by the processes of either education or evangelism or by the relevance of theological concepts. The response of children and adults to the gospel of Jesus Christ is in the last analysis a personal decision that rests in the mystery of God. But that is no excuse for either bad theology or bad education, although it may be an explanation of why we sometimes get satisfying results from poor educational procedures.

THE CURRICULUM OF THEOLOGICAL EDUCATION

One final question is the relation of Christian education to the curriculum of theological education. Courses in Christian education are often electives, or at best perhaps a single course is required for graduation. Being a latecomer to the curriculum, it may be treated as a stepchild. This is bad enough, but what is worse is that it is not considered a theological discipline at all. It is placed in the category of "practical" courses, which means that it is training in techniques. The department of education is expected to provide tools, gadgets, and methods by which the gospel may be taught. When it is just that, and nothing more, it has no independent existence as a theological discipline. It is something that can be learned outside the disciplines of theology by borrowing from the secular educators who know much more about techniques than we do. But this is to commit the heresy of making the Christian religion an adjunct to secular processes. It is this error which led to the excesses of certain followers of progressive education in both secular and religious education. Because no basic educational philosophy stood behind the process, the methods of John Dewey led inevitably to Dewey's instrumentalism. What Christian educators needed to do was to show how Dewey's methodology could be aligned with a theological analysis of human nature and of how we learn. Because of the failure to discriminate between method and theology, some educators got far off the beam at the time when new theological insights were making their way in the thinking of the churches.

The current trend in Christian education indicates that theology remains primary and that method is derivative from both theological and educational insights. In the 1950s, the Presbyterians sensed this, but failed to achieve a complete integration of content and method. The Episcopalians saw it in theory, but faced almost insuperable problems in developing the *Seabury Series*. The editors needed to be immersed in theological thinking and in the ways children and adults think at various age levels; this had to be put together in terms of the understanding of religious needs and religious readiness; this led to methodology based upon an understanding of interpersonal relationships as a basis for theologizing. This kind of Buberian existentialism worked remarkably well for a minority of Episcopal Sunday schools, but the point I am making is that this understanding of the relationship of theology to education is essential at the level of theological education and professional ministerial training.

I would go so far as to suggest that Christian education belongs in the department of theology. It must begin by describing adequately the existential situation, the life-centered problems, the religious predicament, the problem of being human, and the way in which human beings are related to God within a dynamic community. Theology helps to describe the meaning of this relationship in ways that are relevant to the learners. Methods need to be taught, and they are of great importance, but the methods are derived from the situation in which the individual learner finds oneself and not from the secular world outside. The same methods would probably be called on, but because they are derivative they cannot dictate the results.

No one can be adequately trained for the pastoral ministry without an understanding of Christian education. It is against this background that those being ordained are asked: "Are you persuaded that the Holy Scriptures contain all Doctrine required as necessary for eternal salvation through faith in Jesus Christ? And are you determined out of the said Scriptures to *instruct* the people committed to your charge; and to *teach* nothing, as necessary to eternal salvation, but that which you shall be persuaded may be concluded and proved by the Scripture?" The Bible, then, is a primary source of Christian truth, but salvation does not rest on doctrine. Salvation rests on faith in Jesus Christ. Doctrine stands behind faith, and salvation comes through God's grace.

The pastor is an instructor. Her or his responsibility is to teach. And one learns to teach, as far as the seminary is concerned, through courses in Christian education. Therefore, everything one learns in seminary must be relevant, and biblical theology, which describes God's mighty acts in history, becomes a primary source for understanding Christian education. Every course, insofar as it is relevant, contributes to the understanding of Christian education; and Christian education, insofar as it is Christian, is grounded in a relevant theology. Only in this way will the gospel of Jesus Christ be taught to all people, of all ages, in all lands in terms of the relationships between persons and God and between human beings, within the Christian community.

10

Contributions
of Educational Philosophy

Educational philosophy is a discipline in its own right. It deals with the nature of the learner, the ways of teaching, and the goals of education. It operates successfully in a secular domain without regard to religion or theology. It has value as a position in dialogue with Christian education and with various metaphysical and theological positions. It places limitations on some goals of religious or Christian education, especially in the teaching about religion in state-supported schools where there is separation of church and state.

It is an important factor in religious education as well. It has tools for making distinctions that are important for every educational venture. It assists in clarifying the definitions of education, in stating valid objectives and goals, and in the development of theory. It helps to distinguish between education and indoctrination, between closed- and open-ended education, and between teaching for commitment and evangelism. It points to an emphasis on mastering content as against a direction for a style of life. It helps in seeing the values of rational and affective means of education.

I suggest that one way to work through these problems is to look at some of the valid ways in which education has been defined. We may think of education as a discipline in the art of thinking, as an initiation into a value-loaded way of living, as training in the skills of learning and in interpersonal relationships, as a way of evoking insights or disclosures, or as an overall nurturing process within a community. This leads into questions of authority, theology, and worship. All of these activities over-lap in practice, but they may be distinguished from indoctrination, which seeks to provide a ready-made way of thinking, believing, and behaving, or from brainwashing, which uses techniques that deny the freedom of the person to make her or his own decisions.

EDUCATION AS A DISCIPLINE

Marc Belth distinguishes between education and schooling. The school is a creation of the community and fulfills many functions that reflect the concerns of that community or that provide the conditions in which education is likely to be effec-tive. The school is concerned with the health and safety of the pupils, the development of good citizenship and loyalty to the nation, the acquisition of good manners, the ordering of life in the school to avoid chaos, the maintaining of discipline and obedience to the extent that the school may function. But none of these functions, important as they are, has to do with the essential nature of education.

Education, says Belth, "deals with the relationship between concepts and powers nurtured in learners, and with the methods of creating concepts as the inventions of intelligence, in what-ever fields these methods come to be employed."[1] Education is centered in the procedures by which one comes to intellectual conclusions, not on the value of the ideas as such. It is on a different plane from philosophy or theology, although it is rele-vant to the study of such subjects.

Education, then, "becomes a way of raising and answering a question not otherwise asked, a question centering on the prob-lems of improving the ability to think."[2] Education is not limited to the questions students ask; it is more dynamic than this, for it

1. Marc Belth, *Education as a Discipline* (Boston: Allyn & Bacon, Inc., 1965), p. 7.
2. Belth, *Education as a Discipline,* p. 13.

inspires new questions that challenge one to go beyond the previous limits in one's thinking. It makes use of all the knowledge and traditions of previous generations, but it holds earlier conclusions to reexamination in terms of current criteria.

Education takes us beyond the thinking level, however, for it is "concerned with the development of powers of thinking, symbol manipulation, and identification of theoretical bases for the acting and speaking, the exploring, and the describing which identify" us as human.[3] The fully human person is more than a thinking machine, and attitudes and feelings are essential elements in all activity.

If education is defined as a discipline, certain criteria for curriculum follow. All derived and inherited forms of thought are open to scrutiny, so that what is true in them may be assimilated. There will be the possibility of options for the student as competing and comparative systems of thought are examined. Therefore, there will be protection against premature closure of either thought or commitment, and the pupil's thinking will be stimulated to alter and expand. This makes possible further exploration beyond the range of current conclusions, and whatever is available to experience may be considered. The power to compare, test, and evaluate is the major focus at this stage. What needs to be avoided is a kind of nonquestioning literacy that makes possible the acquisition of ideas without critical examination, for such literacy only makes people more likely to succumb to false ideas through the assimilation of propaganda. This can be avoided if the criteria include the power to analyze: to discover and modify the structure and meaning of what is available to experience. One begins to see the interrelatedness of what is learned. "There is," says Belth, "now an abundance of literature reporting that children, even at the kindergarten level or earlier, learn science in a way which enables them to understand the

3. Belth, *Education as a Discipline*, p. 13.

interrelationship of elements in an operation being explored."[4] It is suggested that children at the age of seven can use some biblical material *if* they are helped to distinguish between what is obviously nonliteral or poetic or mythological and what is to be taken literally.

Such a view of education promises exciting consequences, for it points to the creative element in life. The functions of such education include: development of the powers of observation, capacity to operate symbols and models, the use of instrumental skills, the preservation of information in memory, the making of inferences, and finally the testing of inferences in life situations.[5] This is an intellectual exercise, but it is not limited to purely rational and logical developments, for it involves using models derived from myth, science, literature, history, ideology, and religion. Education may be thought of as the use and examination of models in order to illuminate experience. This is consistent with the goals of religious education as normally portrayed, for we need to "do theology" insofar as we are able, and we need to select even those authorities on whom we rely for "expert" help in our thinking and behaving as responsible believers.

EDUCATION AS INITIATION

Education may also be thought of as initiation into a community which has a set of values. The processes of education are understood as containing something worthwhile, including a cognitive perspective and incorporating voluntariness on the part of the learner. A great deal of family education is learning to be and to do what the family stands for. R. S. Peters makes this the center of his analysis of the meaning of education: "'Educa-

---

4. Belth, *Education as a Discipline*, p. 43.
5. Belth, *Education as a Discipline*, p. 75–76.

tion' involves essentially processes which intentionally transmit what is valuable in an intelligible and voluntary manner and which create in the learner a desire to achieve it, this being seen as having its place along with other things in life. Terms like 'training' and 'instruction'—perhaps even 'teaching'—are too specific. Education can occur without these specific transactions and they can take place in ways which fail to satisfy all the criteria implied by 'education.' The term 'initiation,' on the other hand, is general enough to cover these different types of transaction if it is also stipulated that initiation must be into worthwhile activities and modes of conduct."[6]

This implies that a critical consciousness must have something worthwhile to work on. But it is more than a rational exercise. There is also a function of the human person which is called the appreciative consciousness and which, says Bernard Meland, "can best be understood as an orientation of the mind which makes for a maximum degree of receptivity to the datum under consideration on the principle that what is given may be more than what is immediately perceived, or more than one can think."[7] In the educational process conceived as initiation into a value-loaded community, appreciation and critical analysis are interchangeably mixed, without sacrificing the autonomy of either process.

Much that goes on in religious education is initiation. The initiatory rites begin shortly after birth, and there are opportunities along life's way for further initiation into the tradition and mysteries of the community of the faithful. There is a combination of the given and the new, and the student remains free

6. R. S. Peters, in Reginald D. Archambault, ed., *Philosophical Analysis and Education* (London: Routledge & Kegan Paul, 1965; New York: Humanities Press, 1965), p. 102.
7. Bernard E. Meland, *Higher Education and the Human Spirit* (Chicago: University of Chicago Press, 1953), p. 57.

to give or withhold his or her consent. The student also has his or her sense of worth upheld, for in the values of the community one finds a recognition of the worth of each individual.

This approach points to a certain contagion in teaching. A shared search, conducted with care for the vigorous canons of honest thinking and respect for persons, can lead to deep appreciation of the worthwhileness of the task and of the style of life portrayed by religious values. When humor is an essential aspect of teaching, suggests Peters, age, sex, and status cease to be significant factors, and the class becomes a unit in a common exploration. This approach can also be subsumed under the experience of common worship as essential to religious education, for worship may become not only a unifying experience but also may point to those meanings which are essential for any religious education.

EDUCATION AS TRAINING

Education as a discipline or as initiation depends on a degree of efficiency. Training is the process by which one becomes proficient. The best example is the athletic coach, who does not expect the athletes to imitate him or her but to achieve their own goals in terms of their aptitudes. A track coach may train an athlete to run the 100 meters in record time, even though the coach may never have achieved such a goal.

In Christian education, we need "to equip God's people for work in his service" (Eph 4:12,NEB). This leads to at least three types of training. The first is orientation training, by which we learn to relate to other people, become aware of others' needs and concerns, and reflect on the way in which God is at work in our midst. Sometimes this process is carried out by various kinds of participation training, or by the techniques of group process, or by cooperation in some kind of task. It is a socializing process, and the power of the community may be exerted on the learner.

At the simplest level, it is what happens to a child the first day of school. The important element is the sense of value as a person that is gained by all the participants as they discover the value of other persons regardless of cultural accretions.

The second is procedural training. This involves the tools for acquiring factual knowledge, observation training, and utilization of data. At one level is a return to the three R's of reading, 'riting, and 'rithmetic. It is similar to the call of the football coach after a losing game, "Back to fundamentals!" It includes retention of information (memory work), seeking out new information, and relating various data systems to each other.

The teachers especially need a third form of training, based on consultation or supervision of in-service activities. Not even the best secular educational systems have solved this problem, partly because supervision is expensive in personnel and finances and also because no one knows quite how to do it. Certainly we are aware that untrained teachers are a hazard to any educational process, and we know how often Sunday schools and catechetical classes have untrained teachers who do more harm than good. Churches and synagogues are not yet set up to provide good training for teachers, and yet we know that teaching is a risky business. "My brothers," says the author of James, "not many of you should become teachers, for you may be certain that we who teach shall ourselves be judged with greater strictness" (Jas 3:1,NEB).[8]

EDUCATION AS INSIGHT

Another view of education fits in with the first three, but with an entirely different emphasis. It is education for insight, or discernment, or disclosure. Everyone has the experience, from

8. See David R. Hunter, *Christian Education as Engagement* (New York: Seabury Press, 1962), pp. 53-70.

time to time, of having it "come alive" that one knows the solution to a problem. The "light dawns" and one knows what needs to be done. No matter how one struggles with mathematics, or history, or language, or art, suddenly "the penny drops," and there is an answer. When one has gone through all the routes of straight thinking, or entered into the appreciation of values, or been trained to be aware of the concerns of others, there are moments of enlightenment, and these moments are often life transforming.

All education, suggests Ian T. Ramsey, should have as its purpose "to teach insight, to evoke disclosures in which we come to ourselves when and as we discern a world which has 'come alive' in some particular situation."[9] Such a result cannot be guaranteed by the teacher, who works hard for this result but has the patience to wait.

Ramsey suggests several ways in which we can work for this kind of insight. When he looks at ordinary language, Ramsey sees nothing that will enlighten the student. Language about God, especially, always has logically odd qualifiers. By using models and metaphors with logically odd twists, we may evoke a new insight in the student. This approach guards against a too easy and pedestrian identification of God with humanity, for the logically odd use points to the reality for which the word "God" stands. The disclosure that may come does not fit into a neat conceptual scheme, so that we may be sure of God and yet not of our description. As Ramsey says, "being sure in religion does not entail being certain in theology."[10]

Ramsey claims that *all* education seeks to evoke discernment, which may be claiming too much, but certainly education includes moments of insight, and religious education in particular works toward disclosures followed by commitment. As Ramsey

9. In *Religious Education* LVII (January–February 1962), p. 95.
10. Ian T. Ramsey, *On Being Sure in Religion* (London: Athlone Press, 1963), p. 47.

puts it, "what Christian education in particular seeks to do is to create this response and this fullness of life—this commitment—in relation to a discernment which occurs around the person of Jesus Christ as disclosed in the Bible, in doctrine, and in worship."[11] When the right stories are told in an environment which correlates with the stories, when there are logically odd uses of language which parallel the life situation of the learner, it is possible that there may be a disclosure to the learner, but this cannot be guaranteed and the learner's discernment may differ from what the teacher intended.

EDUCATION AS NURTURE

The broadest basis for a definition of education is through the concept of nurture. Education is what happens to a person living in community, whether it be family, neighborhood, school, church, or nation. Instruction may be thought of as the transmission of factual information and its interpretation (as part of procedural training). Nurture is a more inclusive term "to describe the involvement of the pupil in the atmosphere and relationships of a community, including knowledge about it as a means toward loyalty to it. Christian education is the nurture of the total person in all the relationships of life seen from a perspective of membership in the Christian community."[12]

Horace Bushnell, in his *Christian Nurture* in 1847, was thinking primarily of the Christian family and of the influence of parents on their children. He saw clearly the difference that was made by attitudes and emotional climate, even before words could have meaning for the infant. This applies also to later periods of life, so that we can speak of the situation ideally set for

11. In *Religious Education* LVII (January–February 1962), p. 95.
12. Randolph C. Miller, *Christian Nurture and the Church* (New York: Scribner, 1961), p. vii.

Christian nurture as having an "atmosphere in which grace dwells." Thus, the child can grow up as a Christian and never know himself or herself as anything else. This says much to us about the setting for Christian education, which may occur in an environment other than a formal classroom or a Sunday school that imitates a secular school. Maybe it should be a much more free-wheeling atmosphere in which children and adults can enjoy themselves and can be exposed to the "joy and peace of believing" rather than to the harshness of a dull catechetical regimen. Perhaps it says even more about the significance of worship as part of the nurturing process, provided that the worship be meaningful at the level of development being served.

EDUCATION AND INDOCTRINATION

It should not be difficult to distinguish between education, defined as above, and indoctrination. Education implies the right and the power to make inferences, to be open to new insights, and to test what has been learned in experience. Whenever this process is blocked because the teacher is presenting already assured conclusions that are not open to such examination by the student, we have indoctrination. Indoctrination is an alternative to education, or a substitute for it, as a way of producing desired behavior.

Education means that we learn what others think and believe, that we be exposed to the tradition and the history of thought, that we memorize many items from human history (including knowledge of the contents of the Bible), and that we then proceed to choose according to our ability and with adequate criteria among the live options that are forced upon us in order to live meaningfully and intelligently. Information presented authoritatively as the conclusions of experts is not indoctrination. Indoctrination leads to living according to doctrines, beliefs, and values which are handed down without examination, thus denying the autonomy of the learners. These concepts may be the same as we would reach as educated persons, but if we accept them as given we are being indoctrinated and not educated.

We never escape some degree of indoctrination. Simply because a parent, teacher, clergyperson, or political figure is held in high regard or fear, what that person thinks matters greatly to the pupil, disciple, or follower. But if we introduce the ability to make inferences, to question the data, and to choose between live and forced options, we move from indoctrination to education.[13]

Indoctrination at its worst borders on brainwashing, which is the use of techniques to impose agreement with what the authority desires. This may be done by simulating the educational process, by propaganda techniques, and by the use of physical containment, torture, or drugs. Religious teaching, especially in some of its more extreme and fanatic forms, seems closer to brainwashing than to indoctrination or education.

EDUCATION AND AUTHORITY

One learns to accept authority. Freedom and authority are related to each other. Authority in religion is simply rightful power, and it must be recognized as such. It is not coercive power, but rather is like moral persuasion. It is something immediately recognized as such. Jesus taught as "one *having* authority," not as one who taught *from* authority.

Freedom is exemption from *arbitrary* authority or necessity in thought and action. It is a way of acknowledging authority or refusing to acknowledge it. But when authority is rightful power, one may accept it without sacrificing one's freedom. Authority in education, then, is never the denial of the student's freedom to think; it never insists upon agreement; it depends on its own

13. See Belth, *Education as a Discipline,* pp. 77–80.

176   Educational Philosophy

merits to persuade, and it is open to response from the learner. "Only when authority is correlated with freedom, when authority is self-validating because its truth can be demonstrated, when the Bible and traditions and creeds portray and reveal the living God in Christ, is there Christian authority."[14] And this is what we are seeking for in Christian education.

THEOLOGY AND CHRISTIAN EDUCATION

Theology clearly determines to a great degree the content of Christian education. What we teach depends on what we believe. In our pluralistic society we have a great variety of beliefs, and churches and synagogues are providing great diversity of belief as well. If theology is "the-truth-about-God-in-relation-to humanity," it includes both our views of the nature of God and of human beings. This affects not only the content of Christian education but also the theory.

For example, if one takes seriously some of the new developments in theology, such as process thinking, this will provide new models for thinking about God and also new views of human responsibility in relation to God. The emphasis on the persuasive love of a deity who can suffer changes our view of the nature of evil and of chance and opens the door to new views of human freedom. Furthermore, this kind of thinking about theology and education may lead to new approaches to the liberation movements, social justice, and worship.[15]

The center of religious education is God. The problem is to find those words, methods, and activities which point to the reality for which the word "God" stands. Words can point or

14. Randolph C. Miller, *The Clue to Christian Education* (New York: Scribner, 1950), p. 174; see above, chapter 5 and chapter 2.
15. See Gloria Durka and Joanmarie Smith, *Modeling God* (New York: Paulist, 1976); Randolph C. Miller, "Process Thinking and Religious Education," *Anglican Theological Review* (July 1975), pp. 271–288.

show, but they never transfer a concept from one mind to another. Theology helps us to understand the relationship between God and the world, including human beings, and therefore we can be assisted in choosing those ways in which the learner may reflect on those experiences which are identified as being the presence of God. Theology, then, is essential to a theory of religious education as well as to its content.

This does not eliminate the contributions of other disciplines. It should be clear from the analysis we have made of education that we need to make use of the insights of educational psychology, the sociology of learning, and cultural anthropology. But there are great diversities in secular educational theories, and by bringing theology (also with its diversities) into the dialogue we may be able to select with some degree of adequacy what contributes to an overall theory. Some theologies make room for the student's freedom and autonomy, for the development of concepts based on experience, and for a methodology that insists on rational procedures, poetic insight, and a vision of reality as a whole. This approach, I suggest, is consistent with the views of education worked out in the above analysis.

WORSHIP AND CHRISTIAN EDUCATION

Alfred North Whitehead writes that religion is a vision which "claims nothing but worship."[16] Worship, so conceived, is an awareness of the holy, a sense of a "commanding vision," a sharing with others who are also in the presence of God.

In worship, memory and hope are intertwined. This is particularly true in our experience of the sacrament of the Lord's Supper, in which the memory of the Last Supper is brought to bear on the present and points to an unknown future with hope. We

16. Alfred North Whitehead, *Science and the Modern World* (New York: Mentor, 1948), p. 192. See below, chapter 11, for a fuller interpretation of worship and education.

recall the past which is no more except in God's memory, and in our awareness of God this past is re-presented as alive for our present experience. Thus we are in the presence of both the historical Jesus and the risen Christ, and the members of the congregation respond as best they can to this shared vision.

These responses provide raw material for religious education. One response is, What should we do? The moral theology of the church originates in this question, and the results among the people depend on their moral insight into the aims of God for them. Thus education is initiation into a way of living guided by values. Another response is, What does it mean? The doctrines of the church find their sources in this question, for it forces us behind the surface meaning to ultimate meanings. Here is the empirical base for much of our theologizing. A third response is, Do I belong? At the center of our needs is the need to belong, and the church at worship is an expression of our belonging to each other as well as to God. Thus the church at worship is the fellowship of the Spirit (*koinonia*). There emerges a sense of worth on the part of the individual. Such worship has focal points, such as the celebrations of births, confirmations, weddings, and deaths, which highlight both the sense of togetherness and the value of individuals. Finally, worship carries with it a response of euphoria, of the joy and peace of believing, of the comfort of the gospel that accompanies its stimulation.

Such an interpretation of worship, on a level not always experienced in our parishes but occasionally the high point of one's life, is, I suggest, the empirical anchor of educational practice. That is why religious education is more effective in a parish atmosphere than in a school, especially a secular school where worship is divorced from the experiences being analyzed. Church related schools often combine the best of worship with the best of religious teaching, but there is a generation gap between students and teachers, and a lack of family participation.

Worship is both a response to the religious vision and the

cause of it. As Whitehead says, "the worship of God is not a rule of safety—it is an adventure of the spirit, a flight after the unattainable,"[17] and therefore if we are to revise our educational theory and practice we may need to look more closely at the liturgical developments so that we do not lose sight of either the adventure or the unattainable. Then our education may also take wings.

THE OVERALL TASK

Our overall task, in thinking about the nature of Christian education, is to expand and put in order the descriptions of education in the analysis we have made. No one view by itself is adequate, and we need to guard ourselves against turning education into indoctrination. Christian education in most ways is like secular education. It, like all education, is concerned with the development of the art of thinking and the skills that are necessary in order to think straight. Christian education, like all education, is concerned with a value system, and this system is different from some others, although like them in many ways. Christian education, like all education, is a form of coaching or training, both in the essential learning skills and in the socializing essential to living as human beings; as one becomes sensitized to the concerns and needs of others, one may see God at work through interpersonal relations. Christian education, like all education, makes use of models to evoke insight or disclosures, and in Christian education these insights focus on Jesus Christ. Christian education, like all education, takes place in a nurturing environment, and we must make sure that this environment is truly a Christian community. Christian education, like all education, points to essential beliefs, but these beliefs must never be allowed to replace the basic trust in God that stands at the

17. Whitehead, *Science and the Modern World,* p. 192.

center of the Christian life. We must avoid indoctrination simply because it is the nature of education to help students to rethink the concepts about the nature of truth, and openness to new truth is essential to Christian growth. Thus, we must be careful about the kind of authority we assert, and recognize the freedom of the student to reach conclusions at variance with standard belief systems. Christian education, like all education, is rooted in experience, and all experience contributes to the understanding of life, but Christian education has an empirical anchor in the experience of worship which marks it off from systems which ignore this kind of data. Yet Christian education also deals with the data of common experience as well as with selected or unusual experiences, and the problem is to work out some coherent unity for our belief system. Thus, Christian education comes back to theology for its primary content and its organizing principle.

11

Worship and Education

Worship stands at the center of process thought. It is the primary activity that grounds persons in the processes and subjective aims attributed to deity. Behind the reflections that lead to theological speculation and behind the experiences that make religious education possible is the community in worship as felt and shared by members of the congregation. There is response to a vision and to God as an actual entity.

Religion is a vision, and the response to that vision is worship. As human beings have worshiped through the ages, they have refined their beliefs as they moved from barbaric images to clearer forms of belief. "The fact of the religious vision," wrote Whitehead, "and its history of persistent expansion, is our one ground for optimism. Apart from it, human life is a flash of occasional enjoyments lighting up a mass of pain and misery, a bagatelle of transient experience."[1]

The vision is of a persuasive love that never claims anything, never coerces, and never overrules. "The power of God is the worship he inspires."[2] God "is the lure for feeling, the eternal urge of desire."[3] Worship begins with wonder, with an intuition of the overwhelming holiness of that which transcends human life. The worshiper knows that, in the presence of the holy, one is a person of worth, either good or bad. As one worships God,

1. Alfred North Whitehead, *Science and the Modern World* (New York: Mentor, 1948), p. 192.
2. Whitehead, *Science and the Modern World*, p. 192.
3. Alfred North Whitehead, *Process and Reality* (New York: Macmillan, corrected edition, 1978), p. 344 (522).

182   Worship and Education

one is aware of the presence of others, and there is not only a
mutual grasping of feelings in relation to God but also in relation with God and with all who worship together.

In this worship, there is an apprehension of a commanding
vision. This may be found in the scriptures or the preaching, or
in any aspect of the total experience. The response may be a new
sense of duty, a deeper feeling of reverence, or a new awareness
of being loved. The creative and transforming activity of God
working through the worshipers may lead to a sense of newness
or redemption. It is an experience of "transcendent importance."[4]
This adventure of the human spirit points beyond itself to the
unattainable.

There is nothing predictable about worship. The world includes the emergence of novelty, chance, and freedom. The
worshiper may be transformed in ways not expected. The newness of the experience may provide opportunities unforeseen.
The freedom of the worshiper may lead to actions that open up
the future in new ways. This suggests that there is moral responsibility, whereby the worshiper may or may not align her or his
subjective aim with God's. The latter leads to alienation from
God.

There is a hidden power in worship, for it is a means for
unleashing the creative transformation which is God at work
into the world through a specific congregation. It changes lives,
it transforms communities, and it opens up the possibility of the
emergence of new values in the world. William James spoke of
"the nitroglycerine" of the gospel.

FAMILIES AT WORSHIP

One important development in Christian education has been
the practice of a worship service geared to families. The family-
as-a-unit is conceived as parents or parent with children of all

4. Alfred North Whitehead, *Religion in the Making* (New York: Macmillan,
1926), p. 18.

ages. An opportunity for families to worship together at a convenient time may be set at an earlier hour than the conventional service on Sunday. Normally the whole family attends, including babies in arms for at least a portion of the time. Others not associated with families often find this service meaningful.

The service might start at 9:15 and last about thirty-five to forty minutes. It needs to be long enough to allow an unhurried use of a traditional service adapted to those in the congregation plus a fifty-minute class period prior to the next service. Local conditions and the need for use of the buildings will lead to variations.

Because this program is for everyone, there are educational experiences for all. These may be classroom or open classroom experiences. There are classes for parents which may be geared to the interests of their children in various grades. Parents are helped to understand the entire program and their help is enlisted. The class for parents deals with two fundamental questions: (1) What is the meaning of the gospel, to me as a parent? (2) How can I be a mediator of the gospel to my children? There will also be classes for adults who are not parents. An educational program, against the background of worship, it thus available for everyone.

One type of morning service might be as follows:
Prelude
Call to worship
Response from hymn, chant, or unison prayer
Hymn
Scripture (one or more lessons)
Offering, birthday offering, prayer
Hymn
Story, talk, or dramatization
Leader's prayer
Closing hymn
Unison benediction
All go to classes

Another form of service, for more liturgical congregations, might be as follows:

Prelude

Processional hymn, with choir

Opening sentences or Call to worship

Lord's prayer

Versicles

Venite, after which nursery and kindergarten leave

Psalm

Scripture (one or more lessons)

Hymn

Prayers

Hymn

Story, sermonette, or dramatization

Birthday offering, offering, doxology

Closing prayers and benediction

Recessional hymn

Postlude

All go to classes

The success of these services depends on the relevance of the readings, prayers, and hymns, the tempo of the service, and the reverence of the adults. If the service drags or gets too long, normal children will become restless. It is important to keep the structure of the congregation's traditional but longer service. Worship may be modified but not mutilated.

Free churches will make more use of original or improvised prayer, but in all cases there are liturgical expectations and guidelines. The language of prayer is that of poetic simple, with rich imagery, and with a balance of rhythmic prose that is meant to be read or said aloud. The content of the prayer depends on the theology of the leader and the needs of the people. In the family service, the content of prayer should be limited to the attention span and the area of awareness of the younger members of the congregation.

One recent usage is the "newspaper litany," with items

selected from the lead sentences of the major news stories, and with a liturgical response to each item. It is important to dramatize this approach with an actual newspaper and to limit the content to six or seven items. Any position can be included, and if someone asks which side the prayer leader is on, the reply should be that we lift all of our concerns to God. Many other new forms, litany and otherwise, are now available, some with musical responses.

The music chosen for a family service should be from a small repertoire. The hymns, for example, should have some balance between those for children and adults along with those for adults alone. It may be wise to place the simplest hymn first, as the youngest children may leave before the next one. A hymn that can be taught to the nonreaders, so that they can learn to participate in the first stanza or the refrain, may be suitable. It is sometimes helpful to use a hymn for more than one Sunday and then to rotate it out. A junior choir might sing it as an anthem the week prior to its use by the congregation. Theological judgments will eliminate a number of hymns, and sexist language may disqualify others. Both words and music are important, and they need to be fitted together. The words are approved by the rational mind and the music is felt by the appreciative or affective nature of a human being. But there is much music in a service besides the hymnody. Parts of the service may be sung, anthems may be presented by the choir, responses may be set to traditional or modern musical settings. Worshipers respond with their feelings as well as their minds.

The purpose of the sermon, sermonette, talk, or dramatized story is to make the gospel be heard. The Bible is a ready resource for such a presentation, although it may not always be relevant. Modern stories about real-life children, in which the plot parallels the Bible story, are sometimes more suitable than stories left in a biblical setting. It is important to establish a dialogue situation, so that those in the congregation will participate by silent or audible contributions. Proclaiming the gospel is not the same thing as making a point about morality. The sermon is concerned with the commanding vision, the lure for feeling, the sense of wonder at the promise of the gospel, the intuition of holiness, in which the response is the renewal of commitment leading to action. It is not a morality play leading to actions which are respectable.

Parents respond to sermons for children and adults together; they even respond to sermons strictly for children. But children and some adults do not respond to sermons aimed at too high a level. If we have learned to preach to children, suggests Horace Bushnell, we may then learn to preach to adults. The informality of the family service provides an opportunity for dialogue, questions, and quizzes. Various Bible games may be used. A Bible story already read may be repeated with the reader making errors which the listeners are expected to identify, and which can then be used as a basis for interpretation by the preacher.

There are many ways in which we can catch and hold the attention of children, teenagers, and their parents. It is often a matter of being on the same wavelength, and this may lead to changes in traditional practices. Some customs have been introduced through liturgical reform, including the passing of the peace, a physical act which has meaning for children and strangers as well as regulars in the pews. The introduction of folk, rock, or jazz music into the liturgy as well as into the hymnody of the congregation has sometimes seemed revolutionary, but it has spoken to many congregations, especially those with concerned young people. There needs to be a strong feeling of at-homeness, especially among the children, so that they are at ease in the service and are therefore free to respond with wonder when the service actually speaks of God to them. One minister opened the family service by saying, "In this service, no one can make a mistake."

The growing practice of having baptism of infants at the proper place in the family service illustrates a recapturing of the early meaning of baptism. The child is received into the congregation of Christ's flock when the flock is present to receive the child. The children may be asked to gather around the font, and thus they can participate even when the words are beyond them. They can see the child being washed and received, and they can share in the congregation's act of accepting responsibility for the child's growing up as a Christian. They therefore come to a deeper understanding of their own baptism.

Baptism is generally thought of as complete acceptance into the church, so that a baptized person can share in the Holy Communion. There has been confusion over confirmation in some circles and therefore some children have had to wait for confirmation before receiving Holy Communion. The changes in this field are very recent and only apply to some churches. The Roman Catholics have led the way with first Communion coming before confirmation. Many churches have accepted children as recipients of Communion for many years. The most confusion has probably been in the Lutheran and Episcopal denominations where there has been a strong emphasis on confirmation as an adolescent rite and as a requirement for receiving Communion.

With the rising popularity of the family service in the Episcopal church, there has also been an increase in the frequency of Holy Communion, so that children are participating fully in the service of Holy Communion. At first, the nonconfirmed were allowed to come to the altar rail to be blessed but not to receive Communion, but with the theological changes accompanying the new *Book of Common Prayer,* confirmation has become a minor rite that needs theological reconstruction. So whole families come to the altar rail to receive Communion when the parents have decided that the children are ready. In some dioceses, the bishops are involved and in others some kind of training is required. Other denominations have also moved in this direction, some having done so many years ago.

But a service of Holy Communion in the liturgical traditions lasts too long and therefore the criteria of a family service are threatened. Not only is the service too long for children, but it limits the time for classroom or other educational activities to too short a time. In some traditions it will be possible to abbreviate the service without distorting it, but some of the newer liturgical services last more than an hour, which turns it into a "squirmer's mass." The answer is to dismiss children who cannot stand a long service and to lengthen the morning hours for others so that there is still at least a fifty-minute class period. One congregation worked out a program for the whole morning: worship for all at 10:00, classes for all at 11:00, and celebration of what occurred from 12:00 to 12:20.[5]

Children and their parents may come from the family service full of questions about the experience they have just had. These questions are the self-starters for the class session. Usually this will lead into the planned class session for the day, but there is good reason to spend as long as necessary to relate the experience to the daily lives of the pupils no matter what the planned lesson may be. This is also an important consideration in the parents' and other adult classes. Teachers are helped when they receive in advance the hymns, lessons, and sermon topics for the coming sessions at teachers' meetings, where there can be some discussion of the themes. All of this experience and discussion may be shared in the home, for the children, teenagers, and their parents have in common the experience of worship and they will naturally share what has happened in their classes as an extension of their worship. No parents have to ask their children what happened in church school!

Sometimes the service for families-as-units takes the place of the customary late morning service and the whole parish performs as a family. In other congregations there will be a more

5. See William Abernethy, *A New Look for Sunday Morning* (Nashville: Abingdon Press, 1975).

traditional service, mostly for adults, at a later hour. But the family service *is church*! The gospel has been proclaimed, the sacraments have been administered, or worship of God experienced, and the family members have shared in God's gifts of grace as they are mediated at their own level of appreciation. It may lead to the forming of a new congregation without hurting the other one. The two groups may come together for special festivals such as Thanksgiving, Christmas, Easter, and Pentecost if there is room. The total congregation, although meeting at different times, becomes the true family of God. It is experienced as a fellowship of the Holy Spirit where each member is accepted in his or her full humanity.

OTHER FORMS OF WORSHIP

There are customary services of other types which are familiar to those working in Christian education. The old opening exercises are still in existence. There are services set up by departments, age groups, classes. There are special children's chapels in miniature.[6] Then there is the split service for those who want to operate within a limited time schedule, with the children attending the first part of the service and having classes during the sermon period. Rarely is the first part of the service geared to the children, and the class period is too short to be effective. It is a compromise that short-changes everyone.

There is room for imagination in the way worship is incorporated into the overall life of a congregation. John Westerhoff suggests that where the Eucharist is the primary service, it could be preceded by a one-hour catechesis and followed by a parish family meal. This is a procedure followed for many years at the Disciples of Christ congregation at the University of Chicago

6. See Paul H. Vieth, *Worship in Christian Education* (Philadelphia: United Church Press, 1965), pp. 50–67; Iris V. Cully, *Christian Worship and Church Education* (Philadelphia: Westminster Press, 1967), pp. 142–158.

under Edward Scribner Ames. Members of the congregation might meet during the week for Bible study and help plan the upcoming service. Westerhoff suggests that "at this time they could appropriately decorate the place of worship; plan the hymns; prepare the prayers of the people; and plan the sermon as a homily, dialogue, song, story, drama, or dance. They could bake the bread and make the wine to be offered. Further they might plan for an educational experience for all ages before the service to help them prepare to participate in the community liturgy."[7]

There is room for experimentation with small groups within the congregation as well as for the introduction of new forms to the total congregation. But there is always a desire for stability that is interpreted as keeping the status quo. Therefore any new development becomes a threat to a congregation, and a period of transition must go slowly. Witness the resistance to the Roman Catholic mass in English or to the new Episcopal prayer book, mild as these changes were. Small groups are more likely to be open to change, especially youth groups who like to work on their own liturgies, which may be introduced to the congregation as a whole on special occasions.

One example of change is the practice of confirmation. Because it has lost its connection with first communion in almost all denominations, it now exists in a limbo where it has little meaning as a rite of adolescent passage and therefore is dropping into disuse. The meaning of confirmation needs to be reexamined. A likely suggestion is that the symbolism of the laying on of hands, used in ordination, might well be a means of ordination into the ministry of the laity. Just as those ordained into the professional ministry are set apart for special functions, so lay people may see their service in the world as a specialized ministry

7. Gwen Kennedy Neville and John H. Westerhoff III, *Learning Through Liturgy* (New York: Seabury, 1978), p. 106.

and would seek some commissioning by the church. Confirmation, used in this way, would no longer be a rite of adolescence, although it might appear as early as late adolescence or in the late twenties or early thirties as the norm.

EDUCATION FOR WORSHIP

William H. Willimon was dissatisfied with the response to worship in his congregation and worked out an experiment to discover if some kind of education would increase the understanding and appreciation of worship. He wanted to get beyond responses such as "I like it because it looks and sounds pretty," or "I like it because it is the way they used to do it," or "I like it because it makes me feel good inside." These are important responses but they lack the theological depth that makes worship more than an emotional exercise. So he developed "An Educational Project on Worship" as a doctoral project.

The purpose was to teach lay people the key theological, historical, and biblical concepts of Christian worship. By using a control group as well as a participating group, he was able to test the results. The goal was involvement in the deeper meaning of worship through participation based on understanding of what is supposed to occur. By means of a questionnaire used prior to the experiment and afterwards with both groups, he was able to establish the degree to which the participating group increased their understanding and appreciation of the service of worship. He used both personal interviews and a series of two-hour learning sessions. Each session concluded with a worship service utilizing the insights gained from the session. The group then planned and led a Sunday morning worship service.

The program led to a change in knowledge, attitudes, and involvement. There was a direct correlation between the knowledge acquired and the new attitudes, especially with the service of Holy Communion. It led Willimon to the conclusion that "the increased theological, historical, and biblical knowledge of the participants was a major factor in the deeper involvement in worship." Especially when innovation in the service of worship occurred, it was clear that "worship innovation and true lay participation in worship must be preceded by solid, conceptually adequate education."[8] There is a need for lay people to discover the significance of liturgical theology.

This experiment suggests that some kind of liturgical education should be operative at every age level. Children, like adults, do not learn about worship simply through participation and osmosis; they need understanding of what they are attempting to do. This is particularly true when a new theological position is used to interpret worship. If we wish to interpret worship in terms of process theology, it would lead to consideration of specific criteria.

Such a program would begin with an understanding of the relation of ritual, emotion, and myth. Ritual has to do with the performance of acts which are not necessary for well being or survival. It is constantly repeated and in that repetition acquires emotional attachments. Thus the worshiper becomes sensitized to what the ritual stands for and one is taken beyond the immediate experiences of the secular world. Myths and other stories provide ways of giving meaning to one's self-understanding as both an individual and as a member of a community which shares the story, using the vivid fancies of the imagination to provide the feeling of at-homeness in the universe. These stories and myths may or may not be related to actual fact, but they provide symbolic images which enforce our understanding of facts. Thus they provide ways of ordering the life of the individual and the community.

8. William H. Willimon, "The Relationship of Liturgical Education to Worship Participation," *Religious Education* LXIX, No. 5 (September-October 1974), pp. 626, 627.

Ritual and belief without critical analysis lead to stagnation. Worship gets caught in a pragmatic feeling of satisfaction that opposes new concepts or customs, and thus its ritual stands against the world of meaning coming from new experiences. Thus it can result in savage horrors and evil actions. It is not difficult to discover in the pages of history or the events of today savage acts in the name of God.[9]

"Rational religion," writes Whitehead, "is religion whose beliefs and rituals have been reorganized with the aim of making it the central element in a coherent ordering of life—an ordering which shall be coherent both in respect to the elucidation of thought, and in respect to the direction of conduct towards a unified purpose commanding ethical approval.... The relevance of its concepts can be distinctly discerned in moments of insight, and then, for many of us, only after suggestions from without."[10] Thus within worship there must be preaching and teaching, and insofar as religious leaders illuminate "our own best moments, it is reasonable to trust to the evidential force of their experience."[11] The primary source for Christians is what we know of the life of Jesus Christ and the response of the early church, read in worship as the gospel. Here we find the most simple language, free from abstractions, which reveals the power of persuasion as the ideal. It leads to a world consciousness and becomes in its highest state "world loyalty" with a universal claim that dominates our thinking. This is not dogmatic loyalty but a response to our intuition of the holy.[12]

Such worship has as its primary focus the deity who is love, so that "the potentialities of the loved object are felt passionately as a claim that it find itself in a friendly Universe. Such love is

9. See Whitehead, *Religion in the Making*, p. 37.
10. Whitehead, *Religion in the Making*, p. 31.
11. Whitehead, *Religion in the Making*, p. 125.
12. Whitehead, *Religion in the Making*, p. 60.

really an intense feeling as to how the harmony of the world should be realized in particular objects. It is the feeling as to what would happen if right could triumph in a beautiful world, with discord routed. It . . . involves deep feeling of an aim in the Universe, winning such triumph as is possible to it."[13]

We become aware of this only when our senses and intuitions and intelligences are at their highest pitch. It is then that we become aware of the "commanding vision" which is the heart of our worship. We respond with wonder and are overcome by the intuition of holiness in the presence of God, who is with us everlastingly. Because God is love and loves us, we are struck with the realization of our own worth as creatures of God. We realize that we are in a community in which individuals in their own way are responding to the vision and we feel the power of the community worshiping as a group as well as of the individuals, and we know that God in turn is aware of both the individuals and the group in all the possible relationships. There is then a rich multirelational situation which is difficult to portray in the one-on-one relationships described in traditional Western liturgical language. But in spite of the handicaps of limited language, we are able to respond. There is an experience of grace as the free gift of God's love breaks through the linguistic restrictions of our worship. The fundamentally aesthetic experience of worship is communicated to us through music, architecture, art, and interpersonal actions that move beyond the limitations of language, and even language seeks to reach the imagination through metaphor, myths, stories, poetry, and other appeals that stimulate the appreciative rather than the critical consciousness. It is then that we are enabled to respond with a critical consciousness to the needs of others, to ethical imperatives, and thus to align our aims with what we consider to be the aims of God.

The educational challenge to this understanding of worship

13. Alfred North Whitehead, *Adventures of Ideas* (New York: Macmillan, 1933, renewed 1961 by Evelyn Whitehead), p. 373.

could lead to a revitalization of our common liturgies. It might result in experimental liturgies incorporating some of these goals, or it could assist in reinterpreting the more fixed services of the traditionally liturgical churches. Rather than settle for traditional forms, we would seek to express the high hope of adventure, to recognize our flight after the unattainable, and to respond to God as the one who frees us to seek truth, beauty, adventure, and peace.

We would get rid of language that emphasizes the masculine elements in our references to God and recognize that the feminine is equally important. This may eliminate pronouns from some of our prayers. It would cause a revision of many psalms and hymns. It would lead to more ecologically sensitive references to the relation of human beings to creation. It would allow for images that are inclusive of other than the white race, especially in art.

The restructuring of liturgical language would also allow for changes in theological descriptions. The emphasis would no longer be on God as all-powerful or as changeless, as one who predestines people in all of their actions and in their final destination, who wills what seems to us to be evil, who makes wars and destruction, and who causes human suffering. The image of king, dictator, and pharaoh would be eliminated from our thinking. Other aspects of God would be elevated to the center of attention: God's persuasive and forgiving love, God's subjective aim for human beings to which we may align our own aims, God's judgment that opposes us in our disobedience, God's creative transformation of human beings who truly seek to know God and who worship God as the holy one. The stress would be on the enjoyment of God, and on the promise of Jesus that he has come that we may have life more abundantly. There is much more to our theology than this, but this would be a starting point for the revision of our liturgies and our teaching.[14] The

14. See my chapter, "Process Thought, Worship, and Religious Education," in

educational significance of this kind of study would be tremendous.

At the center of any Christian educational program is the Bible. It stands in the most important place in our worship, but we need to learn how to use it. It also is the primary source for the content of Christian teaching, and to this problem we now turn.

Aesthetic Dimensions of Religious Education, ed. Gloria Durka and Joanmarie Smith (New York: Paulist Press, 1979), pp. 107–120.

12

How to Use the Bible
in Christian Education

At the conclusion of chapter 5, David Kelsey was quoted as saying that the church uses scripture "to nurture and reform the self-identity both of the community and of the individual persons who comprise it. Theological proposals are to elucidate what that identity is and ought to be, and what reforms are called for and why."[1] There is a biblical theology that contains the story and from this narrative we can gain a perspective by which to teach the Bible. The Bible is the primary source of our believing and our teaching as Christians. Something is disclosed or revealed that is akin to a vision. We find that secrets of the meaning of being human are unveiled. This sacred literature of both Jews and Christians provides a religious dimension to our understanding of life.

The problem facing educators is to communicate this literature, to transmit to children and adults what the church believes in order to persuade, convince, and move them. The major goal, however, is not to give assistance in the assimilation of the literature as such, which is a proper aim in a course in "English Bible," but to approach the literature religiously, in the hope of evoking insights into the nature of God and God's world and commitment to the Christian way of life.

1. David H. Kelsey, *The Uses of Scripture in Theology* (Philadelphia: Fortress, 1975), p. 214.

DIFFICULTIES

The difficulties are immense. In his *Communication of the Christian Faith*, Hendrik Kraemer wrote: "We must recognize the unintelligibility of the Bible, not only its language, its terminology, but also . . . its . . . picture of the world. This affects people as antiquated, archaic, unscientific. . . . It sounds so strange, so incomprehensible, so distant from their ordinary ways of thinking. It is, at best, to them a 'sacral' language. . . . It is, they think, a book for experts and theologians. . . . It seems an insoluble dilemma."[2]

The problem is to try to get inside the world of the Bible and at the same time to exist meaningfully in one's own secular world. When one can get through the Bible's unintelligibility and incomprehensibility, not an easy task even in New Testament times, one may discern that the Bible is, as Paul Tournier says, "the book of choice. From end to end it sets [one] face to face with the supreme choice which determines all the other choices of [one's] life; from the law of Moses: 'I have set before you life and death . . . therefore choose life,' to the words of Christ, 'No man can serve two masters.' In each of the personal dialogues of which the Bible is full, the Word of God speaks to [each reader], making [one] a person, a responsible being who must answer. The Bible stresses the inexorable and radical nature of that choice: from the Old Testament, where the prophet Elijah cries: 'How long halt ye between two opinions?' to the Revelation: 'Thou art neither hot nor cold: I would thou wert cold or hot.' "[3]

These are adult problems and adult decisions. This raises a horrible thought: Maybe the Bible is not for children at all!

2. Hendrik Kraemer, *Communication of the Christian Faith* (Philadelphia: Westminster Press, 1956), pp. 93–95.
3. Paul Tournier, *The Meaning of Persons* (New York: Harper & Row, 1957), p. 210.

THE BIBLE DRAMA

The Bible presents adult categories involving history and a world view. Although children do not think historically prior to the age of ten to twelve and do not think in terms of logic or abstract propositions until after the age of puberty (if then), it is possible to learn biblically from the beginning of one's Christian education in home and church. The Bible, although written by and for adults, illuminates the world that children live in, provided the story is spelled out in terms of drama, story, imagery, poetry, and the language of relationships.

The universal appeal of the Bible as it cuts across the cultural and historical barriers is that it is a story that proclaims good news about God in every epoch. It is in outline a simple story in five acts: creation, covenent, Christ, church, and consummation, to which our response is commitment. It reaches a climax with the coming of Jesus Christ, for "in Christ God was reconciling the world to himself" (II Cor 5:19). It sees the midpoint in linear time as the coming of Christ. History is seen in a new perspective, with the coming of Christ as a turning point.

This drama has been spelled out in various studies, beginning with G. Ernest Wright's *God Who Acts* and again with Gabriel Fackre's *The Christian Story*. [4] The beginning of the story is creation, and the point of the story is that God gave to human beings both life and power, and this includes their responsibility to make choices which are aligned to God's aims. Adam and Eve dramatize what happens when people deliberately disobey God. Yet even when human beings are separated or alienated from God, God acts to restore that relationship.

4. G. Ernest Wright, *God Who Acts: Biblical Theology as Recital* (Chicago: Regnery, 1952); Gabriel Fackre, *The Christian Story* (Grand Rapids: Eerdmans, 1979); Bernhard W. Anderson, *The Unfolding Drama of the Bible* (New York: Association Press, 1953); R. C. Miller, *Biblical Theology and Christian Education* (New York: Scribners, 1956).

The second act is the story of the covenant. It begins with Abraham, and how God entered into a covenant with Abraham to establish an area of agreement between them, to be supported by the Law. God takes the initiative: "I will be your God, and you shall be my people.... I am Yahweh, who brought you out of the land of Egypt" (Lev 26:12,13). But a covenant is a two-way affair, and both Yahweh and the people are expected to fulfill the agreement. Yet human beings constantly fail to meet the requirements and as the second act draws to a close there can be heard the warning of the preacher, "All is futility" (Eccl 1:2,G). There is momentary hope along the way when the covenant is renewed in the hearts of human beings, but again there is disappointment.

The third act is the focal point of the story. It is the same motif that is disclosed in the first two acts: that all life is perishing and becoming, alienation and reconciliation, being lost and found, death and resurrection. Human beings are separated from each other and from God, and the gift of new life brings all human beings and God together in the community of the Holy Spirit. This symbolism is worked out to the highest degree of understanding and effectiveness in the story of the cross, which is followed by resurrection. The promise of a coming kingdom is underwritten by the event of the resurrection. What God has done in Jesus Christ is made available to us when we have faith in God and share in God's grace.

The fourth act was established as a result of the resurrection experiences of the apostles, and what came was a community of believers. The witnesses to the resurrection experienced a new sense of community as they were filled by the Holy Spirit. They came together for the breaking of bread, prayer, hymn singing, and the recounting of the emerging gospel stories. Thus the church was born as three thousand were baptized on the first Pentecost. This community was known by many names, all of which helped to provide an image of the church as persons related to each other in Christ. Through our baptism we have become members of this ongoing community which finds its roots and its nature in what happened almost two thousand years ago. The family of God is our family and we share its memories and hopes.

Thus we turn to the future from the past which we see through the present. The future is here now and not yet. It is an expression of the purpose of God and still open to whatever emerges. We face our own consummation in death, and we face the consummation of God's purpose for history, and yet we know that God is everlasting. We stand between the hope of a relationship with God and the threat of separation from God. We have the choice, and there is judgment in the light of our choice.

The hope of resurrection into everlasting life is based on the promise of God's grace, and this is the final consummation. There is the good news that we are to be "heirs of God and joint-heirs with Christ" (Rom 8:17). "We are God's children now; what we shall be has not yet been revealed" (I Jn 3:2, 20th).

The response to this story is in terms of commitment. Because of what God has done for us, *therefore* we seek to be worthy of our vocations. Daniel Day Williams saw clearly that the response is ethical: "The living God whose nature and purpose is love calls us to respond in our freedom to the tasks which are set for us by the fact that [God] is at work in our human history both as Creator and as Redeemer."[5]

When we consider each of the five acts of the drama of redemption, we see that each of them reflects a common human experience, even of a baby. Take a baby; a baby is born (creation), depends on the regularity of parental care and love (covenant), experiences alienation and restoration within the family (Christ),

---

5. Daniel Day Williams, *God's Grace and Man's Hope* (New York: Harper & Row, 1949), p. 147.

is baptized into the fellowship of God's people (church), and may and sometimes does die (consummation). The meanings of these five biblical themes are mediated to the baby through the ministry of parenthood long before any words can be used, much less biblical words; but a biblical faith is being built up in the infant as a foundation for the future and as the meaning for the child's life now through the language of relationship. Theodore Wedel wrote that "a child can understand the love story of redemption of the Bible . . . if interpreted by the language of relationships."[6]

Such communication of biblical meanings depends more on relationships than on words, more on atmosphere than on recitation, more on play and games than on discipline. This becomes clear to us when we refer to infants who cannot yet speak and who are having experiences of being lost and found, but this approach is valid for *all* ages, not just for infants, and verbal meanings may be added when and as needed. Thus, our fixation on biblical content can be modified by concentration on biblical meanings expressed in daily living. If we are concerned with evoking disclosures and the resulting commitment, we need to show how various passages fit into the overall view of the Bible in terms of the relationships of daily life.

YOUNG CHILDREN

We know that children below the age of six mix up fantasy and fact. Their cry of "tell me a story" is satisfied with any kind of story, whether it is a "once upon a time" fairy tale, a story of children like themselves, science fiction, or an event from the newspapers. The principle of selection is not always clear. We express our love by telling a story, and that may be enough. There are, however, various biblical motifs that may be com-

6. Theodore O. Wedel, "Leadership Education," *World Christian Education* (Spring 1952), p. 31.

municated indirectly through the choice of a proper story. The selection at this age is not likely to be a story from the Bible, but it may be the retelling of a story in simple words. Often, however, we may prefer to select a story that deals with today, but the theme will parallel a story from the Bible. A "religious" story need not be self-consciously religious. It is important to note that the parables of Jesus are almost always about human beings and their relations to each other, or to a lost coin or sheep, and whatever is religious is derived from the understanding or feeling for the relations. Up to the age of six, or thereabouts, we do not have to worry whether the story is about something that actually happened.

Then comes a period of literalism. The little empiricists ask, "Is it true?" And they mean that the description must be accurate about a concrete event. They say that the Bible is true "because God wrote it," or "because my mommy (or vicar or teacher) says it's true." When they are slightly more advanced, they make the distinction in this way: "The parables aren't true, they are only used to illustrate meaning. All the rest is true." The research of Ronald Goldman[7] and Violet Madge[8] underscores this approach, which leads to a misapprehension of almost all materials from the Bible. They are capable of what Jean Piaget calls "concrete operational thinking" and are inclined to reduce anything that they can believe at all to literalism. As Goldman says, if they do this kind of literal and concrete thinking during the period of seven to twelve years of age, they will be likely to reject everything they have learned when they become thirteen (a common symptom in many Sunday schools).

Children of this age are capable of distinguishing between fact

7. Ronald Goldman, *Religious Thinking from Childhood to Adolescence* (New York: Seabury, 1965).
8. Violet Madge, *Children in Search of Meaning* (New York: Morehouse-Barlow, 1965).

and fancy, but they need help and guidance in carrying out such judgments. They can appreciate poetry, parable, folklore, story, and myth if these categories are properly labeled. They must be protected against the literalizing of such literary forms. Many passages from the Bible, when properly identified as myth, or folklore, or just a story, may be used with children, and they can reflect on such stories in meaningful ways.

When they think in concrete terms, they need opportunities for dealing with their own experiences. This is what Father Divine called "tangibilizin'." Halford Luccock put it this way: "When someone asked Mr. Averill Harriman how his French was, he said, 'My French is excellent, all except the verbs.' Quite an exception! It often happens that our Christianity is excellent, 'all except the verbs.' The nouns are wonderful, 'Master, Saviour, Redeemer.' The adjectives are inspiring, 'noble, divine, sacred.' The verbs are often missing. No action. Yet the verb is the sinew of speech. It is the sinew of the gospel, great verbs, 'come, go, follow, serve, give, love, share.'"[9]

This suggests that selections from the Bible must be in terms of what children can do about them. Children prior to adolescence do not connect things up as adults do. Yet they are capable of making discoveries about the meanings of their own lives as they work on stories having some degree of relevance. This means that children need to operate on their own terms and at their own speed.

In many Sunday schools we are guilty of "overkill." We give the children too much too soon, and as a result they misapprehend some of the material, parrot back some of it without comprehension and become immune to the possibilities in the story at a later time. Usually, insofar as they believe a story, they

9. Halford Luccock, *Communicating the Gospel* (New York: Harper & Row, 1954), pp. 150–51.

literalize it and therefore eliminate the possibility of discerning its religious significance.

Ronald Goldman is insistent on this point. Many Bible-centered teachers and parents keep the pressure on for more Bible, because "it cannot hurt them." But Goldman writes, "To say that a child will 'grow out of [one's] misunderstandings' is not an accurate statement, since all the evidence points to the fact that most children carry their misunderstandings through with them into early adolescence. They then find the crude ideas untenable, and because the alternative is not put before them or left until it is too late, they then may reject religion as intellectually untenable."[10]

BIBLE STORIES

This brings us to the crucial point of what to do with various age groups. With infants and kindergarten ages, very little can be used, even as retold stories. Ethel Smither, in *Children and the Bible,* suggests a simple retelling of the Christmas stories, something about Jesus and the children, and stories of Jesus and the outdoors. If we are concerned with the biblical message, however, we can tell stories of real children in today's world whose experiences are such that they reflect biblical stories. One would not tell Jesus' parables as they stand to a three-year-old, for example, but we would tell them about a little boy or girl who helped another, or about a boy who felt alone even at home, or about a girl who was overjoyed when she found a lost toy.

At the primary age, Goldman believes that we should stick to the factual and the literal, which eliminates most of the interesting material. But if they are helped to distinguish between the literal and the parable or "just a story" literature, they may be

10. Goldman, *Religious Thinking from Childhood to Adolescence,* p. 223.

helped in reaching insights into the nature of religious language. A second grader is likely to ask, "Which came first, Adam and Eve or the dinosaur?" The question cannot be answered in literal terms, for the dinosaur would win every time. But if the primary child is helped to see the purpose of the Genesis story *as a story*, there will be room for both Adam and Eve and dinosaurs in God's created world, as long as Adam and Eve are restricted to the "just a story" category.

The primary child can handle a few stories that are interpreted literally. Some of the gospel stories about Jesus, especially his relations with his family (Mk 6:1–6) or with his disciples, might prove valuable. When dealing with death (a perennial issue with seven-year-olds, although they usually join the adult conspiracy of silence), the story of David when his and Bathsheba's son dies is relevant and religiously significant. The story of Peter's mother-in-law has possibilities when dealing with illness. The varieties and contradictions of the death and resurrection stories are too complex for this age, and the teacher needs to guard against premature literalism by favoring one story. If the Easter event is to be taught at this age, the teacher should use the many stories that arose because of the mystery surrounding what happened.

Some stories previously popular with children of primary age would be questioned by this approach. When Moses' mother leaves her baby in the bulrushes, what is this saying to the young child who is insecure in relation to his or her own mother? Or how would a six-year-old react to the story that Samuel's mother had him locked up with a group of monks when he should have been playing with other children? Or what would a seven-year-old think of a father who let his boy go off to the big city alone, for if he loved him wouldn't a father have gone right after him? And what value has "a zoo at sea" against the background of a flood based on God's judgment and a Noah who got drunk after a safe landing? Where are the religious values in such stories at this age level?

Juniors, age nine to eleven, move into a more advanced form of concrete thinking. This is the age of concrete knowledge, such as baseball statistics or trivia games. They sometimes have a desire for concrete historical knowledge, especially when they are stimulated by competition or curiosity. It is an age when the discovery of background information is legitimate, provided it also has a basic interest-catching action and content. A great deal of this can be in the form of stories, with action, vigor, and significant deeds at the center. David the "super boy scout" is a poor caricature of David the lovable scamp. So we need to work through the whole story of David near the end of this period. If boys and girls of 8½ to 10 have special friends or chums, a careful study of David and Jonathan should come at this time. Paul's interest in athletics, both track and boxing, should surface during this period. Stories of the Exodus and Exile have some significance, and they can be related to some of the psalms. About the sixth grade, a serious approach to the life of Jesus is appropriate; one that tells the story in an unusual and dramatic way is likely to be appreciated. The Old Testament stress on law ties in with their distinctions between right and wrong, and yet they are also ready to face the fundamental motif of being lost and found, which can be approached through parables, incidents in their own lives, and the death and resurrection language of Paul, provided they understand such language as figurative and not literal. In the fifth and sixth grades they can approach the text of the Bible, and therefore it is helpful to expose them to the many translations now available.

Something happens to junior-highs (unless they suffer from premature stifling of their development—which may carry over to adulthood). There is what Goldman calls a "watershed." Thirteen-year-olds can begin to see "truth" in a nonliteral manner; they begin to form generalized and abstract concepts; they see "one world" from a variety of perspectives; they distinguish between different uses of language, especially between the poetic or imaginary and the prosaic and literal; they even develop theological concepts about God and Jesus—if they want to.

When the teacher is fully aware of the exciting changes taking place, a whole new approach to religious thinking can be built on the foundations of earlier good teaching. F. H. Hilliard writes: "The teacher now has to begin deliberately and consistently to help [the] pupils to explore the inner meaning of stories, incidents, history in the Old Testament, and of parables, miracles, and overt teaching in the New Testament. This does not, of course, imply that [the teacher] can afford to ignore the difficulty of helping adolescents to see why these profound religious truths are sometimes conveyed, in the Bible, in terms which no longer make sense in the twentieth century. Myth, magic, and miracle (in the sense of a suspension of 'natural law'), angels, evil spirits, and heavenly voices, all these phenomena must be discussed in terms which a thoughtful adolescent can accept as aspects of the thought-worlds of the Hebrews and early Christians. . . . But [the student] must be shown, at the same time, how to keep for [one's self] and how to clothe in a more acceptable framework of thought the profound truths about God, [humanity], the world and . . . salvation, which [those] of old expressed in their own way."[11]

This statement by Hilliard brings us back to the one from Hendrik Kraemer with which we began. It makes clear that the adolescent is entering into a process of critical and creative thinking that needs to go on as long as a person lives. The approach suggested by Hilliard is needed for senior high, college,

11. F. H. Hilliard, "Implications for the Secondary School," *Learning for Living* (May 1963), p. 14.

and adult groups as well. By the age of fifteen, there is not much that a young person cannot do provided one has access to the skills, contents, and opportunities to develop as a Christian.

SENIOR HIGHS

Senior high pupils, unless already ruined or lost to the educational process (as often happens and for good reasons), have special religious concerns. The Bible is appealing only if they can find ways in which it speaks to their particular concerns. In recent years, some high school students have sensed the futility of much modern culture, and the cynicism and wisdom of such a book as Ecclesiastes appeal to them. Others may be challenged by the problems of frustration and suffering, and they may move through the writings of Sartre and Camus to the book Job and the play *JB*. They may deepen their understanding of sex by comparing David and Bathsheba with Susanna (in the Apocrypha). The problem of loneliness is faced in some of the psalms. The recurrent concern for social justice finds strong support in the writings of Amos, Micah, Hosea, and II Isaiah.

Some introduction to the processes and results of biblical scholarship, presupposed throughout this whole approach and introduced wherever it seems helpful, can be handled more directly with high school junior and seniors. Especially if they learn to appreciate the situation in which the passage arose and to compare it with their own situation, they will find in such parallels (when they occur) a deepening of their own understanding.

Any curriculum that is Christian is going to deal with the nature of Jesus as the Christ. As one gains adult stature and moves toward Christian maturity and responsibility, one needs to have some idea of what Christ means in today's terms. The early church went through three stages in appropriating faith in

Christ: (1) he was remembered, (2) he was known still, (3) he was interpreted.[12] We begin with stories about Jesus as he was remembered. Until the middle-teen years, the emphasis remains on the human and historical Jesus. To "know him still" as risen Lord or in the power of the Spirit does not come early, even though some children are sufficiently brainwashed to use such language. To evoke such a disclosure followed by commitment in Christian terms is a matter of Christian maturity, something more than "discerning the Lord's body" in the Holy Communion, although it includes that. I believe that the experience of "knowing him still" is an ongoing process open to a variety of interpretations. If we remember Jesus and come to know him as living Lord, we are ready at last to interpret the data in terms of reasoning and commitment. Perhaps this is the point at which confirmation would be meaningful, as one consciously accepts the commission of Christ to be his disciple in the secular world.

The educational process may lead up to this decision about confirmation. We are claiming that in Christ the disciples become a new creation. They not only acquire new skills but they also develop a new loyalty. They know that they are living by grace through faith, and therefore they are to be loyal to God in their callings. Their education becomes centrally relevant as they develop new capacities to think about concepts related to God. This is why, in the 1960s, the "death of God" movement shook some churchpeople in and from their "comfortable pews" and set them on new paths of theological exploration. They became concerned about "the secular city" as a place where the Bible can be relevant, for the strange new land of the Bible is primarily secular and therefore religious in a profound sense. So modern Christians are learning how to "do" theology by looking at their own world and at the Bible and then comparing the

12. See John Knox, *Christ the Lord* (Chicago: Willett, Clark, 1945), p. 60. See above, chapter 2.

situations and seeing how God "speaks" anew in this year of our Lord. Because this world offers new moral challenges in new situations, they are learning to "do" moral analysis (and they find both sound and unsound moral analysis on campus or in the political arena). They are asking, as perhaps they never asked before, how one lives as a Christian in the world and in the church. At this point, straight thinking depends on their biblical backgrounds more than on their direct study of Bible content. If they lack this background, they are not likely to become mature Christians in the modern world; and this background began to be acquired or not in the crib.

There has been more "what" than "how" in this chapter. Method is primarily the way in which teachers assist pupils to connect their situations with relevant subject matter. There is no surefire method, just as there is no guaranteed subject matter for a given situation. The wide range of suggestions on the nature of the age group, the variety of possible methods and the freedom of choice in some of the best curriculum materials seem to me to provide superb resources for a relatively intelligent and devoted teacher. The good teacher does not need to be anxious about methods, for any method that treats the pupil as a person is valid. The prior question is when and where to use what portions of the Bible with what children and at what age. To this I have given primary attention in this chapter.

13

Anxiety and Learning

There is a theology of relationships underlying the way we interpret anxiety and its place in the learning process. The great words of Christianity describe relationships: love is the establishment of a relationship, sin is a breaking of relationship, forgiveness is the restoration of relationship, anxiety is a situation where one is out of relationship. Martin Buber has made popular the "I-thou" relationship as essential to human communication, where one treats another as a person and not as a thing; but Buber points beyond the interpersonal on the human level to the divine "I-Thou" relationship. When this relationship is right, there is "the joy and peace of believing."

We cannot command this relationship. When we are filled with anxiety, with the isolation and loneliness that accompany it, we are helpless. We do not understand that this anxiety is fundamentally religious. We look first at all the secondary causes, such as childhood conditioning, poor environment, evil companions, the pressure of competition, the danger of war, and the complexities of daily living, all of which are involved in the development of anxiety. But when we see that alienation and meaninglessness are a form of perishing, we can discover that anxiety is religious at its source. Anxiety is a condition of separation from God and from other human beings.[1]

There is a religious answer to anxiety. Paul wrote: "Have no anxiety about anything, but make all your wants known to God

1. See my *Living with Anxiety* (Philadelphia: Pilgrim Press, 1971), pp. 33,73.

212

in prayer and entreaty, and with thanksgiving" (Phil 4:6,G). "Throw all your anxiety upon God, for God cares for your" (I Pet 5:7), paraphrased).

> "Be not anxious about tomorrow,
> Let tomorrow be anxious about itself;
> Surely there are troubles enough today" (Mt 6:34,E).

"If God is for us, who can be against us?... Who, then, can separate us from the love of Christ? Can trouble do it, or hardship, or persecution, or hunger, or poverty, or danger, or death?... For I am certain that nothing can separate us from God's love... there is nothing in all creation that will ever be able to separate us from the love of God which is ours through Jesus Christ our Lord" (Rom 8:31b,35,38a,39b, TEV).

There is ministry to anxious persons as part of the life of the church. Wherever people have believed in Jesus Christ, works have been done in Christ's name to make people whole. With this kind of shared faith in the God of Jesus Christ, Christians develop a mature faith that leads to poise and stability in the face of the pressures, crises, and tortures of life. They belong to a community of faithful people, participate in its life, find strength for living by means of the grace provided by the sacraments and worship, and know that Christ loves them, although they are still sinners and therefore separated from God. They know that God has entered the arena of history in a unique way through Jesus Christ, and that God is present today as the Holy Spirit works through us. This new beginning, renewed from day to day or time to time, is nurtured by the congregation of faithful people.

This love of God is mediated through people. Thus, our anxiety is overcome in so far as those around us serve to remove the obstacles that we cannot remove by ourselves. Grace comes to us from others, and therefore ministry by the nonanxious is essential to the overcoming of anxiety. Teachers are frequently perceived by anxiety-ridden pupils as authority figures, as things or objects which stand in the way of the students' pleasure. There is no genuine interpersonal relationship upon which to build an anxiety-free classroom environment. Teachers are sometimes free to imagine how the students feel, but they are helpless until they understand what can be done about it. As teachers gain self-awareness and increasing sensitivity, they gain humility and lose the status of dominance. Teachers learn to accept the students as they are, and each one is different. This acceptance builds up a feeling of confidence among the students and resistence to being taught or being organized is overcome. The students accept the teachers as persons; they trust the teachers because the teachers are taking part in the students' lives. It is then that the students learn to ask questions.[2]

The "I-thou" of teachers and pupils can never be one of absolute equality. The responsibility given to teachers makes any claims of equality seem phony. There can be times when there is genuine meeting on an equal basis, but the role of teacher must assert itself if there is to be learning. The important aspects are the creation of mutual trust and respect, and the recognition that all the pupils are equal in the classroom situation. As Buber writes, the teacher "sees them crouching at the desks, indiscriminately flung together, the misshapen and the well-proportioned, animal faces, empty faces, and noble faces in indiscriminate confusion, like the presence of the created universe; the glance of the educator accepts and receives them all."[3] Only this rarely happens. The student who is most unlovable is also least likely to call out the love in the teacher. The need for acceptance makes acceptance more difficult. The fundamental antagonism to love that resists love brings out the latent anx-

2. See Martin Buber, *Between Man and Man* (London: Routledge & Kegan Paul, 1947), pp. 83–117.
3. Buber, *Between Man and Man*, p. 94.

ieties in the teacher. Thus there is hostility in the classroom that permeates the atmosphere. Human love becomes ineffective when unloveliness becomes dominant. In the face of such unrest, a high degree of maturity on the part of the teacher, probably rooted in religious faith, is needed and is sometimes available.

THE NATURE OF ANXIETY

"The first of all learning is, I think, beyond doubt in immediate connection with anxiety," wrote Harry Stack Sullivan.[4] He was referring to a particular kind of interpersonal anxiety, which he described as an "uncanny" emotion linked to dread, horror, loathing, and awe. Such anxiety was uncomfortable and in some ways paralyzing in that it got in the way of achieving anything worthwhile. It could be compared with Kierkegaard's interpretation of dread and Tillich's of *angst*, but without the religious overtones. Anxiety has no direct object, it is opposed to the satisfaction of needs, and it destroys foresight. And what is worse, "the circumstances conducive to anxiety cannot be removed, nor destroyed, nor escaped."[5]

We can see the connection, although a negative one, between anxiety and learning if we look further at what anxiety does. If anxiety becomes severe enough, it is paralyzing. Like a blow on the head, it leaves the sufferer helpless. Less severe anxiety, almost as unpleasant, leads to certain kinds of negative learning as one comes to discriminate between increasing and decreasing anxiety. A child learns how *not* to annoy Mother. The avoidance of unpleasant feelings is more important than learning anything positive. If a situation is likely to lead to anxiety, the child escapes, so he or she thinks, through apathy, sublimation,

4. Harry Stack Sullivan, *The Interpersonal Theory of Psychiatry* (New York: Norton, 1953), p. 152.
5. Sullivan, *Interpersonal Theory of Psychiatry*, p. 53.

"compulsive selective inattention," or disparagement. These activities are forms of learning, but the results are negative and protective rather than positive and adventuresome.

Anxiety on the interpersonal level is a threat to one's security. But it may strike a deeper note and become a threat to one's existence. No matter how much security one has, there is always the threat of death. There is no ultimate security until the problem of death has been faced with an attitude of maturity. We may fear being killed or being in a fatal accident or the process of dying, but death means that we cease to be; and this nonbeing or nothingness is not an object and therefore creates anxiety and not fear. So we become anxious about the fact that we will become nothing.[6] Paul Tillich speaks of "the courage to be" in such a situation. At this point, we need to "throw all our anxiety upon God, for God cares for us" (I Peter 5:7, paraphrased).

As we approach any situation which may cause anxiety, we tend to modify our behavior so that the result will be decreasing rather than increasing anxiety. We make use of an anxiety gradient which becomes almost a calculus of what values we will sacrifice in order to avoid anxiety. The emotional distress of anxiety is not worth the satisfaction that would result from deeper interpersonal relations.

Some theologians, especially Kierkegaard and Tillich, have stressed the relation of anxiety to religious doubt and faith. If the dynamics of faith are properly understood, Christianity may serve to help people overcome their anxiety. "Be not anxious," said Jesus, and he was emphasizing the positive aspect of confidence about God in this world. If, as Sullivan says, anxiety is related to negative learning, we may assume that education grounded in Christianity may help in overcoming anxiety. Religious growth

6. See my *Live Until You Die* (Philadelphia: Pilgrim Press, 1973), p. 28; Paul Tillich, *The Courage to Be* (New Haven: Yale University Press, 1952), pp. 37–38.

may be understood as "growth in grace," as we respond to the "lure of feeling" that attracts us to God. With the emphasis on interpersonal relations as the situation in which religious nurture takes place, it is possible to work out a theory of Christian education related to anxiety as a means of illuminating the whole process.

Anxiety, as interpreted by Sullivan, is a condition that we cannot overcome by ourselves; we cannot simply throw off anxiety by an act of the will. It is, rather, a matter of grace. We need help from the outside, as someone is enabled to remove the conditions that make for anxiety. Our own efforts will meet frustration and only increase the anxiety.

DEVELOPMENTAL STAGES

Let us turn to the developmental stages and observe how anxiety operates either to increase or decrease, depending on external circumstances and interpersonal relations. This will lead to some clues for how to operate an educational program in church or synagogue. It will give us clues to the way we handle groups of boys and girls in church school classes, to ways of meeting the needs of parents, and the interpretation of life from a religious perspective for all ages.

Infant baptism, whatever its sacramental significance, is a sign of the acceptance of the child as a child of God and as a member of the body of Christ. It is the child's introduction to a community in which certain needs are asserted and met: We promise that the child will be loved and accepted, that there will be a structure of dependableness for life in the community, that the child will be free to grow, and that the awareness of the sense of holiness and mystery will be shared. When these needs are met, there is not likely to be much anxiety. Yet baptism may make no difference to the child unless the mother is helped to become relatively free from anxiety, for anxiety in the mother induces anxiety in the infant through some sort of empathy. The mother is the key figure, and if she is free from anxiety there is every expectation that the infant will be also. The church's ministry to expectant and new mothers, when seen in this light, is of great importance; and it is an area in which very little work is done.

If anxiety develops in the infant, and if it continues to develop, we can observe several processes. Potential development is hindered at this level, often by sublimation, which unwittingly settles for a second-best that does not cause anxiety. There is escape into apathy, fantasy, and other undesirable forms of learning. As language develops, there is need for continued play with the parents, for experiencing the parents as an approving audience, and for reassurance of love through emotional expression. If these supports are not provided, the child soon learns to use words which are not sincere, to conceal information, and to play roles which are hypocritical. These false learnings, as attempts to protect one against anxiety, lead away from positive learnings and nothing benefits except the self-system which becomes more rigid and thus less open to learning. As Basil Yeaxlee summarized the situation, the parents "are actually interpreting or misinterpreting God to the child in the only medium possible, though often the parents have not the faintest notion that religion enters into the matter at all, whether they account themselves religious or not."[7]

The church's educational program needs to proceed at two levels: First, there is the need to assist the parents in their ministry to the child; this can be handled through pastoral visitations, counseling, and parents' classes, but there may be special sessions for parents of infants primarily as help for their anxiety problems. Most parents are not aware that religious faith begins in the

---

7. Basil A. Yeaxlee, *Religion and the Growing Mind* (New York: Seabury, 1952), p. 44. See Horace Bushnell, *Christian Nurture* (New Haven: Yale University Press, 1947) for a full theory of development through relationships.

parent-child relationship. Most fathers are not aware that they become the models for a child's concept of God as Father. Second, the nursery and kindergarten classes provide an atmosphere in which anxiety may be overcome or additional anxiety may be stimulated. This is even more crucial in secular school, but because the church school is directly related to religion even this briefer experience is important. Anxiety may lead to a fantasy mode of thinking and feeling which is an escape from reality, and this must be differentiated from that fantasy mode of creative imagination in which myth, legend, fairy tale, and story are proper means of communication and sources of security in a world that may prove threatening. There is a fine line between the sense of the holy and the sense of dread which Sullivan does not take account of. When the sense of mystery results in wonder and awe, we may be sure that the response is healthy; but when it leads to dread or loathing or increased anxiety, we may be alarmed at the negative response. Much depends on the kinds of relationships the child has prior to hearing stories that inculcate the sense of mystery.

CHILDHOOD

In 1943, one of the best church school courses for the first grade was *Now We Are Going to School* in the Cloister Series. It recognized that first grade was a changing point in life, an opportunity to overcome, correct, or supplement the influence of the home. It is the beginning of a socializing process sponsored by forces outside the home. Many new authority figures enter the children's world. They come into new relationships with their peers in new situations that are less structured in some cases. Their crudeness in personal relations is overcome by learning subordination and accommodation. Their parents are cut down almost to size. If the children make satisfactory adjustments during these primary years, their anxiety will be decreased; if they fail to do so, their anxiety will become greater. There will still be some sublimation, partly unwitting. They learn about ingroups and outgroups and may end up outside all groups, ostracized by their peers. If this ostracism is sensed as defeat, they may find ways to cover it up, even for themselves, usually by disparagement and often with an assist from their parents. Such experiences are obvious to a sensitive church school teacher and steps can be taken to provide an atmosphere in which this ostracism may be overcome. In many church schools, however, it may be increased, for often the local congregation has no resources for accepting the unacceptable.

Sullivan's treatment of interpersonal anxiety holds out the hope that a change may take place. It is never too late for hope, and one must never give up on a potential delinquent. Sullivan believes that the experience of having a chum (who also may be ostracized) may lead to the discovery of personal worth of the chum and of one's self. This exploration of intimacy and value provides a validation that formerly was impossible, and thus the two chums are able to function with their peers without anxiety. This chumship may develop into small gang experiences, and the fact of being and having a chum may make one more acceptable, and thus one's anxiety is lessened or overcome. Occasionally, the chumship may prove malignant, but usually it only seems that way to those threatened by a twosome in class. Some teachers consider two chums who are whispering in class as a challenge to their authority, and the solution may be to split the chums. The question needs to be faced: What can be done for the redemption of these two in their chumship? Some children, even as preadolescents, know neither chums nor gangs; they only know a loneliness that eats at their insides. There comes a time when, as Sullivan writes, "loneliness in itself is more terrible than anxiety."[8] They therefore seek companionship, even though the

8. Sullivan, *Interpersonal Theory of Psychiatry*, p. 262.

seeking increases their anxiety and makes them less fit for companionship. Yet, says Sullivan, there is still hope. The church school finds it more difficult at this stage because the new symptoms indicate a more deep-seated anxiety, yet the self-centered preadolescents usually lack the resources or the will to help the helpless among their peers.

Until adolescence, the growing persons have Christian faith mediated to them by significant adults in the home, school, and church. They have intimations of faith, but it is never their own. They may want faith, but they are not yet capable of decision in the face of a divine-human encounter, and they lack the capacity for formal operational thinking that provides abstract religious concepts. They can share in the community that lives by this faith, and thus they are nurtured in it so that it comes to them gradually and almost naturally; but only in adolescence can they make the decision which gives them a faith of their own.

ADOLESCENCE

As they move into adolescence, they are seeking to stand on their own feet. We can help them to cultivate what Yeaxlee calls a "master sentiment, . . . which gathers all others into a purposive unity dependent upon both their affinity to itself and its ability to give them full effect as parts of a splendid dynamic whole."[9] As they become aware of themselves as persons, they seek for some kind of integration, either around some kind of values, around a community of persons, or around a divine person. Often it is a mixture of all three. They may come to a new self-awareness and pass through a conversion experience either gradually or suddenly. It may not be religious in any conventional sense, and it may be a turning away from conventional religion. It may be part of their breaking with their parents, or it

9. Yeaxlee, *Religion and the Growing Mind*, pp. 131–32.

may be identification with them from a more mature perspective. It may come at early, middle, or late adolescence or run through all three sub-stages; and it may run through such a period of time that decisions are made which contradict each other.

They may carry all the old anxieties into adolescence, or perhaps some of them will have been eliminated. But a new cause for anxiety has arisen. Sex is here at last in obvious and overt form. Learning to live with the sex drive, especially in our present culture, may cause a new type of anxiety to arise. Running away from the problem is no solution, for boy-girl relations are essential for the continuous exploration and experience of personal worth. The problem is how to handle the sex drive without either anxiety or guilt. Some kinds of religious teaching intensify the anxiety, the guilt, or the yearning. Yet the church, when it is aware of the interpersonal anxiety which includes the problems of sex, may do much to alleviate the anxiety and to assist the young people to find a center for living that provides an antidote to anxiety. The church should provide the opportunity to explore, experiment, doubt, and make decisions within the framework of faith in the one who said, "Be not anxious."

Adolescents are about half-way to maturity, although they think they are further along than that. They may develop a sense of the holy and be capable of responding with wonder and reverence or awe. They may begin to develop a clear set of ideals, or be more consistent in one of the many ways of behavior. They need to do something about a purpose in life, perhaps in terms of higher education but surely in terms of discovering what it means to be human and an adult. They need something to do and someone to love, and they are beginning to point toward work and marriage. They are not sure what the male and female roles are in the society that is emerging, and this may increase their anxiety. Some of them are unable to face up to any of these decisions, for they are handicapped by continuing interpersonal anxiety. At this point, what Paul Tillich writes is relevant:

Genuine Christian faith begins with the realization that "you are accepted, accepted by that which is greater than you, the name of which you do not know. Do not ask the name now: perhaps you will find it later. Do not try to do anything now: perhaps later you will do much. Do not seek for anything; do not perform anything; do not intend anything. Simply accept the fact that you are accepted. This is the experience of grace. Everything is transformed. We are able to hear him as by grace we accept others, who have not accepted themselves or us. Our broken relationships are restored. We may not be better than we were before, but our relationships are transfigured."[10]

This, I believe, is what *may* occur in adolescence when a change is made pointing in the direction of the Christian faith. Adolescents may not understand that God in Christ is the one who accepts them as they are, and they may not understand that there is no other demand on them except to accept this acceptance. But when once this revelation comes to them and their relationships are transfigured, they become new persons in the Christian sense and begin to understand that "in Christ God was reconciling the world to himself" (II Cor 5:19), and that they are part of that process and fellowship of reconciliation. They experience the redemptive and persuasive love of God, and their vocation is to witness to that love in human relationships. They begin to know what Jesus meant when he said, "Be not anxious," for through faith their anxieties are overcome and they are free to live as disciples of Christ. They are on the threshold of that maturity which is "the full measure of development which belongs to the fullness of Christ" (Eph 4:13b, Moffatt).

When we examine the process by which people grow away from anxiety or sink more deeply into it, when we understand that how we treat our children and young people makes a dif-

10. Paul Tillich, *The Shaking of Foundations* (New York: Scribners, 1948), p. 162.

ference at every stage and that hope is not lost, our responsibility for Christian nurture in terms of anxiety as found in interpersonal relationships becomes obvious. If we are to be free from anxiety and therefore free to align our wills with God's will in effective ways, we must set up the conditions whereby these goals may be achieved within the Christian community. Anxiety is only one element in the learning process. Although it can stop all positive learning, we need to understand how it operates and what we can do to provide anxiety-free learning. The work of the Holy Spirit and our understanding of growth in grace may unlock meanings of the gospel that we did not know were there.

ADULTS

Unless things have gone reasonably well, so that the personality is not badly warped, adults continue to have problems with anxiety. This is why Sullivan's view that anxiety is handed down through some kind of empathy from mothering one to child makes sense. New anxieties sometimes develop with new crises or responsibilities. One of the great crises is marriage, and more frequently today the experience turns out to be devastating. But when one has weathered the increased complexities of interpersonal relations in marriage, there soon comes the crisis of childbirth, involving both parents in at least the three-way relationship of parent to parent, parents to child, and child to parents.

It is clear that the developmental tasks of adulthood keep changing as new transitions are faced. Each transition must be met with new ways of doing things and with a change in the emotional structure. Accompanying these transitions and decisions are new and sometimes unexpected anxieties. When one is a novice, at any age, the transition will not have the backing of experience or the emotional balance of maturity. But one also has interpersonal relations to deal with, and a change in one's lifestyle may threaten the ongoing relationship. The new studies of adults are providing a broader base for good adult education.

The goal of adult education is to foster or nurture adult development as we do for children and young people. The crises that develop may be handled by proper therapeutic procedures available in mental health centers and sometimes in churches and synagogues. But such programs only help the person adapt to the current institutions and we need to do more than that if we are to assist in eliminating the anxieties that persist in spite of a caring ministry in mental and emotional health. In his massive study of male adults, Daniel J. Levinson concludes that "if we are to support adult development on a wider scale, we will have to modify the social institutions that shape our lives. Industry and other work organizations, government, higher education, religion and family—all of these must take account of the changing needs of adults in different eras and developmental periods. What is helpful in one era may not be in another."[11] Steps need to be taken to eliminate excessive stress during the middle and late twenties and early thirties if development is not to be undermined. Adequate guidance and some degree of mentoring are necessary as the young person seeks and fulfills job obligations.

This suggests that in dealing with adults as with children and youth, "Christian education must be personal; it must take place in a personal encounter *and, only secondarily, is it transmissive.* On the other hand, Christian education is responsible for the continued recital of God's saving acts and of the transmission of the subject matter of the historical faith and life of the Christian community," writes Reuel Howe.[12]

11. Daniel J. Levinson, Charlotte N. Darrow, Edward B. Klein, Maria H. Levinson, Braxton McKee, *The Seasons of a Man's Life* (New York: Ballantine, 1978), p. 337.
12. Reuel L. Howe, *Man's Need and God's Action* (New York: Seabury Press, 1953), p. 114. Howe's italics.

The emphasis on interpersonal relationships, approached in different ways by Sullivan, Buber, Levinson, and Howe, points to a common conclusion: we can be helped to overcome stress and anxiety primarily by the way people are ministered to in various institutions. For teaching to take place, interpersonal relations can help us be free from anxiety so that we will not settle for an anxiety gradient that hinders our learning but will participate in a community of mutual trust approaching love where we are free to learn. This basic trust, when it grows out of human community, prepares us to trust in God who is at work in our midst. When we see our worth in community, we are assisted in coming into the presence of God whom we judge to be the source of our worth.

Adult education takes us beyond the professional and practical training that we need in order to get along in the world of work. It is concerned with the human situation of the learners, who have accumulated a number of anxieties and who have not acquired a security of faith in God that makes it possible to deal with the anxieties. The purpose of education at this point when technical knowledge is no longer essential to promotion in one's work, is to create the possibility of a certain style of life, to develop the kind of person needed for today's world. The program so envisaged would be different for those epochs and areas where there are special needs. Martin Buber, dealing with the situation in Israel, set up a program for the training of teachers to work with those in immigration camps, primarily individually or in small groups. What was sought, typical of Buber, was "reciprocal conversation." "Adult education," says Buber, "is concerned with character, and character is not above the situation, but is attached to the cruel, hard demand of this hour."[13]

13. Maurice S. Friedman, *Martin Buber: The Life of Dialogue*, 3rd. ed., (Chicago: University of Chicago Press, 1976), p. 183; from "Adult Education in Israel," *Torch*, June 1952.

Adult education, dealing with the relationship of anxiety and learning, is to deal with character. As one moves toward maturity, one is released from the limitations of anxiety and acquires a style of life that can deal with the stresses and strains of various transitions accompanying adult living. This is a task which churches and synagogues can carry out through a caring and loving ministry, but from a theological standpoint this would be seen as the grace of God at work.

14

Religion Is Any Subject

We have been thinking about Christian education with a theological base as it occurs in church-sponsored Christian education. It is here that most of us have been exposed to the Christian religion to some degree. Experiences have led to deep commitment in some cases and in reaction against religion in others. There is the study of religion, sometimes with the expectation of commitment, outside of the churches, however, especially in Christian families. There has been a minority of young people, especially fortunate in many ways, who have had experience in parochial and private schools, and an even smaller number in independent schools which focus on resident or boarding students. In this chapter we are concerned with the unique opportunities offered by church-related independent schools, either denominational or nondenominational in orientation.

Some of these schools offer courses in religion and include chapel services in the round of events. But because the school is permeated with religious interests, religion may appear in almost any course of study. It is for this reason that the emphasis in this chapter is on the topic: *religion is any subject.*

COMMUNITY

This approach depends on how we think of the school population as a community. The word "community" has many meanings. If we go back to the Greek usage, *koinonia*, it means "fellowship," which has many implications for the life of the school.

Community means simply living together. It points to likeness, or similarity, or identity. It may mean joint ownership. People work together because they have a community of interests. Every school has a degree of community, enough like-mindedness, to reflect a common purpose of faculty and students and a capacity to share these goals in much that they do.

A second meaning is closely related to the first: communion, which means having in common. It also means intimate talk. It means the exchange of thoughts and feelings on a person-to-person basis. It means a close spiritual relationship. This can be either good or bad. "Communion with the bad corrupts good character," as we are warned about our companions while growing up.

A third meaning is fellowship, companionship, friendship, taking part with others, brotherhood or sisterhood. The word can be ruined, as when there is talk about "fellowshipping together," but it expresses at its best a depth of communication and relationship that is significant for any education.

A fourth meaning is more active, meaning to share, to use together, to enjoy together, to have in common, to divide in parts with each taking part. Cooperation, teamwork, and the feeling for organic unity come into the picture at this level.

Finally, koinonia means to participate, to take part, to have a share, as when "the teacher participated in the children's games."

Community may be on almost any level. The illustrations we have suggested point to a high level. But community is never consistently maintained. We fail to share, to participate; our fellowship is broken, our community ceases. Or at least the fellowship or communion is shallow. There may be a certain amount of community in a gang, but gangs may refer to gangsters and a low level of activity or to a group of teenagers having a wonderful time. The sense of community may be strong in both cases, but the value structures are different. The word community does not describe what we are trying to say. If we return to the New Testament, we find that *koinonia* has a second reference; it is a community *of the Holy Spirit* or the fellowship *of Jesus Christ*. It is a community that points toward a value, a goal, a process. It is an organic unity in which all the parts are interconnected and it is a body which has a head.

We are faced with the question: To what extent can a school be a Christian community? This question is relevant whether or not the school is church-related or nondenominational or nonsectarian or humanistic. Can a school be an extension of a church or a home?

Some years ago I tried an experiment with a small boarding school. The faculty, and where possible the spouses, were asked to be present for a two-day conference before school opened. The school was church-related only to the extent that the chapel was recognized by a certain denomination; the chaplain was of that denomination but the headmaster was not. It was a school that wanted to be a Christian community without being church-related. So the question was posed: "To what extent can this school be a Christian community?" The leader sat down with the group and listened for two days. All sorts of things happened. Here was a group of faculty members drawing on their own resources, their own faith—a faith that was deeper in many cases than their colleagues suspected—combining that faith with honest skepticism concerning the church; others had a strong faith combined with a firm attachment to the church; others reflected their confusion about faith and community; others responded in a luke-warm manner to the whole idea. The group struggled with the problem of trying to find ways in which the school could operate not as a pious but as a Christian community. This led to questions about sacred studies and the chapel program, but it was already clear that the key questions concerned what was *happening* in the classroom. What was the relation of the teacher to the pupils?

The conclusions of this faculty are not particularly relevant, although they were the conclusions I hoped for. Let us try to describe a community of the Holy Spirit (not in terms of church-relatedness or spirituality) as a form of community life. The Holy Spirit does not belong to the church; although we can say that the church belongs to the Holy Spirit. But there is also what might be called "the secular work of the Holy Spirit," a spirit which like the wind "bloweth where it listeth." The creative process which we call the work of the Holy Spirit is as likely to be found in a chemical laboratory as in a chapel, more anonymously, perhaps, but maybe more effectively.

If we keep this in mind, we can start asking about the community of the Holy Spirit. In any community life there are certain person-to-person relationships. These relationships are built up or torn down; they are broken and they are restored. Sometimes they are broken because of person-to-person conflict; between two students, between a student and a teacher, between two teachers, or along a pecking order that is either overt or covert. Many students go through the etiquette of saying "I'm sorry" and are well behaved for the moment, but they don't mean it; or broken relationships may be successfully disguised so that we are not aware of them. At other times they break out into the open. No longer can the temper be withheld, the repressive forces break down and the animosities come into clear view. Sometimes the expression of feelings is sufficiently therapeutic to effect a catharsis, especially when the one against whom the feelings are expressed accepts them. But where a pound of flesh is required, no healing takes place.

In these relationships, we want performance. The school's job is to educate, to make students do their best; and this is right. Everything legitimate should be done to stimulate them. But when we ask for the basis of this motivation, we may be disturbed by the discovery that for them to do their best the glory lies in the parent or the teacher who are manipulators. We, as persons in authority, use them for our own good. We cease to treat them as persons and think of them as things. The parent, for example, may say that it is good for the child to dance for the edification of visitors. This may very well be true; it may be the very thing that the child needs for his or her own development. But it may be true that the child does not want to do this; so the child acts under compulsion, and the parent has a self-satisfied smirk. The parent has used the child as a puppet. One would hesitate to call this an "I-Thou" relationship.

Where there is genuine community within the life of the school, we will guard against broken relationships and seek ways of healing them. The teacher may ask, "I recognize that the pupils have broken relationships among themselves, as well as with parents and teachers. What can I do? What is my ministry to heal these relationships?" The teacher has a ministry of reconciliation, which means to take up the sufferings and the sins of the pupils. This is hard to do, even when it is recognized as within the responsibility of the teacher. But if we do not do it, we fail as teachers. Assuming that a school may be a community of reconciliation, we need to be open to a ministry of healing.

BASIC NEEDS

Another way of approaching students within a school community is in terms of their basic needs. These needs have been described in a variety of ways, and what follows is my own classification that I have used for many years. What I am doing here is to classify and correlate them with the idea of community and with the basic religious concepts that stand behind it.

First is the need for *love and acceptance.* Love and acceptance are closely related concepts. To accept someone as that person is, to love without qualifications, is difficult, but the recognition of this leads ultimately to the religious insight that God loves me as I am, accepts me even when I am unacceptable. Love cannot be earned. The teacher realizes that God loves each pupil, not as that pupil ought to be, but as that pupil is. This I understand to be a central Christian doctrine at the heart of the gospel. It is symbolized in the fact that God loved the world so much that he sent his Son; or again, we are told that Jesus did not die *after* human beings had reformed, but that while we were still sinners Christ died for us. There are many ways to express this insight, but the point is that God's love expressed through the suffering of Jesus stands as a model for human love in a Christian community. This is a theological issue, not just a sociological one, that permeates every situation; and thus religion is any subject.

Second is the need for some kind of *structure or discipline.* This love that is accepting is not an easy-going Pollyanna kind of love. Love has sharp edges; it provides direction and law. Law is subsumed under love, not the reverse. There is discipline, structure, correction, limitation, guidance, or else processes get out of line. Yet many of the restrictions on school life and community do not seem to be structuring of positive actions. Are all of the silly little rules and regulations that we use to run our schools just or necessary? Or do we have to get behind the surface laws to an ultimate question: "Is not the structure of the universe due to the fact that we believe that God who is love is a God of justice?" A God who demands righteousness is a deity of the moral and natural law, and thus we are driven to a God who is the principle of limitation. Again, religion is any subject.

Third, every person needs *freedom to grow.* The best the teacher ever does is to set up the conditions, provide the guidance, and hope to evoke insight. No matter how much structure we provide, no matter how much love we offer, no matter how well we plant or water, *God provides the growth* (I Cor 3:6G). But it is not quite this simple, for unless there is student motivation as well as creative teaching, the growth does not occur. It is the old story of the farmer who was told by a pious minister that he should thank God for the wonderful crop. The farmer replied: "I don't know whether to thank him or not. You should have seen the mess that was here last year when God was running it alone." And so it is with education. There is no growth unless the conditions have been met.

Fourth, and finally, there is the need for some satisfaction of the *sense of mystery*. At the center of life there is this feeling of mystery, something we can point to but cannot explain. Little children have a sense of wonder, and it never completely vanishes among adults. It takes on all sorts of forms and shapes, and is expressed in myriad ways. It may be simply a wondering about life. It is often expressed in terms of aesthetics, as in the beauty of a sunset, or a great painting, or music. We can respond in this way to human creations as well as to natural beauty. We find it in worship sometimes—even in worship in chapel at school.

This yearning for the sense of mystery goes back to what Rudolph Otto called the sense of the numinous, the sense of the holy. We cannot achieve this experience by any tricks. There have been attempts to create atmospheres of worship which are spooky enough to evoke a response; the leaders dim the lights and light the candles and play sentimental music and somehow the Holy Spirit is supposed to come. The sense of the holy cannot be contrived in this way. It is an experience which is awe-inspiring, which arouses responses of wonder, reverence, and sometimes dread, and ultimately it points to the reality of God who is the holy of holies. This is mediated through persons but points beyond them. It is expressed in community life and worship, not so much verbally as in the relationships that develop.

KEY QUESTIONS

Another approach is through key questions. For example, a boy was hit on the head playing football and went to the hospital. The report was that he was fine, but he still didn't know who he was. This leads to the key question: "Who is he when he doesn't know who he is?" "Does God still know who he is?" The familiar question, "Who am I?" becomes "Who am I in relation to God?" The answer begins: "I am more than a name. I am more than a number. I am more than my parents' child. I am more than a biological creation of my parents. But, who am I?" So they progress to other questions: "Where did I come from? Where am I going? What is the world like?" These questions are asked at every level from childhood to maturity. They are basically religious questions. And there are no easy answers.

If religion is any subject as far as needs and questions are concerned, how about the classroom? Do we find in the classroom the kind of community we described at the opening of this chapter? The subject matter in any classroom is mediated through the personality of the teacher. Every teacher has a number of biases that influence how the subject matter is presented. Bias is evident in all teaching. There is no such thing as "immaculate perception" in our grasp of subject matter. If we did succeed in being free from all bias, our teaching would be sterile. The question is not whether the teacher has a bias, but whether or not we can recognize the bias and correct it so that we do justice to the positions of others. Chiefly, and we cannot command this, there needs to be a relationship of trust between teacher and pupils. If there is an atmosphere in which grace flourishes, there can be effective teaching in spite of bias. This requires of the teacher some skills in human relations and the capacity to work with group process, recognizing the particular problem of an individual within the group, and developing those personal relationships in which trust and communication between teacher and pupils are developed.

The danger of this approach, if we leave it at this point, is that it can evaporate. We must have verbalized pegs on which to hang ideas and identify relationships. We require the capacity to use words in order to evaluate and criticize what we are doing.

But words are meaningless without relationships; relationships may be meaningful without words, but the meaning can evaporate. There are certain kinds of communication where words seem to be unnecessary. A husband doesn't have to tell his wife that he loves her; it is more important to kiss her; but there still needs to be some verbal direction to their life together. Likewise, there needs to be some verbalized understanding of the school and its life as a community. The students need to know what we and they are trying to do. For a school to seek to be a community such as we have been describing, it needs the sympathetic understanding of most of the faculty and students. This may be achieved partly by telling them what we are trying to do.

We are beginning to understand how religion may be part of any subject. Religion as a way of life within a community certainly affects everything the school does. But religion also is related to the subject matter of any subject. This is obvious in any study of history, where religion plays such a large part. It is equally clear in geography. It is obvious to some extent in language, where religious terms play a large part. Schools may prefer Platonic Greek and seminaries may prefer *koine*, but religious terms are significant in both. In the sciences, we have the problem of the creation of the world seen from the standpoint of biblical fundamentalism as opposed to theories of evolution, something we thought we had resolved in the 1920s. As we move toward a scientific world view, we have problems of theological reconstruction at every age level.

This can be put another way. William G. Pollard suggests that the problem is not so much science versus religion as it is a question of a dual educational emphasis. The educational system of Western culture rests on the Greek classical tradition, with only a bow to the Judaic-Christian tradition. The Greek classical tradition provides a wealth of insight into all aspects of life. We have reduced our own religious heritage to a subject within the curriculum that operates as a foreign body and an irritant. Our

culture is Greek-Jewish-Christian, but our educational philosophies on the whole have carried out the Greek tradition only.
Thus, the Jewish-Christian tradition is seen as an extra, to be
taught as a special subject within the public schools in purely
objective fashion or in released time classes, as an isolated sacred
studies course in many private and parochial schools, and
centered in chapel and nowhere else in some other schools. The
curriculum problem depends on how we see the relationship of
the Greek and Jewish-Christian educational traditions and on
whether we can treat religion as any subject.[1]

NONPUBLIC SCHOOLS

Religious subjects have been taught in nonpublic schools with
varying success. The products of such classes have been identified in many ways. Some students have become "prep school
atheists" who have been exposed to compulsory courses over a
period of years. They are sick and tired of the whole thing. If
they have had compulsory chapel as well, the chances that the
college or university chaplains will capture their interest are
slight.

But the situation is not all gloomy. There are private schools
throughout the country with voluntary religious and chapel programs and courses that gain positive responses. The graduates are
favorably disposed toward further religious studies in higher education. There are now many excellent courses in public high
schools that have aroused intellectual interest and have fed religious needs. Teacher-training programs in several states are now
geared to the objective teaching of religion.

There are students who become what I have called the
"church mouse" type. They have accepted a dogmatic approach

1. William G. Pollard, in Edmund Fuller, ed., *The Christian Idea of Education*
(New Haven: Yale University Press, 1957), pp. 1–22.

to religion and have not been exposed to critical questioning. I remember what happened to them when I was a college chaplain. We usually started with a discussion of *what the chaplain doesn't believe,* which captured the interest of the doubters and searchers and all who wanted to think. But all the church mice quit.

This suggests that we need to challenge our students to think clearly and critically about religious studies, and especially the literature of the Bible. But the Bible often ends up as just that: literature. It may be taught by a Shakespearian with a love for the King James Version, and this has value as a study of Elizabethan ways of writing. But Elizabethan is a foreign language today. The King James Version was written in order that the common people might read it; it grew out of Tyndale's effort to make sure that the boy behind the plow could read it.

Today's problem is the same as it was in 1611. We need a translation in the language of the people. I am not certain that the Revised Standard Version does the job. If you have tried to teach out of Phillips, or Goodspeed, or the New English Bible, or Today's English Version, you may have discovered that your course suddenly became alive. The question becomes, "What does the Bible say to me in the language [in the case of Goodspeed] of a Chicago American?" The story of Simon the magician, who tried to bribe Peter with money in order to do Christian tricks, ends with Peter saying (according to Phillips), "To hell with you and your money" (Acts 8:20,P). Most students will appreciate the directness of the language, and it becomes a way into an understanding of unmerited grace versus works.

Another perspective on the Bible is to place it in a theological framework, so that we interpret the mighty acts of God as a drama of redemption not only in the history of Jews and Christians but also in our own lives, as suggested in chapter 12. Thus the Bible's cutting edge can become a reality in the lives of the pupils. The Bible is not primarily a record of *ideas* of God, although it is that; it is the story of a living deity at work in our history as dramatized in the creation, the covenant, the coming of Christ, the gift of the church, and the consummation of all things.

So what do we do? We get lost in the "begats" or the kings of Israel. Or we get David as a model Boy Scout and omit Bathsheba. David is an interesting character if you let the students have all of him. Most students will appreciate the great poetry of the song of Deborah, even though it includes some nail pounding through Sisera's skull by that sweet young thing named Jael. Have you thought of analysing the story of Cain and Abel so that the punch line becomes, "Am I my brother's baby sitter?" The Bible is alive and is taught in this way in many schools.

The Bible also ministers to our underlying anxiety. We can conveniently examine two types of anxiety to which the Bible addresses itself. First is the anxiety of *status,* based on the desire to be accepted by our peers. This status comes when one knows one's self as one is and is assured of God's love in the midst of life's problems. This is the kind of status that no one can take from us, for it arises from the ultimate meaning found in a relationship with God. This relationship may be mediated through other persons, but the loss of another person does not destroy the relationship with deity. Some couples are happily married, and the death of one spouse leaves the other completely desolated, because the security was in the spouse's love rather in God's love. They need to learn not to fear those who can kill the body but only those who can destroy both soul and body (Mt 10:28).

There is a second kind of anxiety expressed in terms of *existence.* Who am I if I cease to exist? This is a personalized anxiety in the face of the threat of nothingness, and it is clear that I will die. A child learns this at about the age of six, but adults usually have a conspiracy of silence about the possibility of death. After one dies, is there a future existence? How can we help students move beyond the anxiety of status to the anxiety of existence and then find the religious sources for overcoming both kinds of anxiety? This is the profound religious teaching that may underlie good sacred studies. It leads to an understanding of the experience of grace.[2]

Grace leads to ethics as the human response to God's love. There can be ethics without faith in God, as is evident from the results of various studies in moral education. But the religious dimension has its own integrity, and the motivation for ethical living is derived from a biblical faith. The problem becomes the existential one of deciding what to do in a specific situation. What do young people do at that point in a necking party when they are tempted to give in? This is the point at which their own resources are inadequate unless they know God's aim for them. This is the kind of ethics that has power in a crisis. It leads to good citizenship, and to good social and political morality. It becomes evident in the lives of students within the school community.

SCHOOL WORSHIP

Worship emerges out of the life of the school and at the same time may become the central factor in the meaning of life together in the school. If religion is every subject, as we have suggested, worship is something geared to the needs of the community. The preaching in such worship will emerge from school life. This makes me suspicious of the effectiveness of visiting firemen, no matter how big their names may be. Occasionally the outsider may be a welcomed change, but the members of the community are the ones who know the community and are best prepared to address it. The prayers and hymns and lessons are tied into the overall picture. There might be a chance afterwards

2. See above, chapter 13, for a fuller treatment of anxiety.

for a chaplain's hour to reflect on the sermon. So appreciation and analysis and decision go hand in hand in the presence of the Lord.

Worship is much more than preaching. We expect to meet God when we go to chapel. But is this a possibility? It cannot be done by architecture or by false aesthetics. It can be done only insofar as the community life of the school becomes alive in terms of its religious predicament and sense of reverence. This is the school at worship.

We can overdo this business of worship. If we are going to have it every day, by all means make it voluntary. Massey Shepherd once suggested that if chapel is compulsory it should be so only for the faculty[3] Of course, there need to be rules about chapel and worship, but they should be for minimum exposure.

Private and parochial schools are free, as public schools are not, to practice the Christian faith. The denominational schools, however, are sometimes frustrated by inherited practices or restrictions written into the charter, while the nonsectarian schools are sometimes timid because of those in their midst who belong to differing religious communities. In one case there may be extreme formalism and rigidity and in other cases religion can be watered down to practically nothing. We need to remember that the demand for Christian community includes the stranger within the gates: Jews, other Christian bodies, non-Christian religious groups, and nonbelievers. All students are to be accepted as they are within the community, and they are to be included as far as possible at all levels.

Community means communion, fellowship, sharing, and participation at the deepest levels of existence. We seek to create "an atmosphere in which grace flourishes." We believe that God is at work in such a community, providing the growth, healing

3. Massey H. Shepherd, in Fuller, ed., *Christian Idea of Education*, p. 147.

power, and emerging novelty that makes life meaningful. When faith is at work in such a community, it is caught and not taught.

The relationships of a community of the Holy Spirit may seem rather vague unless we have the words to tell our story. When we are aware of the basic needs of our pupils, *religion is any subject*, for it is taught in terms of the integrity of the learner as a child of God. The learners come to see the significance of their religious heritage as it provides meaning for their day-to-day existence. In subject matter, in worship, and in preaching they *may* come to see the relevance of the gospel for their daily living. Through the chapel program, they *may* come to a mature decision to be a Christian, or, if that decision is already made, it will be enriched or strengthened.

Chiefly, they will become what they will be through the relationships of everyday living in the school community and through the interpretation of these relationships in the light of the gospel. It is our task to equip them, and religion is any subject.

15

The Discipline of Theology
in the University
and the Divinity School

"Religion" as a topic of study has become accepted in most of the state universities in the United States, especially since the Supreme Court decision of 1964. The situation has been expanding and changing rapidly, so that current surveys are immediately out of date. Because this is where the action is, some careful thinking about the significance of religion in the humanities should precede a consideration of theology in the university, and both of these developments may provide new insights for doing theology in a divinity school or theological seminary.

The significance of the study of religion in state universities is at least twofold. First, within a few years it is estimated that ninety percent of students at the college and university level will be in state universities. Therefore, one might welcome the development of religious studies because it is the only way in which a majority of students will receive any knowledge of religion at an academically respectable level. Second, the study of religion apart from denominational allegiance or professional training within a pluralistic society now becomes possible in a new way.

THE PLACE OF RELIGION IN THE UNIVERSITY

Within the scope of a secular university, religion is a discipline which includes the study of both the quality of human experience designated as religious and the beliefs that constitute the

244 The University and Divinity School

structure of religions. It is a recognition that there is a realm called sacred open to secular examination. The phenomena of religion are subject to public scrutiny. Claims that religious beliefs are based on revelation may be examined, but there can be no insistence on the acceptance of such claims. As a humanistic field of study, it has no distinctive methodology but makes use of methodologies from many disciplines and fields. However, it is a subject of study in its own right, although it may also be studied within the scope of other disciplines and fields, such as sociology, psychology, history, anthropology, and philosophy. Clyde Holbrook writes, "Stated in comprehensive terms, religion embraces the study of those forms of conviction, belief, and behavior and those systems of thought in which [people] express their concerned responses to whatever they hold to be worthy of lasting and universal commitment."[1]

Such study is to be "objective." That is, although the need for imaginative projection and perhaps empathy for the experiences being analyzed is recognized, such teaching is not confessional. Whatever is taught needs to be intelligible to both the believer and the nonbeliever. Such teaching needs to be free from charges of indoctrination or of antireligious bias, so that both the believer and nonbeliever take a risk by being exposed to such teaching, although the content is not loaded in either direction. Objectivity is not sterility or indifference.

The objective teaching of religion operates on three levels. The first is a descriptive and analytical approach to the many phenomena that are called religious. There is little involvement at this level, but it may be the best approach to the foundations of religious study. The scope may be wide or narrow; the approach may be through a variety of methodologies; the emphasis may be on anthropology, sociology, or psychology; the cultural

1. Clyde A. Holbrook, *Religion, A Humanistic Field* (Englewood Cliffs, N.J.: Prentice-Hall, Inc., 1963), p. 36.

roots may be explored; the impact on daily living may be examined; the belief structures may be compared.

The second approach takes current religious traditions and in the light of their histories seeks to discover the sources of their energies. Here one may turn to myth and cult, to the power of community, to the place of law, to the scriptures and sacraments. This information is to be sought in historical data, for religious meanings arise in history and can be understood in their cultural contexts. In such a study one discovers the similarities in the various traditions. If this element is overemphasized, one may miss the distinctiveness of each major tradition. However, if this element is underemphasized, the uniqueness of each tradition may be considered as different in kind (so that one may say that Christianity, for example, is not a religion and therefore cannot be compared with other faith systems).

Religion is marked off from other disciplines and religions are distinguished from each other in terms of religious language. Today, when even the possibility of religious language has been questioned, the historical evidence is that the category of religion has its own language or languages. Within the scope of religious thinking, one finds a logic that is internal to the language, and this makes it difficult for the outsider to understand the meanings. One element of involvement that the nonreligious person must risk in attempting to understand religious behavior and thought is to acquire some capacity to grasp the self-involving and performative nature of religious language.

The third approach is a comparison of and analysis of belief systems. Here one comes close to "doing theology," which will be discussed later; but there is a place for looking at theologies and meanings of life as a purely academic procedure. The self-understanding of human beings in relation to God comes to the fore at this level of study. In some situations, this cannot properly be called theology and should be considered as philosophy of religion; but in other cases philosophy and theology overlap in both methods and conclusions; and yet, in contrast, in the thinking of some theologians, theology has no clear relationship with philosophy. These distinctions are important and will be considered in any broadly-based comparative study of belief systems. It would be proper, also, in this regard, to make a careful study of a single system of thought, such as Protestant thought after the reformation, or Catholic thought since Vatican II, or Moslem theologies of the Middle Ages.

Religion, then, offers a complex field of study with a variety of methodologies and approaches. Most of the elements making up the total field can be categorized in different ways: the religions of the world, the textual study of the scriptures of all the religions, historical, psychological, sociological, and anthropological approaches to all the religions, comparative theologies, and specialized approaches. No university can hope to cover the whole field, and some subjects will be omitted because of the lack of trained personnel. Possibly, because of the pluralism of American religions, an attempt should be made to cover most of the live options for American students, and this may be done to the degree that there are competent scholars on the faculty, without concern for representation of committed members of all the churches and synagogues and other institutions. Some degree of specialization must be expected, or else all teaching will be watered down.[2]

What marks off teaching in a state university from a divinity school or even from some church-related or Jewish colleges is that the state university seeks specifically to avoid evangelization, conversion, and indoctrination. Holbrook has an excellent chapter on "Purposes of Religious Instruction." He stresses both the materials and methods of the field and the needs of the student. The first objective is stated as follows: "To acquaint the student with the perennial questions which [people] have raised and attempted to answer concerning their meaning and destiny as these are reflected in systems of thought, cultic acts, and characteristic attitudes and beliefs."[3] This approach is to be both descriptive and evaluative, and the criticism should be on the basis of internal logical and moral consistency.

The second objective, according to Holbrook, is to dispel ignorance and to assist the students in formulating their own views of the meaning of life. This involves some degree of appreciation and understanding of human experience in the field of religion combined with freedom to make their own decisions. In other words, guidance of the students' self-development is at the center of the university's concern, and the teaching of religion may contribute to this guidance. Many students hope to develop a philosophy of life during their educational experience, and they also want to become competent in their fields of knowledge. To achieve this, students need "practice in criticism and the self-esteem and confidence that will enable" them "to stand in opposition to pressures of authority and of the immediate social group." They also need "models of independent thinking, a general climate of freedom in [the] college, and a rule structure that is appropriate to" their stages "of development."[4]

There is a risk that the result will be commitment to the religious goals of the teacher. But where the teachers are fulfilling their roles with enthusiasm for the subject, change in the students is to be expected as a by-product. The important element is that the students be challenged to face the issues and to make decisions, and therefore to develop as persons. That they may decide to accept the positions of their teachers is a risk that has to be taken, whether the subject is political science, philosophy, ethics, or religion.

3. Holbrook, *Religion, A Humanistic Field*, p. 71.
4. Nevitt Sanford, "Aims of College Education," in Charles W. Havice, ed., *Campus Values* (New York: Charles Scribner's Sons, 1968), p. 16; see pp. 1–16.

In order for such a possibility to exist, not only must religion exist as an academic pursuit on the campus but the field must be representative of the live options of the day. The danger does not come from the opportunity for commitment, for any living subject includes this possibility, but in the limitation by those in authority as to the acceptable form of commitment. At this point, the university has a freedom and integrity that is not often possible for a denominational college or a theological seminary, and perhaps the freedom of the university might serve as a model for other institutions of learning.

There is another set of purposes that needs recognition. So far, we have talked about the nonprofessional concerns of students of religion. However, there are groups within the university who are planning on graduate work in religion, teaching in elementary and secondary schools, or entering training for the Christian ministry. These students normally have some degree of commitment and some kind of vocational plans. Decisions about course offerings need to be made with these students in mind, just as courses are planned for premedical, prelegal, and other preprofessional students. This will not change the focus of university teaching of religion, but it may broaden the base of course offerings, especially in the area of theology which is often neglected in current university faculties.

WHO SHOULD TEACH?

There is a great deal of discussion concerning departments of religious studies as the proper organization for teaching religion at the university level. Some would prefer to have religious subject matter included in other academic disciplines. There is much to be said for both approaches, but perhaps the warning of E. Thomas Lawson should be noted: "When religion is taught as an aspect of other academic disciplines it is not adequately done.

Even if a person is a trained historian, it requires specialized training in theology, which few historians have, to teach a course in the history of Christian thought."[5] There should be a faculty of religion, whether in a department or not, and at the same time it needs to be recognized that religion has always been involved in any understanding of the economic, political, literary, artistic, and philosophical approaches to human activity and therefore should appear in any course where it is relevant.

But what of this faculty of religion? In the American scene, with its pluralism carelessly classified as Catholic, Protestant, and Jewish, some faculties have followed what is called the "zoo" approach. Representatives of each of the three faiths serve as exhibits A, B, and C and are exponents of their own positions, and students can make an "eenie, meenie, minie, mo" approach. This is a distortion of what actually happens, and in the best example of this approach, at the School of Religion at the University of Iowa, one finds highly qualified representatives of a fully academic approach to religious studies.

What the issue comes down to is qualified personnel, without too much concern for denominational or faith commitments. When a policy has been developed concerning offerings in religious studies, with recognition of the richness of the field and the limitations of the university, each institution must decide where to specialize. This decision in turn is qualified by the availability of trained instructors. The requirement for faculty is based on academic expertness and involvement rather than commitment. As Holbrook writes, "a distinction not always noted is that between the professor's enthusiasm for the study of his [or her] field and the religious commitments which may or may not underlie

5. E. Thomas Lawson, in Milton D. MacLean, ed., *Religious Studies in Public Universities* (Carbondale, IL: Central Publications, Southern Illinois University Press, 1967), p. 48.

his [or her] interest in the field."[6] The experts in religious
scholarship and teaching have not always been exponents of the
faith they have studied.[7]

Many competent scholars have received their graduate degrees
from church-related institutions and theological seminaries.
They are likely to have commitments, but this does not disqualify them. In the future, as graduate departments of religious
studies in the universities develop, not only will there be a supply
of trained scholars and teachers for university faculties, but it is
to be expected that they will also teach in divinity schools. This
interchange back and forth will be a good thing.

ON DOING THEOLOGY

So far we have dealt with the scope of religious studies in the
public university, which is where most of the action is today. But
a casual study of the offerings at these universities exhibits a lack
in theology, even when one discovers some courses in the history
of Christian thought, contemporary Christian thought, and occasionally in the theology of Aquinas, Barth, or the Niebuhrs.
There is even less evidence of such teaching concerning Jewish
theologians.

Part of this, I think, is due to misapprehension concerning the

6. Holbrook, *Religion, A Humanistic Field,* p. 33.
7. Marvin Fox writes: "George Foote Moore was a scholar of Judaism of the
first rank, though he himself was a Christian. Ignaz Goldziher, a Jew, was a
distinguished student of Islam. Joseph Klausner was a Jew who produced outstanding studies of early Christianity. Harry A. Wolfson of Harvard is a Jew
who has written one of the most important studies of the church fathers.
. . . Why should we demand of teachers of religion something unique?. . . If
it is because the subject matter is peculiar then perhaps this is an indication that
the subject matter has no proper place in the university curriculum. If the
subject matter is not peculiar, then I see no argument in favor of this demand"
("Who Is Competent to Teach Religion?" *Religious Education* LIV [March–
April 1959], p. 113).

nature of theology, which is often thought to be a closed system of indoctrination based on a revelation not in the public domain and not open to analysis in terms of the human experience of religious phenomena. That some theology fits such a description is obvious. Theology is simply "the truth about God in relation to persons." For the Christian, it has its roots in the Bible and the history of the church, but it operates in terms of verification based on history, reason, and spiritual experience. Although theology has a narrower boundary than the field of religious studies, it is a specific discipline within that field.

William Temple suggests that "*the primary assurances of Religion are the ultimate questions of Philosophy.*" He goes on to say that religion has three central convictions: (1) "the conviction that Spirit is a true source of initiation of processes," (2) "the conviction that all existence finds its course in a Supreme Reality of which the nature is Spirit," and (3) "the conviction that between that Spirit there can be, and to some extent already is, true fellowship, at least such as is involved in our conscious dependence on that Spirit."[8] "Theology starts from the Supreme Spirit and explains the world by reference to Him. Philosophy starts from the detailed experience of [persons], and seeks to build up its understanding of that experience by reference to that experience alone."[9] This leads to an uneasy but necessary alliance between theology and philosophy, which is theological philosophy or natural theology. Temple goes on to establish this on the basis of revelation, which he defines as "the coincidence of event and appreciation," something possible in every aspect of knowledge and therefore not limited to theological issues.

In this view, no propositions are revealed. They are the result of thinking about events which have aroused appreciation, sometimes of a unique sort. This approach eliminates any dogmatism

8. William Temple, *Nature, Man and God* (London: Macmillan, 1934), p. 35.
9. Temple, *Nature, Man and God*, p. 45.

in theological statements, although it allows for such statements as significant propositions interpreting events. Ian T. Ramsey speaks of moments of discernment or disclosure, where the "light dawns" or the "ice breaks." Ideas "come alive" in specific situations and then are tested in daily living. For Ramsey, these experiences occur in "characteristically personal situations,"[10] while for Temple " all occurrences are to some degree revelation of God."[11] For both, the certainty lies in the discernment and not in the propositions. Ramsey says that "being sure in religion does not entail being certain in theology."[12]

Bernard Meland, in a chapter on "The Appreciative Consciousness," develops the first part of the claims of Temple and Ramsey, utilizing William James' claim for the depth in immediate awareness that underlies conscious experience but that an attentive act as such can never achieve.[13] As a regulative principle in thought, says Meland, "the appreciative consciousness . . . can best be understood as an orientation of the mind which makes for a maximum degree of receptivity to the datum under consideration on the principle that what is given may be more than what is immediately perceived, or more than one can think. . . . Call it what one will: intellectual humility, wonder, reverence, or simply open awareness, some such mood is essential to the orientation of the mind we are describing."[14] Tillich, who claims to be no empiricist, makes the same point at the beginning of his *Systematic Theology*: "The theological concepts of both idealists and naturalists are rooted in a 'mystical a priori,'

10. Ian T. Ramsey, *Religious Language* (London::SCM Press, 1957), p. 20.
11. Temple, *Nature, Man and God,* p. 306.
12. Ian T. Ramsey, *On Being Sure in Religion* (University of London: The Athlone Press, 1963), p. 47; see *Christian Discourse* (London: Oxford University Press, 1965), p. 89.
13. Bernard E. Meland, *Higher Education and the Human Spirit* (Chicago: University of Chicago Press, 1953), p. 57.
14. Meland, *Higher Education and the Human Spirit,* pp. 63–64.

an awareness of something that transcends the cleavage between subject and object."[15]

There is, then, a dual nature to theology. First, there is a concern with the appreciative consciousness as such; second, there is concern with the object of that consciousness. When put in the language of faith, there is faith as trust or commitment and there is faith as loyalty to the one who claims such faith, which involves a critical analysis of faith both as an activity and in relation to the object or objects.

The critical function of theology is the crucial one in the current scene. Verification in terms of scientific checks or the appeal to sense experience seems to many to be impossible, and yet the empirical anchor, as Ramsey calls it, cannot be ignored without reducing theology to some kind of impossible speculation that is not open to adequate analysis. It is no accident that van Buren's approach in *The Secular Meaning of the Gospel*, using a strict theory of verification derived from logical analysis, seems to turn Barth's theology on its head. As against both van Buren and Barth, there are those who claim that theology provides a complex presentation of evidence demanding some kind of decision that takes account of many subtleties and includes the attitude of the one making the decision. A theology calls attention to a way in which facts may be seen and understood.[16]

Theology has been a way of analysing and evaluating faith systems. This has been its most important function. In doing this, it has often operated in terms of seeming authority that in due time has been undercut by new insights and new formulations. Partly this has been due to increased information and new techniques of investigation, which may supplement or improve some theological systems and threaten others. Today, most of

15. Paul Tillich, *Systematic Theology*, Vol. I (Chicago: University of Chicago Press, 1951), p. 9.
16. See John Wisdom, "Gods," in *Logic and Language*, First Series, ed. Antony Flew (Oxford: Basil Blackwell, 1951), p. 192.

the pressure is in terms of serious questioning of all theological formulations. As one commentator has put it, we no longer have viable systems, we do not even have foundations, and all we can do is to take soundings once again.[17] The death-of-God movement was evidence of this vital reexamination of theological method and systems, and it has now moved on to new ways of formulating theological questions which may produce new propositions or resurrect theological positions that were in temporary eclipse.

Theology is also concerned with communication. It is at this point that it has often failed miserably, especially with the lay person and the undergraduate student. Although many people are eager to consider what their life means and to ask questions about the nature of God, they do not find intelligible answers among the professional theologians. When someone writes a book like *Honest to God*, its popularity surprises the professionals not only in theology but in other disciplines. The popularity of Paul Tillich, Hans Küng, and James A. Pike on university campuses was another significant factor, for these men were not popularizers or interpreters of religion in general but spoke on theological issues. The developments in linguistic philosophy, especially the writings of Ian T. Ramsey, Donald Evans, and Dallas High, may lead to new ways of communicating what theologians wish to say.

APPROACHES TO TEACHING THEOLOGY

Obviously, there are many ways to teach theology in a secular university. The simplest way of introduction for many is to do a study of existing theological systems, in terms of the history of Christian thought or comparative current systems. Such courses

17. See Alec Vidler, ed., *Soundings* (Cambridge: At the University Press, 1962), pp. x–xii.

are being taught successfully, often as survey courses. They may deal only with the results of such thinking, so that one compares Barth, Buber, and Rahner in a manner similar to a comparison of a Corvette, a Ferrari, and a Mustang, not in terms of how they were made or how they perform or what they cost but only of how they look. But if one gets inside the system, discovers the principles of construction, the methods of handling the evidence, and the criteria for judging the final model, one is on the way to doing theology. It is this involvement that the students need in order to free their own abilities in the field and to make decisions. Many students make this kind of effort in deciding what car to buy, although some are satisfied with advertising claims or the amount of chrome on the car.

This approach may be used with any theology derived from any religious tradition. Those universities which can provide adequate personnel may offer courses in the theologies of various Moslem schools of thought—or others. There also are the many varieties of Christian theology. In all cases, the purpose is the study of any theology and theology as a whole as an academic discipline in its own right.

In the case of Christian theology, this means adequate critical acquaintance with the scriptures as the basis for theology. This is the point at which almost all curricula seem to be adequate, although not necessarily in the focus of being a foundation for theologizing. The check on such teaching should be only in terms of professional competence, not in terms of some institution's orthodoxy. It might be hoped that both believers and nonbelievers would find such courses helpful. At Oxford University, it was said that "for believers the present performance of the faculty of Theology is not constructive enough, while for unbelievers it is not open and relevant enough."[18]

18. David Jenkins, "Oxford—The Anglican Position," in John Coulson, ed., *Theology and the University* (Baltimore: Helicon Press, 1964), p. 152.

Bernard Meland describes an approach in philosophy of religion that applies also to "doing theology." He writes, "I am trying to point a way between a purely objective procedure and an overburdened subjective concern with knowledge, realizing that a serious loss of perspective follows when the personal equation intrudes too zealously."[19] This means taking seriously the "appreciative response," seeing it in action in the human experiences which may be recounted. This is the note of elemental religion, as seen at a high level in some of the psalms. This principle of selection could be applied to primitive religion, to Medieval Christianity, to great personalities, and to the current scene. With this beginning, Meland takes his students through relevant literature and on to the existential issues of today's world, using art and poetry and music as well as theological works. Such an approach, Meland believes, gives philosophy of religion a sense of function, moves it out of a negative atmosphere, accepts the modern secular mentality at the start, and makes such study restorative. Chiefly, though, the students "are there to develop reflective powers, to inform the mind, to widen the imagination; but all this so that they may sharpen their capacity for insight, that they may be both critically and appreciatively aware of data which bear significantly upon those crucial inquiries which come to [them], either in moments of solitary reflection or in situations of extremity, or in society when one finds other human beings confronting one."[20]

When philosophy of religion or theology is taught in the way that Meland describes, the student is on the way to "doing theology." Meland is quite clear that he is talking of theology that operates within "the human level of meaning," and this may be a severe limitation for some. It is one thing to insist that theologi-

19. Meland, *Higher Education and the Human Spirit*, pp. 82–83.
20. Meland, *Higher Education and the Human Spirit*, p. 108.

cal meanings carry one beyond human limitations (as do most of the sciences) and another to insist that theology relies on other than human propositions or tools in order to accomplish its goals. Some theologies, if seen in this latter way, could very well appear in a course in the history of Christian thought or even in a course in contemporary theology, to be looked at with the tools and attitudes proper to humanistic learning. One can learn that the doctrines promulgated are not considered open to human enquiry, that authority may not be questioned, or that this is a command from on high. Such claims are frequently found among some of the sects and occasionally among the major theologians of some traditions—Christian and otherwise. But normally, this understanding is not "doing theology" as far as one learns to use the tools proper to a university setting.

In the United States today, most of the research and creative thinking in the field of religion have occurred in the theological seminaries and private universities and colleges. This has been so primarily because there was no home for the professionally trained religious scholar in the universities. But a new day has dawned. The resources for research and creative scholarship are gravitating toward the graduate departments of religious studies in the great state universities. Already, some of the best research is occurring in such institutions. This will not eliminate research in the seminaries but will provide healthy competition. It also means that competent undergraduates and graduate students will be participating in such research and scholarly activities. The geographical movement of the seminaries into university communities is partly a recognition of this development. Furthermore, the free university may have fewer restrictions on its research than a denominational seminary.

Of course, this movement toward the university community is also a recognition that the church cannot live apart from the world. "Academic theology," says Howard E. Root, "has lived on its own fat."[21] There is a whole new world to be explored by theologians in a worldly setting, and out of it may come a bolder natural theology that has a proper place for the Christian revelation. This is the kind of thinking one finds in books by John Cobb, Schubert Ogden, David Griffin, and Charles Hartshorne,[22] in which metaphysics regains its place in theological reconstruction.

Theology is taught out of situations for dialogue. Such dialogue can be between those representing various viable theological positions or between those in theology and those in other disciplines. But for such dialogue to be effective, certain conditions must obtain. First, dialogue is not achieved when there is an interchange of ignorance. Herman Wornom suggests that participants must be advocates of the position they defend, but others would claim that good teachers can represent various positions with empathy and understanding.[23] Second, the curriculum must provide enough religious knowledge to make dialogue fruitful. The basic courses in today's universities usually provide this. Third, there needs to be some common basis of agreement about epistemology, so that what counts for knowledge can be discussed. Sometimes this is a question of what "language game" is to be used, for among theologies one finds language used in different ways.[24] Fourth, there must be freedom

---

21. Howard E. Root, in Alec Vidler, ed., *Soundings* (Cambridge: At the University Press, 1962), p. 19.
22. John Cobb, *A Christian Natural Theology* (Philadelphia: Westminster Press, 1965); Schubert Ogden, *The Reality of God* (New York: Harper & Row, 1966), Charles Hartshorne, *A Natural Theology for Our Time* (LaSalle, Ill.: Open Court, 1967); David R. Griffin, *God, Power and Evil* (Philadelphia: Westminster Press, 1976); Randolph C. Miller, *The American Spirit in Theology* (Philadelphia: Pilgrim Press, 1974).
23. Herman E. Wornom, "Critical Issues," *Religious Education* LIV (March–April 1959), pp. 99–101.
24. G.E. Hutchinson, "Religion and the Natural Sciences," in Erich A. Walter, ed., *Religion and the State University* (Ann Arbor: The University of Michi-

to explore ideas. Since this is basic to the university, one would hardly think that this requirement needs mentioning; but it is a fact that many state universities have not permitted free discussion of religious issues.

Such dialogue should continue between theology and other disciplines. This could be done strictly on a comparison of disciplines dealing with theological questions, or it might involve the ways in which leaders in various disciplines approach crucial issues in politics, social ethics, race relations, community living, medicine, technology, or church life. This is not a question of making theological pronouncements about the other disciplines, although this also is within the province of theology, but of assisting the theologian in making theology more relevant and communicable in the modern world. [25]

The objections to the approaches suggested are not likely to come from the academic community, except among those who are avowed secularists, or from the religious community, except for extreme conservatives among Catholics, Protestants, and Jews. Because "religious studies must be liberal and open, seeking to understand as a part of the community of learning rather than the community of faith," [26] the universities will not be doing the jobs of churches and synagogues and will offend those who are not open to the humanistic study of religion and theology. Most approaches to religious studies will satisfy neither the religious

gan Press, 1958), pp. 170–171. See John A. Hutchison, "Language Analysis and Theology: Present and Future," *Journal of the American Academy of Religion*, XXXV (December 1967), 323–336; See Randolph C. Miller, *The Language Gap and God* (Philadelphia: Pilgrim Press, 1970).

25. See Philip Scharper, "The Relevance of Theology to the University," in Katharine T. Hargrove, ed., *On the Other Side* (Englewood Cliffs, N.J.: Prentice-Hall, 1967), pp. 12–13.

26. Robert A. Spivey, "Modest Messiahs: The Study of Religion in State Universities," *Religious Education* LXIII (January–February 1968), p. 12.

conservative nor the nontheist, and this is the risk that must be taken because religion is properly an academic subject within the community of learning.

THE PROTESTANT DIVINITY SCHOOL

Traditionally, the Protestant divinity school has conceived its purpose as training of men and women for the parish ministry, with little concern for other possible ministries or for the work of women and men in Christian service. Within this framework, theology was a major subject of academic study, but this study was oriented to a denominational tradition and to an acceptable point of view. Some competent theologians were on seminary faculties, but many professors taught theology as something received from the tradition.

Today, all this has changed. The seminaries are not sure of their purpose; the vocations for which men and women are being trained are not clear-cut; curricula are under radical revision; clusters of theological schools, both Protestant and Roman Catholic, are being located near major universities.

The students entering these seminaries are not sure of why they are there. Some of them disavow the parish ministry but have romantic ideas about other forms of ministry; they are uncertain about the nature and function of the church; they are doubtful about the truth of many theological statements; and yet they are attending seminaries in increasing numbers in order to find out what it is all about. Not all of these students are carefully selected, however, and often they are incapable of work at the graduate level which seminaries claim for their post-B.A. degree (B.D. or M. Div.).[27]

In such an avowedly confused situation, seminaries are at-

27. See Nathan M. Pusey and Charles L. Taylor, *Ministry for Tomorrow* (New York: Seabury, 1967), p. 71.

tempting to rethink their purpose and to restructure their curricula and organizations, even moving into new geographical areas or considering mergers. Although we cannot deal in any detail with such complex situations that vary from one institution to another, we need to keep them in mind as we look at the emerging sense of purpose and the place of theology in the life of a Protestant divinity school.

At the academic level, the purpose of a divinity school has been described as educating men and women in theological thinking, which includes "development of the student's awareness of the relationships between theological conceptions and the historical experience of the community, its present life, and its hopes and thrusts into the future." Essential to "education in theological thinking" is "practical contact with the changing world."[28] The theological school is the "intellectual center of the Church's life, . . . a community of students in communication with one another, with the common subjects or objects studied, and with companions of the past and present in like communication with the objects."[29]

It also has as its purpose education for service in and to the church and to people, including the professional and ordained ministry but also the lay ministry. It is vocational and professional, as well as academic and graduate, training in religion. It lacks the secular neutrality of a state university, although it seeks the same degree of objectivity and scholarly competence.

Because it is in the service of the church, a divinity school, even if part of a university, has as part of its function concern with commitment of its students. It aims at what is called *formation* of its students for their work of ministry. This is a point at which Protestants can learn much from Roman Catholic practice. There is a community of committed faculty, a life in some

28. *Theological Education* IV (Spring 1968), pp. 675–676.
29. H. Richard Niebuhr, *The Purpose of the Church and Its Ministry* (New York: Harper & Row, 1956), p. 117.

kind of Christian community including worship and fellowship, and a sense that this is the church in action, but often this has led to withdrawal from the secular world and therefore from concern for the needs of humanity.

This points to the seminary's need of the university at two levels. First, the recent development of religious studies at the university level leads to the expectation that students will come to the divinity school with better preparation in religion at the undergraduate level, some with background in comparative religions and the relation of religion to culture, some with increasing expertise in doing theology, some with a broad outlook on the secular scene, some with a great intellectual interest in religion but with no commitment except for academic excellence, and some already capable of dialogue between theology and secular disciplines. Second, when a theological school is related to a university, the university is a resource for theological education. Students may take many of the courses needed to make up deficiencies in any subject including religion, they may take secular subjects that are needed for a broad training for their particular ministries, and they may use the resources of university life and library for greater breadth and depth of learning. Furthermore, the university faculty may become agents of dialogue with the divinity faculty. When there is a cluster of seminaries in the vicinity, such dialogue may cross various denominational and faith lines.

In our discussion of doing theology at the university level, we dealt with the appreciative consciousness. It is expected, in a theological school, that personal involvement will exist to an unusual degree, even when there is confusion about beliefs and vocational goals. H. Richard Niebuhr suggests that such "study is hazardous; the involvement may become so personal and emotional that intellectual activity ceases and the work of abstraction, comparison, and criticism stops."[30]

30. Niebuhr, *Purpose of the Church and Its Ministry*, p. 118.

If in the university there is the risk of commitment in an academically neutral community, in the divinity school such commitment is expected or hoped for as part of the process. Not only what goes on in the classroom but the support of the community impels the student in this direction, often to the accompaniment of indoctrination rather than doing theology.

Granted the differences in environment and commitment, I cannot see that the purpose in teaching one to do theology in the seminary is different from what it is in the university. One learns to reflect theologically on the meaning of experience, dealing with the ultimate issues of life in all of its forms. Theology includes the study of "God and [humanity]-before-God in their interrelation," including reflection on the life of the church and the world.[31]

Seminaries have not done a good job of helping students to think theologically, even when they have filled them with theological systems and ideas. Charles Feilding writes, "I have persisted . . . in asking how theology is learned, how the faith of the communities of Christians in past history is learned today, how it is apprehended as something with which present Christian faith and life is continuous and by which it may be illuminated and criticized, and how that faith may illuminate our own time and become the ground for living the Christian faith now. I have found it difficult and often impossible to find articulate replies to questions of this kind."[32]

Students today, we are told, want to start with basic questions. They are moved by the liberation theologies, by the radical and secular theologies and moralities that are popularized, by the relevance of some of the ideas they have accumulated in university life, and some of them are turning back to conservative evangelical traditional thinking, but all are dissatisfied with the outmoded methods and approaches of most theological systems.

31. Niebuhr, *Purpose of the Church and Its Ministry*, p. 113.
32. Charles Feilding, "Education for Ministry" in *Theological Education* III (Autumn 1966), p. 9.

If we are going to reflect theologically upon the current scene, we may need historical knowledge for perspective but we need new methodologies in order to relate the Christian interpretation of reality to daily life. Feilding suggests that the theology which comes alive for many students is that taught through clinical training or field education, but that this is often a theology different from what is taught in a theology class.[33] A theology that is the private property of theologians and clergy is not likely to become a functioning part of ministry among lay people. This suggests that theology needs a pastoral orientation, with communication to lay people, both verbally and through ministry, as basic. This may involve a new kind of scholarship and research every bit as demanding as the mastery of abstruse and abstract ideas. Theology must be functional without losing its academic respectability. This is what "doing theology" or "thinking theologically" really means.

To some extent, this marks off seminary theological teaching from both the undergraduate and the graduate programs in the university. Except for the students who are continuing beyond seminary into a graduate program, most of the students need to learn how to do theology within the Christian community, with an emphasis on the functional aspect, as the minister becomes a teacher of teachers.

DOING THEOLOGY IN A DIVINITY SCHOOL

If theology is no longer the queen of the sciences, it is still the chief topic in a theological education. No matter what the subject taught, that subject's primary value in a theological school is that it contributes to doing theology. This focus is primary, for all that the students learn is for the purpose of assisting them to reflect theologically on the meanings of all aspects of life and to

33. Feilding, "Education for Ministry," pp. 30–31.

act on these reflections in terms of ethical decisions and obedience to their Christian consciences, which may be stated best under the model of "the will of God."

To do this adequately requires some degree of unity of purpose on the part of the faculty, so that they are agreed on what they are trying to do. Theologizing underlies every subject and every subject contributes to the process of theologizing. The school is dealing with "the truth about God in relation to persons" at every level of learning activity.

Such agreement as to purpose does not entail agreement on the results of theologizing or even on the methods. The chaos in the field of theology today, which many consider to be a healthy situation, means that there is an openness as to both methodology and subject matter that promises new insights and degrees of commitment.

Our concern in this chapter, however, is with theology as a discipline. We may recognize that other elements in the curriculum are intimately concerned with theologizing, but we are concerned primarily with doing theology. Much of this endeavor will be identical with what goes on in the university at both the undergraduate and graduate level, but in the theological seminary other approaches and other claims may be recognized and emphasized.

In the secular approach of the university, most theology will be examined in terms of natural theology or philosophical theology. In the seminary it is possible to start with the claim of revelation as something distinctly other than natural theology, as in the thought of Karl Barth. In the university, Barth's position may be presented and examined, but in the seminary his theology may be presented as conviction or at least shared as such by the students. The freedom of the university may permit acceptance of Barth's position, but in the seminary it may be presented by an advocate without considering the philosophical or metaphysical conditions.

In the seminary, also, where there is genuine academic freedom, the students and teachers are free to reject any specific theological system. The primary goal is not indoctrination, even in a seminary closely controlled by a confessional denomination. For the seminary as for the university, we cannot escape the fact that theology must operate in the public domain. On the other hand, both institutions need to recognize the validity of the use of language of belief even when there may be no evidence of verification on humanistic grounds. It may be that involvement is essential to getting at the meaning of a theology, although, as we have said, there can be involvement without commitment. In a survey course, one may become involved in a number of theologies without being committed to any of them, just as one may become involved in the meanings of other religions without sacrificing one's Christian commitment. But, in the seminary, it is expected that the result of doing theology will be that students not only think straight but also illuminate their commitments.

For many in the seminaries, the beginning point of such theological involvement may be in terms of Christology. The focus of much theology today is Christology; the response to questions about belief in God has been that we must start with Jesus Christ. Pusey and Taylor state this clearly: "Christ is the message, contemporary, basic, urgent, underlying all theological endeavor."[34] But others will ask if this can be so unless one already believes in God. Does Christology precede or follow belief in God? Does the special revelation of God in Christ have priority over the revelation of God in the experience of humankind? As students deal with such questions, they begin to develop their own methodologies in terms of perspectives that come from their prior ways of examining reality.

For others, the beginning point for theological reflection may be the current doubts of what has been called radical theology.

34. Pusey and Taylor, *Ministry for Tomorrow,* p. 25.

This requires what has been called "apologetics," a consideration of the evidence for Christian belief. But such an approach will be entirely different from traditional apologetics. One approach is through language study, as described by Dallas High: "When *looking at and seeing* language at work (not idling), it is the case clearly that we do not give 'reasons' in quite ordinary ways for the beliefs we 'own' and 'own up to' including religious (creedal and doctrinal) beliefs. Moreover, performing an act of believing or holding a belief implies that we will not entertain such utterances, at least seriously, unless we are also willing to 'back them up,' 'give reasons,' 'justification,' or 'grounds' if asked or pressed, or if we think about it."[35] When one says, "I believe," there are involvement and commitment and a willingness to stand back of the statement or proposition. One anchors one's beliefs in experience, history, authority, or scripture, and this is open to the examination of others.[36] What one is working for is not agreement about what is true or false but agreement in the language one uses which points to a form of life. This style of life is illustrated by the theology one holds, and often one's theology is commended more by a style of living than by a logical system.

Competence in doing theology relies on two kinds of internal discipline, the historical and the comparative. Both deal with the sources of faith, but from different perspectives. The history of Christian thought needs a broad base in the development of the culture and the church. Within this framework, students can learn both how theology was done in those days and what the results were. There is as much to learn, for example, from Augustine's or Anselm's methodology as from their conclusions, and in some cases the methodology may be borrowed and different con-

35. Dallas High, *Language, Persons, and Belief* (New York: Oxford University Press, 1967), p. 207.
36. See High, *Language, Persons and Belief*, pp. 210–211. See also Randolph C. Miller, *This We Can Believe* (New York: Hawthorn-Seabury, 1976), ch. 1 and 2.

clusions be reached. Historical continuity and discontinuity in the development of method and doctrine need to be understood. Theologians from the same or different periods can be compared. The dynamics of theological conflicts, as exhibited in the early councils, the Reformation, the modernist-fundamentalist controvery, and other conflicts will be helpful.

The comparative study of theology can be looked at historically but will be more fruitful when concerned with the live options in today's world. Theological opinions are changing rapidly, and in some cases there have been revivals of positions prematurely pronounced dead. The negative criticisms of the more radical theologians, for example, have turned some thinkers back to the empirical theological methods of the 1920s and 1930s. The new hermeneutics may be a revival of some earlier kinds of biblical study with new twists. The developments in linguistic philosophy, at first detrimental to theological study, have become an invaluable tool in the hands of such men as Ian T. Ramsey and Dallas High. As background for the current scene, one could take the theologians from Schleiermacher down to the present and with a selection from such lists and the use of the original writings of these theologians, a comparative approach to methodology and belief could lead to exercises in doing theology.

Besides the use of historical and comparative approaches to theological thinking, there are also the dogmatic and the systematic. In some vocabularies, these two approaches either overlap or are identical, but if dogmatics is the presentation in a systematic way of a given theology of the church, we can consider systematic theology as the building of a system of theological thinking. When one is a member of a denomination with a distinctive theological heritage, this can be learned through a study of dogmatic theology. Granting that there are variations in dogmatic emphasis, Catholic, Eastern Orthodox, and Lutheran theologies are more suitable for dogmatic presentation that those of the free churches or Anglicanism.

Most theologians today would not claim to be explicating the official doctrine of the church. They have their own systems of theology. The study of any of these theologians, especially when one gets inside the point of view and grasps the methodology, is an invaluable discipline as background for doing one's own theology. But there is the danger that such theologizing will be of the "hot house" brand if it is purely an intellectual exercise. Charles Feilding has warned us that theology comes alive for many students within some kind of practical situation, and that this theology may have no relation with what is taught in the more traditional classroom approach. This suggests that in the systematic theology classroom there should be concern with a methodology that takes account constantly of the world of daily living, that theologizing be a continuing process in relation to all that happens to the student in the seminary and outside, and that this kind of theologizing be recognized as the chief purpose of the divinity school. For unless theology provides an interpretation of the meaning of the world, can operate in the public domain, and can do this for lay people as well as for technically trained leaders, it will be sterile and deserve the opprobrium from which it often suffers.

Theology, then, is neither an intellectual nor a practical exercise but a combination of the two. The distinction between theology as content and practical theology as found in many seminaries is a false one and guarantees sterility, irrelevance, or shallowness. With all the varieties of ministry now open to seminary graduates, the theological school must assist them to reflect theologically on what is involved in a broad field of activity. In religious education, for example, theology provides perspective and guidance, but in turn the findings of educators *as educators* may modify the theological approach. There is here a kind of dialogue between disciplines and even between interdisciplinary fields that provides the possibility of some kind of unity in one's approach to ministry.

This leads to a final point: the need for dialogue. First, there needs to be opportunity for dialogue between representatives of various theological traditions. In the larger seminaries, this is possible, and in the move toward clusters of seminaries even greater varieties of dialogue may develop. In the isolated small seminary, however, the one professor of theology may be found talking to himself or herself unless he or she is enough of a scholar to bring many possible positions into the classroom through books and has the ability to make objective and yet impassioned presentations of others' positions—obviously a mark of a great teacher not often found in a small seminary. Those seminaries near colleges and universities have access to theologians on other faculties. All seminaries can provide the setting for dialogue among students, either in classes or in nonclassroom activities.

Second, there needs to be dialogue between representatives of all the disciplines on the faculty. All teachers in theological schools are dealing with theology in their own way, and their subjects contribute to the process of theologizing. Multiple teaching teams, conceived in terms of genuine interchange of ideas, especially with small classes in which students can participate in this discussion, may be especially illuminating. Students may be encouraged to meet informally with faculty and outside guests to discuss their own choices of issues. The problem is both to overcome the pigeon-hole effect of the average curriculum and to achieve an overall view of what it means to do theology against the background of the complex riches of the curriculum.

Third, there needs to be dialogue between theology and the world. This involves dialogue between the theological school and the university, between theology and secular disciplines. The Niebuhr, Williams, Gustafson study puts it this way: "If the Christian faith must enter a dialogue with contemporary thought and culture, a student has not been introduced to the core of theological education until he [or she] has entered into this conversation between Christian thought and the many disci-

plines which are concerned with [humanity] and [its] world."[37]
One cannot assume that this has happened in the student's previous training. One cannot simply hope that it might happen. It
needs to be built into the curriculum. Here again the cluster of
divinity schools around a university suggests a way out. When
students are encouraged to take courses with a purely secular
orientation, the seminary can provide periods of theological reflection on what has been learned. The student needs many
secular subjects, including psychology, sociology, and philosophy
as a basis for ministry, but these are not adequate resources until
they are part of one as a theological person.

Some of the most interesting experiments of the seminaries are
in terms of knowing the world. Intern years are more likely than
before to be in secular situations. Students are encouraged to
participate in summer-in-industry programs. It is suggested by
some groups that students should spend a year between college or
university and seminary in some kind of secular occupation. Students are being offered, for one year of their training, housing in
inner-city situations, where their field education and classroom
work are centered. It has been suggested that such centers of
training for ministry be mandatory, with focus on a life cycle
ministry, institutions, business and industry, political process,
crisis (civil rights, poverty, war), and the arts.

We have talked about clusters of seminaries. One purpose of
such clusters is the establishment of ecumenical dialogue, which
may be between various brands of Protestants, between Catholics
and Protestants, or between Christians and Jews. Already there
are clusters of these kinds, providing rich resources for dialogue
and for cooperative education. The interdenominational seminaries, especially when university related, already have these
resources, but they need much greater exploitation. The isolated

37. H. Richard Niebuhr, Daniel Day Williams, James M. Gustafson, *The
Advancement of Theological Education* (New York: Harper & Row, 1957), p. 87.

divinity school could consider adding a faculty member of another faith (although this reflects the "zoo" approach) to teach within the existing framework or seek an expert on the other faith as one does in presenting the comparative study of religions.

CONCLUSION

Theology, when properly conceived as doing theology, has its proper place both within the university curriculum and that of the theological school. The foci of the institutions differ, however, for the university is a secular institution in which religion and theology have proper academic standings and the seminary has an overriding theological purpose for education in theological thinking. The university accepts commitment among students and professors but does not expect increasing or new commitments from the academic approach, although the involvement necessary for any appreciation of religious reality and doing theology involves always the risk of commitment. The theological school is supposedly a community of the committed, although increasingly this is not so, and works for fuller, stronger, and sometimes different commitments. The university is concerned with the welfare of its students and hopes for the development of an overall view of the meaning of life, but does not think of this in terms of Christian faith. The divinity school is concerned with the formation of its students for Christian ministry, lay or ordained, in its many varieties and new developments. Everything that happens in the theological school is for the development of theological reflection about all the dimensions of the world in which we live. Theology is the dominant interest, and all other subjects have value primarily as they feed the process of doing theology.

There is continuity between theology as taught in the university and seminary. Doing theology involves methodology and reflection, no matter what the environment may be. Furthermore, the sources are the same in both instances. In many cases, the syllabus for a course in the university at either the undergraduate or graduate level could conceivably be the same as in the seminary. The difference could come at the level of attitudes toward revelation in a secular university, or in the possibility of teaching dogmatic theology as a single option, or in the expectation or requirement of commitment to the object of study.

The development of religious studies in the university frees the seminaries to do more advanced work with its incoming students, although the university courses are conceived in humanistic and not in professional or preprofessional terms. The university is concerned primarily with religion, including theology, as a proper academic discipline for all who elect such subjects for any reasons whatever. Such endeavors may or may not provide intelligent lay people for the churches or seminaries. What will result is a sector of the public that is not religiously illiterate, and this in itself justifies the efforts of the university. Through its graduate programs, some teachers for seminaries and universities will be developed, but again this is for the enrichment of the teaching profession as such, not for the good of the church or seminary as a primary objective. But the side effects, in terms of commitment and professional competence, may prove in the long run to be as valuable as the achievement of the primary goal.

16

The Crystal Ball

Any process theologian knows that the future is open and that the creativity which makes life a flow of becoming and perishing moves toward emerging novelty. Anything can happen and probably will. Because identity runs through the process, it is likely that there will be continuity as well as contrast as characteristics of forthcoming events. The theory will probably change somewhat, and the practice may or may not change radically.

A theological school, writes H. Richard Niebuhr, has a "double function. On the one hand it is that place or occasion where the Church exercises its intellectual love of God and neighbor; on the other hand it is the community that serves the Church's other activities by bringing reflection and criticism to bear on worship, preaching, teaching and the care of souls."[1] This leads Niebuhr to claim that there is a *theory of practice* which applies to Christian education and other activities of the Christian community. This process breaks down when there is an inadequate theory or one that is based on an intellectualist or pragmatic treatment of theory and practice. What Niebuhr stresses is "the conviction that reflection and criticism form an indispensable element in all human activity, not least in the activities of the Church, but that such reflection cannot be independent of other activities, such as worship, proclamation, healing, et cetera. Reflection is never the first action, though in personal and com-

1. H. Richard Niebuhr, *The Purpose of the Church and Its Ministry* (New York: Harper & Row, 1956), p. 110.

274

munal life we can never go back to a moment in which action
has been unmodified by reflection. . . . Reflection precedes, accompanies, and follows action but this does not make it the
source or end of action."[2]

Behind such theory is experience, with the data selected on
the basis of previous theory. One does not learn by doing, as
Niebuhr reminds us, but "we do not learn the meaning of deeds
without doing."[3] There is a constant interplay between theory
and practice, and there are times for the intellect to play with
new ideas and abstractions before it returns to the testing ground
of experience. So we learn *now* what comes to us from the past
and present, plus our current theory, plus the anticipation of the
future.

THE PAST

Christian education has been viewed with critical eyes for
many years. Horace Bushnell in 1847 was aware that much that
is called religious education made "the subject odious, and that,
as nearly as we can discover, in exact proportion to the amount
of religious teaching received." Some parents may be doing an
excellent job of nurturing their children in the faith, but they
fear what may happen in the churches, which may be "rent by
divisions, burnt up by fanaticism, frozen by the chill of a worldly
spirit, petrified in a rigid and dead orthodoxy."[4] In Sunday
school, Bushnell wrote in 1869, we find "jolly no-religion songs,
the amusing stories and droll illustrations that illustrate nothing,
the uncaring manner of memorizing, school training recitations—

2. Niebuhr, *Purpose of the Church and Its Ministry*, pp. 127–128.
3. Niebuhr, *Purpose of the Church and Its Ministry*, p. 129.
4. Horace Bushnell, *Christian Nurture* (New Haven: Yale, 1947), pp. 11,
39–40.

all these produce, when taken together, an atmosphere of general unchristlikeness."[5]

In 1903, the situation was no better. Already there were complaints that the Bible was being removed from the public schools. There was little evidence of the use of the new educational principles and methods. There was less home training of children than in Bushnell's time. Religion was becoming an isolated subject, separate from life. These undesirable changes had been going on for at least twenty-five years. The Religious Education Association was founded in 1903 to seek to reverse the trends by bringing professional expertise and up-to-date biblical scholarship to the field.

Much was hoped for. John Dewey had written in 1903 of the ways children understand at various age levels. Uniform lessons were considered obsolete. Curriculum materials were being written to match the capacity of age groups; both group-graded and closely-graded lessons were being developed on a cooperative basis. The theories of secular educators were taken seriously and applied, sometimes uncritically, to religious education. Teachers were carefully recruited, adequately trained, and sometimes paid. There was a vision in 1903 that provided hope for the future.

The developments since 1903 showed some promise. Graded curriculum became the norm for the larger mainline churches, and in many of them teachers were trained to a high level of competence. As a result, attendance at Sunday school increased and going to Sunday school became more popular. There was a slowing down of this trend in the 1940s, but it was due to a drop in the birth rate and not to a growing indifference. By the 1950s, there was a general feeling of euphoria over the wide development of study materials and the use of the best methods and

5. Horace Bushnell, *God's Thoughts Fit Bread for Children* (Boston: Noyes & Nichols, 1869), p. 24.

equipment. All of the major denominations were involved in this development of materials, and morale remained high until the 1960s.

But something had happened. In some states, the Bible had been read regularly in the schools, and this was stopped by a decision of the Supreme Court in 1963. The new idea of teaching *about* religion in public schools caught on very slowly and did not draw large numbers of students. The surge in family cooperation began to reverse itself and enthusiasm dropped. There was an increase in the number of broken and one-parent families. And the churches faced a failure of nerve, symbolized by the announcement in *Time* that God had died! The momentum was stopped, the morale dropped, confidence among parents in the capacity of the churches to teach their children and adults almost vanished. A whole generation was failing to know much about the Bible, to understand how faith works in today's world, and to care very much one way or the other. They seemed to be bored with most forms of Christianity, except for the Jesus freaks and some of the communes which represented a variety of religious claims. There was growth among the evangelical churches, who were reaching out to the world on the one hand and back to a private individualized faith on the other. Some of these conservative educational programs grew rapidly.

In late 1979, a congregation at a funeral was asked to join in the 23rd psalm, although no copies were in either the service sheet or the hymnal. Yet the large congregation recited the psalm in the King James Version. In another fifteen or twenty years, such an experience may be impossible, for many people will be ignorant of the psalm or will know it in another translation but not well enough to recite it, or will be unable to handle even the rich imagery and metaphors that have spoken to countless generations.

One other problem is faced by the educators. The churches

confront difficult economic decisions. The new materials cost money, and churches have their priorities as to where their funds will be spent. Educational materials have always been at the bottom of the totem pole, and as the economic squeeze gets tighter and the materials more expensive, there will be serious shortages of the tools for education.

A PROJECTION

If one takes seriously the charts of some sociologists, it can be shown that in the light of the recent decline of Protestant Sunday schools there will be no Sunday schools by the year 2001. The charts indicate that the decline of enrollment in parochial schools will not be quite so sharp, but there will be fewer schools. The charts also show an increase in the number of courses about religion in the public schools, although the upward movements is slight. The largest incline is in courses about religion at the universities, and at present the rate of increase is such that we might predict that most students will be religion majors by 2025 A.D!

There is evidence to counteract the charts, however, and some have concluded that we will have Protestant Sunday schools for some time to come and that there will be Catholic schools of a similar type in many parishes where the children do not attend parochial schools. There will be some drop in the number of parochial schools, especially in areas where public schools are doing a first-class job. Religion classes in high schools and universities will show increases.

The sociologists are predicting what will happen to traditional Sunday schools. But if there is a new model for religious education, all the charts will become useless. There is some ferment at this point. The old "most wasted hour of the week" is going into deserved oblivion and new, mostly homegrown, ideas are taking hold. Continuing traditional Sunday schools have been doing good jobs and they will continue; others have been woeful failures. Out of both success and failure have come new ideas about worship, interest centers, ministry to the family-as-a-unit, professionally trained teachers, and teaching to invoke insight followed by commitment rather than to transmit dogma and concepts.

Within the parochial schools, new ideas about religious education became prominent with the rise of concern with the proclamation or story of salvation (*kerygma*) rather than with propositions about faith found in a catechism. As the story became correlated with the issues of religious living in the world, teaching came alive. Moralism in the pejorative sense was not completely done away with, but the emphasis was on creative decisions in the light of genuine and live options rather than artificial cases.

Behind all such teaching was the desire for conversion or increased commitment. No church ever teaches in a completely open-ended manner, and its educational theory has been mixed with indoctrination, so that the desired result is predetermined. Many students have rebelled because their freedom to think has been abrogated. So they turned from church-sponsored education, and, at the university level, at least, flocked to courses about religion where they believed that the teacher had no axe to grind. Feeling free to compare live options either within the Christian communions or between Christianity and other competitors, they acted as autonomous learners.

This has left professional religious educators in an ambiguous position. They are in no position to influence very much of what goes on in a secular situation, whether public school or university. The professionals are criticized by traditionalists in parochial schools or CCD, who think that tinkering with *kerygma* has undercut sound catechetical methods. Even when they seek out new approaches, they are caught with the need to indoctrinate rather than leave students free to choose between live options. This question is not new, however, for it is the question of whether religious education has ever been educational.[6]

Robert W. Lynn and Elliott Wright have demonstrated that the Protestant Sunday school has been healthy only when it was dominated by a strong evangelical motive. The purpose was to "make Christians" out of all learners, no matter what techniques were needed to bring it about. Measurement of success was in terms of conversions, confirmations, declarations of faith, or believers' baptisms. A large confirmation class meant a good Sunday school. No matter that within three to five years almost all of the confirmands had vanished; no matter that there was no correlation between winning a prize for memorizing the most Bible verses and Christian behavior; no matter that such Sunday schools never looked beyond the private sphere to social conditions of the neighborhood and beyond.[7] The parochial school likewise, especially when the emphasis was on the catechism and confirmation, measured its success in numbers. The stress was on performance rather than motivation. Evangelism was the means to catch believers.

Because of this emphasis on evangelism, transmission of tradition, and indoctrination in the Sunday school movement, professional religious educators were suspect because they were concerned with helping learners to solve problems and to think straight about the Christian faith. This threatened not only the tradition-oriented teachers but also the hierarchy with its stress on numbers. The professional educators want students to learn to think against the background of evidence, but this does not lead

6. See Charles Melchert, "Does the Church Really Want Religious Education?" in John H. Westerhoff III, ed., *Who Are We?* (Birmingham: Religious Education Press, 1978), pp. 250–263. Reprinted from *Religious Education*, LXIX, No. 1 (January–February 1974), pp. 12–22.

7. See Robert W. Lynn and Elliott Wright, *The Big Little School* (Birmingham:

to guaranteed results. The educators want teachers to be imaginative and to resort to poetic imagery, so that there might be evoked in the pupils new insights or disclosures about God, but because no one can control such disclosures the risk seems too great. The educators want students to be initiated into a value-oriented community by their own free will, but students cannot be trusted to use the insights of the New Testament to support the status quo in church or society. The educators, encouraged by Vatican II and by the freedom in the Protestant churches, want to open up the teaching of the Bible and the ways of worship, but the Bible does not always ratify the teachers' or the congregations' prejudices, and worship opens up all kinds of possibilities, including the use of new forms.[8]

A key problem facing us today is the influence on the church of professional educators and theologians with the views just outlined. Of course, the educators themselves are divided. They do not agree on the right age for teaching portions of the Bible, for confirmation, for exposure to theological concepts, or on the right methods for effective teaching. But there are many professional religious educators who are defining education in religion to include freedom of choice, the development of intelligibility in terms of age-level capacities, and of selecting options within or beyond the tradition of a given set of doctrines. The present, then, is one of facing questions, with some significant and creative ideas about religious education floating around and waiting to be incorporated into a philosophy of education. There are confusion and hope, becoming and perishing, the emergence of novel ideas in the midst of fixed procedures, the use of experiment and creativity in tension with recognition of the values of tradition.

FRUITFUL DEVELOPMENTS

The most effective way of handling the economic squeeze is to act ecumenically. Some denominations are cooperating in "joint educational development" (JED) and are producing "shared approaches" materials. These are supposed to meet the needs of all varieties and sizes of churches and their educational projects at a cost that is within reason. These materials are not closely graded because most Protestant Sunday schools are now so small that they need more flexible materials. As a result, the materials are group-graded for smaller operations, which is a far cry from the hopes of the Religious Education Association in 1903 or from the achievements of the 1930s and 1950s.

This ecumenical thrust is important, however, even if it emerges from fiscal weakness. Insofar as the new materials are useful in various kinds of churches, there will be a common corpus of subject matter to be considered by the students. Perhaps we can hope that a group in the future can say the 23rd Psalm together in some translation. Furthermore, the use of a common lectionary in many denominations will help relate the lessons read in worship to the consideration of the Bible in classes. This means that there is an important body of knowledge, ecumenically arrived at, which will be available to all students in the major cooperating denominations. There is danger, however, especially in the series cooperating on the Bible, that standardized passages will be used without regard to age group capacities, and thus we will be back in the pre-1900 stage of uniform lessons.

There have been sufficient developments in Catholic curriculum materials to raise the hope that these materials may be used ecumenically. Already some Protestant educational programs are making full use of Catholic materials of all kinds, including not only written lessons but audio-visual sources as well. This may lead to further ecumenical interchange. At least it raises the sights of those responsible for creating and using the materials.

THE FAMILY

Any consideration of the future of Christian education must take account of the changes in family life. Since the time of Horace Bushnell we have known that the family plays a crucial role in the religious development of children. What happens in the first three years of a child's life is a determining factor for future religious development. Yet families are fractured in many ways; the mother is no longer necessarily the mothering one, and a male parent may not be available. This does not in any way invalidate Bushnell's observation; it just makes it more difficult to achieve what is essential for the child's religious growth. It may be that the most important function of a local congregation where there are working mothers is to provide for child care in which the emphasis will be on the role of the mothering one, perhaps a parenting type teacher for each three or four children. The selection of such teachers will be crucial for the success of such a program.

Other families achieve something approaching the ideal. The two-parent family, with proper sharing by mother and father, and sometimes a one-parent family, can provide the atmosphere in which grace dwells, where the child grows up as a Christian, where the family worships together in a church that recognizes the child as a person with rights, status, privilege, and duties. There are such families and parishes, and when they function effectively the chances are that Christian education will take place, leading in time to a decision for Christ.

BEYOND THE SUNDAY SCHOOL

The future, however, does not depend on the school model. One weakness of the Sunday school has been its subservience to the secular school model. Perhaps we need to de-school the Sunday school. Then the emphasis will not be exclusively on knowledge and concepts and right doctrine, but on those relationships by which one grows in faith and understanding toward an attitude of trust in God. The focus may turn to affective rather than cognitive learning, to attitudes of loyalty and trust rather than credal statements, although a sound theology must necessarily stand behind the grace-faith relationship. This approach can lead to many new experiments, such as intergenerational learning, informal activities, use of drama and music, and a breaking away from fixed curriculum material.

WORSHIP

Throughout this book there has been an emphasis on worship both as an end in religious living and also as an essential part of the educational experience of church members. It may be that worship is the most significant factor in sound Christian education. The continuance of the church in Russia, where overt teaching has been outlawed, suggests the importance of worship. If religion is primarily a vision of the rightness of things, of the process by which we are assisted in achieving a creative relationship with God, then the response to that vision is worship. We have repeated several times that Whitehead has said that "the power of God is the worship he inspires,"[9] and through worship children and adults together come into the presence of God, who, in Christ, is reconciling the world to the divine.

9. *Science and the Modern World,* Mentor ed., p. 192.

TECHNICAL ADVANCES

In the future we will be assisted by the many technical advances that have been or are being perfected. We in the churches are slowly learning ways of using audio-visual tools so that they will be more than entertainment for students or crutches for incompetent teachers. As far back as 1946, Paul H. Vieth was perfecting the use of the tools then available for creating interpersonal relations in which education could take place.[10] The kind of education issuing from audio-visuals that function to create interpersonal relations includes reflection, straight thinking, discrimination between right and wrong, the move toward new insights, and acceptance of new commitments. Any kind of information can be fed into the mind so that such processes of thinking are assisted and enriched. Good teachers know how to utilize any source of data, including audio-visuals and other new technical developments.

Computers are coming into the picture. They are already available in secular education, but for the present few churches think they can afford them. They are primarily helpful in providing the data for reflection, but they also assist in checking knowledge, analyzing data and concepts, reviewing the entire learning process, and proposing new fields for exploration. They are expensive and unless used to their full capacity the cost becomes prohibitive; the result is that cooperation, probably with secular organizations which can use them during the week, is mandatory. Also, it takes skill to program computers, and there is a question whether amateurs will acquire such skills.

By 1977, nine Roman Catholic dioceses were operating huge television systems, and some were tied in with satellite transmission. There is a claim that by proper use of TV we can provide

10. See William L. Rogers and Paul H. Vieth, *Visual Aids in the Church* (Philadelphia: United Church Press, 1946).

the expertise that is nationally available and locally limited, thus making that expertise come alive for individuals and small groups in any location. By this kind of management of human resources, it will be possible to bring the church's educational and spiritual formation skills to larger numbers while they still remain in their small groups for discussion afterwards. When to such programs are added the possibilities of videotape and even instant replay, it can be seen what possibilities there are for reinforcement in learning. With the proper theory for bringing about personal involvement, we can use these tools for the nurture of human beings in the Christian faith.[11]

LANGUAGE

About the time that Horace Bushnell was struggling with *Christian Nurture*, he was working on the problem of language. He was concerned that too much theology was descriptive, exact, literal, and wrong. Religious language, he said, was metaphorical, a second stage beyond words used for the physical world. When the word "wind" is taken metaphorically, we can speak of "spirit." When we think of "reaching forth," we can begin to understand what "hope" is. When we speak of "turning in our bonds" for their profit earned, we can think of "redemption." There is, then, an analogical connection between physically based and spiritually pointing words, so that our more poetic, metaphorical, and imaginative uses of language do not get out of control. As we deal with these analogical uses, we come to a revelation of God as that intelligence which guarantees the connection. The gospel is a gift to the imagination.

In this way, we can move toward the center of Christian faith,

11. See Michael J. Dempsey, "New Grounds in the Catholic Educational System," and Frances Forde Plude, "New Networks: Sharing Resources through TV and Technology," *Religious Education* LXXXIII (January–February 1978), pp. 42–51, 51–59.

which is trust in Christ, who "was called a door to be entered, a bread from heaven to be fed upon, a water of life to quench the thirst, life, way, shepherd, healer, teacher, master, king, and rock."[12] There are many more such metaphors, and even the parables may be considered drawn-out metaphors. As we help children and adults grow in faith, we point to the multiplicity of forms and images, presenting opposite sides, partial truths, and conflicting images, a rich and riotous mixture of words without regard to consistency, finding in the Bible no system of thought but a variety of ways of touching human souls. Communication in this sense is the use of words so that the student will respond to the image or form evoked by such disclosures. We use many words, many images, many creeds in order that there might be a moment of discernment or disclosure. The event of revelation is so rich that no selection of words is adequate.

When we look at contemporary criticisms of Christian education, with the inert ideas that bore the students, we recognize the need to get away from such oppressiveness. Bushnell was trying to get away from inane activities and abstract concepts which cannot lead to decisions and commitments that matter. The Christian education of the future, if it comes to grips with the varieties of language offered not only by Bushnell but by others since then, will be more effective both in communication of images and in the process of straight thinking.[13]

SOCIALIZATION

"Socialization," writes James Michael Lee, "is that process by and through which a person is initiated into the life meanings

12. Horace Bushnell, "Our Gospel a Gift to the Imagination," *Building Eras* (New York: Charles Scribner's Sons, 1881), p. 260. See my "God's Gift to the Imagination," *Perkins Journal* (Spring 1979), pp. 9–16.
13. See my *The Language Gap and God* (Philadelphia: Pilgrim Press, 1970), pp. 94–100.

and life patterns of interaction characterizing a particular group."[14] John Westerhoff has modified his emphasis on "intentional social-ization" because it implies doing something to someone, so he has chosen the term "enculturation."[15] Neither "socialization" nor "enculturation" is very different from the socializing process described by Ellis Nelson. One becomes a product of culture who wishes to be different from that product.[16] This indicates a degree of tension between the larger culture that stamps it-self on our personality and the nurturing process of the church that provides models, including Jesus Christ, as influences within the smaller social process which directly influences us. The socializing function of the church as a nurturing environ-ment more than an institution hinders and restricts certain func-tions of the natural person, but it also provides the fertile ground for creative personal growth and a deepening relation to God.

FAITH AND WORKS

Christian education is centered on an understanding and ap-preciation of the grace-faith relationship, on forgiveness and rec-onciliation, on redemption through the persuasive love of God in Christ, but it moves quickly beyond this to the recognition that Christians are followers of "The Way." Theologically, this was expressed a generation or so ago by the social gospel. More recently, it was illustrated by the battle for civil rights and racial equality. It has come down to the present as the fruits of libera-tion theology: black, feminine, ecological, and Third World. It is a recognition of the legitimate application of the command to

14. James Michael Lee, *The Shape of Religious Instruction* (Birmingham: Reli-gious Education Press, 1971), p. 24.
15. John H. Westerhoff III, *Will Our Children Have Faith?* (New York: Sea-bury, 1976), p. 79.
16. C. Ellis Nelson, *Where Faith Begins* (Atlanta: John Knox Press, 1967), p. 11.

love one's neighbor. It is a response to the claim of the sovereignty of God's love on earth.

Theologically, the prayer, "not my will but thine be done," is central to the response of faith to God's grace. When we get beyond the milk of elementary teaching to the strong meat of the gospel, we are involved in moral and social and political and economic responsibility for the welfare of all people. At the present time, the focus is on race relations, especially those of blacks and whites but also of various minorities, and we must not lose sight of this issue as others impinge upon us. The move from a patriarchal to a feminist theology, which will possibly move beyond that to a simply human one, should lead morally and socially to an effective understanding of male and female roles under a deity who provides the image for both. Equally demanding on our attention is the need to revise our theology of nature so that we will come to new understandings of the problems we face in terms of natural resources and energy. The church has been slow in developing an adequate understanding of ecology or even to see it as a religious issue. There is also a new theology of liberation emerging in the Third World, which is most evident in Latin American countries and among Roman Catholics. Because this theology arises within an alien culture and political system, it takes creative imagination to be able to share in the basic problems. All of this is a response to the cries of the oppressed in all cultures. The theology underlying the approach of this book, especially the first three chapters, is an attempt to meet this need.

These issues do not exhaust the possible applications of the gospel to the human situation. We need to discover the ways in which Christians respond to the problems of hunger and over-population. The simple figures are frightening as we examine the limited food supplies and the increase in human beings. What is responsible parenthood in today's world? If the problem of hunger is related to population, only a completely rethought theology of sexual relations can lead to integrity in the light of the food problem. Such questions spill over into issues such as which people should have children, abortion, and the right to die.

THE FUTURE

We come back to the crystal ball, with predictions about the future. But all the crystal ball does is to illumine some informed guesses.

(1) The Sunday school, in both Protestant and Catholic forms, will stay with us. If the downward curve of a few years ago had continued, the Sunday school would already have vanished, but other factors played their part in keeping it alive, even if in a different form. Sunday schools will be smaller, partly because of the birthrate and partly because the mainline churches have lost their hold on a segment of the population. The Catholic Sunday schools will continue to develop, especially in those areas where the parochial schools have closed. As long as the conservative mood affects Protestantism as a whole, the evangelical Sunday schools will remain large.

In some instances, there will be healthy experiments (such as described by John H. Westerhoff III in *Values for Tomorrow's Children*, Pilgrim 1970). Some will think along the lines of Ivan Illich and try to "de-school" the Sunday school, seeking for a more radical model. Others will pick up ways of teaching the oppressed in terms of helping them to understand what it means to be human under God. Many will seek new and creative teaching methods that will strive to evoke insights or disclosures rather than master a batch of material. We will find a very informal type of education, with interest groups crossing age barriers, with activities for families who will think, act, play, and pray together, with teachers being hired for limited periods to use their special skills, with social action as a focus for biblical teaching, with the use of music, art, drama, audio-visuals, and television built into the curriculum rather than as aids, and with much education going on outside the church building. There will be many new kinds of adult education on a much wider base, and in some cases the Sunday school will only register families-as-a-whole. It can be predicted that most of these things will happen somewhere. It can also be predicted that some congregations, Catholic and Protestant, will discover what kind of worship should occur when children and adults can worship together. Some of them will also learn how to correlate their worship with the curriculum goals so that one will carry over into the other and vice versa. The whole parish will be seeking to educate the whole parish.

(2) Religious educators will learn from secular educators to be more "educational." Because human beings learn in the same way under any auspices, we need to be sure that no discoveries about effective education miss our attention. An analysis of what makes an effective learning environment is helpful at this point. James Michael Lee works from a cluster of the learner, the teacher, the subject matter content, and the environment.[17] He suggests that "a facilitational environment is one which is (1) purposively planned; (2) selective; (3) rich in stimuli; (4) evocative of a total response from the learner; (5) reinforcing; and (6) warm in climate."[18] These are nontheological factors, but they could be theologically significant if they contained elements either supportive of or antithetic to the specific religious goals.

(3) Out of the ferment of Vatican II, the secular attacks on or reconstruction of religious belief, and the posttraditional thinking of the current period may come a new blooming of theology. Some of us can see this development in the thought of Teilhard de Chardin, Gregory Baum, Ewart Cousins, Eugene Fontinell, Gloria Durka, Joanmarie Smith, and Hans Küng among Catholics, and of Alfred North Whitehead, Charles Hartshorne, Bernard

17. James Michael Lee, *The Flow of Religious Instruction* (Birmingham: Religious Education Press, 1973), pp. 233–248.
18. Lee, *Flow of Religious Instruction*, p. 243.

Meland, John Cobb, Daniel Day Williams, David Griffin, Norman Pittenger, and others among Protestants. Theologians are turning to experience as a source of data and to a scientific view of the universe; they are learning from the new understanding of dynamic process in nature and in God; they are concerned with the nature of the human person and the meaning of community; they see the redemptive and transforming work of God in our midst, incarnated in Jesus Christ and let loose in the world by the power of the Holy Spirit. The new generation of students can respond to this kind of theology and make it their own.

(4) With such a background of theology and educational theory, the teaching of religion in parochial schools will undergo radical changes. Some of the security of the hothouse will be replaced by a sense of risk and a vision of reality that can be planted anew in the world of politics and social action, where the human animal moves in order to survive and to find meaning in life. The liberation theology that has been produced by both Catholics and Protestants in Latin America sees theology emerging from the experiences of being oppressed and from the revolutionary hopes that the churches pray for. Paulo Freire speaks of *The Pedagogy of the Oppressed* (New York: Seabury, 1970), and both Christians and non-Christians have responded to his teaching. I doubt if many parochial schools will use Freire's *Education for a Critical Consciousness,* but it represents the goal for this kind of teaching and learning.

(5) The movement among university students continues to be one of seeking. As long as religious courses continue to provide reasonable explanations and appreciative meanings for the events of history and of the current scene, students will flock to their courses. And where the courses are geared to the interior life without regard to the social whirl, there will be those who prefer these less disturbing courses. In spite of the general restrictions on growth of departments, university departments of religious studies are not hurting unduly.

(6) For the past two decades, outside the churches and some-

times outside of the conventional society, there have been those who search for meaning in nontraditional ways. Whether it is Zen or drugs, social action or revolutionary violence, communes or burnings, it has been a call for help without trust in the Establishment. These movements have surged and retreated, like the surf, and it is hard to cite which ones will be dominant tomorrow. Some of the more untraditional ones have begun to move toward the main stream. This is often a more social and economic movement than it is a religious one. "Perhaps," says Robert Bellah, "the major meaning of the sixties was not anything positive at all."[19] Most of the movements have fallen into decay or have become institutionalized and lost their vision. A few other movements, like the Unification Church, are surviving and are seeking to become respectable, as did the Christian Scientists and Mormons in an earlier day.

(7) At a consultation on the future of educational ministry, five of the outstanding theorists and practitioners of Christian education dealt with the shaping of the future, assuming that we can work together to take responsibility for creating a future that will account for the current cultural situation in terms of the gospel. In Sara Little's reflections on what happened, she said that "the shape of the future is one with many dimensions," including some of the points already mentioned. She continued by pointing to the need to "make use of the gifts given to people," "telling our stories," and developing mutuality. But this is not enough. She quoted from a friend:

> Where there is no vision,
>   the people perish.
> Where there is only vision,
>   the people have a nervous breakdown.[20]

19. Charles Y. Glock and Robert H. Bellah, eds., *The New Religious Consciousness* (Berkeley: University of California Press, 1976), p. 341.
20. *Religious Education*, LXXIII (July–August 1978), pp. 447–448. The Yale-Hartford-Berkeley Consultation featured addresses by Maria Harris on the prob-

Whitehead writes that the response to the religious vision is worship. Sara Little tells us that the further response is doing something about it. Disclosure leads to commitment and commitment leads to action. The connections are there, and when they are broken there is frustration. The final test of theory is action.

Christian education faces a future of continuity and contrast. It has many good things to build on, and the changing cultural and religion scene will require new developments.[21] Donald E. Miller summarizes the picture in this way: "In the stories we tell to children and youth we glimpse the transformational structures that reflect the way in which God's will comes ever anew to humankind as a transforming and saving possibility."[22]

(8) There is one final point. No matter what happens, we had better be able to speak of God so that those who hear will understand. The educators themselves are just beginning to face up to this challenge, which came originally from the logical positivists, who claimed that religion is "non sense." If there is a deity about whom we may speak, and of this many of us are convinced, our talk about God must be effective in its power to point to God and to show who God is by what God does.[23] Hearing about the transformational structures of which Donald Miller speaks helps us to understand this process by which persons learn to believe *in* rather than have beliefs *about* God.

---

lems of language, Sara Little on belief and behavior, John H. Westerhoff III on catechesis and evangelism, Stephen Schmidt on the prophetic element, and Charles Melchert on the query: "What Is the Educational Ministry of the Church?" See pp. 387–448 for the complete report.

21. See my "Continuity and Contrast in the Future of Religious Education," in *The Religious Education We Need*, ed. James Michael Lee (Birmingham: Religious Education Press, 1977), pp. 28–54.

22. Iris V. Cully and Kendig B. Cully, eds., *Process and Relationship* (Birmingham: Religious Education Press, 1978) p. 105.

23. See my *Language Gap and God* (Philadelphia: Pilgrim Press, 1970).

Theology remains in the background and faith and grace are in the foreground of Christian education. The future is open but God is present and everlasting.

A brief chapter cannot point to all the questions facing Christian education in the future, but the ones we have mentioned are of supreme importance. Christian education cannot survive unless it is related to life situations. The people will become dull of hearing if they are fed inert ideas, whether it is in the field of ethical decisions or theological distinctions. Both concepts and commitments depend on prior experience, which may arise out of what happens to the learner in a worshiping congregation, or in some mutually sustaining dialogue with another, or in the solitariness of the divine presence, which leads to a degree of creative transformation. The priority of God in the grace-faith relationship is essential to sound Christian education leading to both belief and action. This is as it should be, and it is the basis for hope for the Christian education of the future.[24]

24. For two delightful articles on the past and future of the Sunday school, see Boardman W. Kathan, "The Sunday School Revisited" and D. Campbell Wyckoff, "As American as Crab Grass: The Protestant Sunday School," *Religious Education* 75 (January–February 1980), pp. 5–14 and 27–35.

Index of Subjects

(The most important references are in **boldface** type.)

298   Index of Subjects

304   Index of Subjects

pragmatism, 14, 55
prayer, 51, 151, 184
preaching, 240
preadolescents, 220–221
precision, 19, 21
predestination, 17, 23–24
prehension, 25, 40
Presbyterian Assembly, 86
Presbyterians, 163
pride, 142, 147
primary age, **205–206**
private schools, 228
procedural training, **171**
process paradigm, **13–15**, 17
process theologians, 16, 28, 29, 44
process theology, **22–30**, 96
professional religious educators, **279–281**
progressive education, 154
Protestant divinity school, the, **260–273**
Protestant Episcopal Church, **89–94**
Protestants, Protestantism, **80,** 83, 84, 85, **89–94,** 104, 129
psalm, 23rd, 277, 282

Quakers, 87
Quantum theory, 25
questions, **234–235**

race relations, 146, 289
racial equality, 288
racial problem, 105
radical empiricism, **14,** 66
rational, the, 65–66, 193
realism, epistemological, 66, 72
reality, 49, 64–68
  social nature of, 17, 25, 37

Reality of God, The (Ogden), 12
reason, 69
reconciliation, **40–41,** 158, 200
redemption, 40, 155, 157
reflection, 272, 274–275
relations, 66
  external, 119
relationships, 38, **156–157,** 159, **212, 223, 231,** 236, 242
  interpersonal, 225–226, **231**
  I-thou, 67, 157, 160, 212, 214, 232
  language of, 202
relativity, 25, 38, 136
relevance, 156, 157, 161
religion, **19–21,** 27, 67, **228–242, 243–248, 251**
  and philosophy, **251**
  as a humanistic field, 244, 273
  objective study of, **244**
  rational, **193**
religious consciousness, 10, 69, 70
religious education, 11, 19, 20, 21, **30–45,** 165, 178
Religious Education, 153
Religious Education Association, 276, 282
religious experience, 54, 65–70, **70–71**
religious object, 68
religious readiness, 156, 158
religious studies, 259, 262, 273
religious way, 53
remarriage, 146
responsibility, **149**
resurrection, 86, 87, 200, 201
revelation, **7–9,** 15, 23, 49–51, 54, 57, 65, 78, 90, 96, 109, 244, 251, 265, 287
  supernatural, 23, 49, 51, 55, 78

reverence, 18, 19, 21, 30, 32
right religious adjustment, 160
ritual, 192, 193
Roman Catholic Church, Roman
    Catholics, 58, 80, **81–85,** 86,
    89, 134, 139, 145, 187, 268,
    285–286, 289
root metaphor, 95, 96, 135
Russia, 284

sacraments, 17
salvation, 90, 164
sapentia (wisdom), 126, 127
school, 166, **228–242,** 277, 278,
    279, 284, 290, **292**
    boarding, 228, 230
    independent, **228–242**
    parochial, 228, 241, 278, **279,**
        290, **292**
    Sunday, 39, 154, 174, 275,
        276, 278–279, 280, 282,
        284, **290–291**
science, 236
scriptures, 255 (see The *Bible*)
Seabury Series, 163
secular education, 153, 163,
    179–180, 284
Secular Meaning of the Gospel, The
    (van Buren)
senior highs, **209–211**
sense of worth, 26, 36, **41–43,**
    107, 110, **111,** 170, 178, 194
sentiment, master, 221
Septuagint, 77
sermon, 185, 186
"seventh inning stretch," 103
sex, 124, **222**
sexual relations, 290
sin, 102, 139
slavery, 35, 41

small groups, 190
social action, 17
social change, 146
social nature of reality, 17, 25, 37
social process, 155
socialization, **287–288**
Spirit, **251**
Spirit and Forms of Love, The
    (Williams), 12
"squirmer's mass," 188
stories, Bible, 203, **205–209**
structure, **233**
students, 214, 263
style of life, **148–151,** 226, 267
suffering, 34, **35–37, 150**
    Christ's, **150,** 233
Sunday schools, 39, 154, 174,
    275–283, 284, **290–291**
supernaturalism, 48, 49, 51, 54
Supreme Court, 243, 277
synagogue, the, 107, 110
Synoptic Gospels, 135
Systematic Theology (Tillich), 252

teacher, teachers, 1, 208, **214,**
    220, 232, 233, 235, 247,
    248–250, 276, 283, 290
teaching, 160–161
    theology, **254–260**
technical advances, **285–286**
television systems, **285–286**
Ten Commandments, 124
tension, 142, 144, 147
theism, naturalistic, 51, 56, 57,
    59
theodicy, **33–35** (see *evil*)
theological discipline and
    method, 2, **156–164**
theological education, **162–164**
    (see *divinity school*)

Index of Names

(The more important references are in **boldface.**)